SURVIVING THE WINTERS

C&C
CAMPAIGNS & COMMANDERS
GREGORY J. W. URWIN, SERIES EDITOR

CAMPAIGNS AND COMMANDERS

GENERAL EDITOR

Gregory J. W. Urwin, *Temple University, Philadelphia, Pennsylvania*

ADVISORY BOARD

Lawrence E. Babits, *Greenville, North Carolina*

James C. Bradford, *Texas A&M University, College Station*

David M. Glantz, *Carlisle, Pennsylvania*

Jerome A. Greene, *Denver, Colorado*

Victor Davis Hanson, *Hoover Institution of Stanford University, Stanford, California*

Herman Hattaway, *Leawood, Kansas*

J. A. Houlding, *Rückersdorf, Germany*

Eugenia C. Kiesling, *United States Military Academy, West Point, New York*

Timothy K. Nenninger, *National Archives, Washington, DC*

Frederick C. Schneid, *High Point University, High Point, North Carolina*

Timothy J. Stapleton, *University of Calgary*

SURVIVING THE WINTERS

Housing Washington's Army during the American Revolution

STEVEN ELLIOTT

UNIVERSITY OF OKLAHOMA PRESS : NORMAN

Chapter 5 was published in an earlier form as "Hills, Huts, and Horse-Teams: The New Jersey Environment and Continental Army Winter Encampments, 1778–1780," *New Jersey Studies* 3 (2017): 107–36.

Library of Congress Cataloging-in-Publication Data
Names: Elliott, Steven E., 1987– author.
Title: Surviving the winters : housing Washington's Army during the American Revolution / Steven Elliott.
Other titles: Housing Washington's Army during the American Revolution
Description: Norman : University of Oklahoma Press, [2021] | Series: Campaigns and commanders; volume 72 | Includes bibliographical references and index. | Summary: "Provides a comprehensive study of the Continental Army's winter encampments, arguing that improvements to camp construction and administration proved crucial to both the health of the soldiers and an important role in strategy during the War of Independence" —Provided by publisher.
Identifiers: LCCN 2020028775 | ISBN 978-0-8061-6858-6 (hardcover)
Subjects: LCSH: United States. Continental Army—Barracks and quarters—History—18th century. | United States—History—Revolution, 1775–1783. | Soldiers—Billeting—United States—History—18th century. | United States—History—Colonial period, ca. 1600-1775. | United States—History, Military—18th century. | Washington, George, 1732–1799.
Classification: LCC E259 .E55 2021 | DDC 973.3/44—dc23
LC record available at https://lccn.loc.gov/2020028775

Surviving the Winters: Housing Washington's Army during the American Revolution is Volume 72 in the Campaigns and Commanders series.

The paper in this book meets the guidelines for permanence and durability of the Committee on Production Guidelines for Book Longevity of the Council on Library Resources, Inc. ∞

For my parents

CONTENTS

ACKNOWLEDGMENTS

The completion of the book would not have been possible without the support of a number of individuals and institutions. First and foremost, Gregory J. W. Urwin championed my project from initial concept through the final draft of the dissertation and then helped shepherd it through publication. He challenged me to better myself as a writer and researcher, and to whatever extent this book is clear and engaging to read is due in large part to his persistent critiques and revisions. My dissertation committee members Andrew C. Isenberg and Jessica Roney took time away from their own busy schedules to give ample suggestions to improve my work. Mark Edward Lender likewise proved generous with his time in reading several chapter drafts and offering his enthusiastic support. James Kirby Martin and T. Cole Jones contributed valuable suggestions to the book manuscript prior to publication.

Completing my dissertation and book would have been impossible without the financial support of several institutions. The Temple University Graduate School awarded me a four-year teaching fellowship that covered the costs of tuition and provided a stipend for living expenses. The David Library of the American Revolution awarded me a one-month fellowship that allowed me to conduct extensive and uninterrupted research in that institution's holdings. A one-week fellowship at the Society of the Cincinnati likewise permitted me to mine that organization's collection. The New Jersey Historical Commission and North Jersey Heritage Trail Association each provided an award that covered travel and research costs. Finally, a three-month residential fellowship at the Fred W. Smith National Library for the Study of George Washington afforded me time to write and explore archival holdings in the Washington, DC, area.

The support of my colleagues made the entire process of writing this book a pleasant one. The staff at Morristown National Historical Park made for wonderful companions during my summers working and researching at the park. Sarah Minegar and Jude Pfister in the curatorial department aided me with every research request. Park historian Eric Olsen deserves a very special thank-you for the numerous insights and tips he generously provided from his own experiences studying Morristown's role in the Revolution. Every conversation with him yielded new ideas that found their way into this text. Adam Kane and J. Kent Calder at the University of Oklahoma Press provided all the support one could ask for in the editorial process.

Finally, I could never have written this book without the help of my family. My partner, Rabeya, consistently offered to read drafts of various chapters and happily accompanied me on numerous research trips. My brother, Doug, contributed his photography expertise as I sought out illustrations for the book. Lastly, my parents supported my studies with hot meals, a roof over my head, and numerous fixes to computers and cars. I dedicate this book to them.

Introduction

"All the Views and Designs of a General in the Choice of His Camps"

In December 1779, the Continental Army's main force under Gen. George Washington appeared to be entering a quiet phase of the struggle for independence that it had been waging for four and a half years. With British and Hessian troops ensconced in New York City, Washington's men would spend the following cold months holding their position in the hills of northern New Jersey and New York's Hudson Highlands. Ebenezer Fitch, a schoolmaster from Connecticut, passed through the army's primary winter quarters at Jockey Hollow, a tract of hills and woodland southwest of Morristown, New Jersey, and described the quarters: "The log-house city [is] on the declivity of a high hill, three miles south of Morristown. There the Connecticut Line dwells in tabernacles like Israel of old. And there the troops of the other States lie, some at a greater and some at a less distance among the hills in similar habitations."[1]

Fitch's description of the Jockey Hollow camp as a log-house city is apt. More than ten thousand men and several hundred women and children occupied a few square miles of ground around Jockey Hollow. This single camp had a population comparable to the young country's largest cities.[2] The camp comprised more than one thousand log huts, most of them housing twelve enlisted men each. They were of uniform dimensions and neatly arranged in rows along the New Jersey hillsides. A contemporary description printed in a New Jersey newspaper proclaimed, "The huts are all of a size, and placed in more exact order than Philadelphia."[3] The huts fulfilled a vital function, providing soldiers with shelter. An army without protection from the elements would quickly suffer a decline in morale and a deterioration of health. Shelter was even more crucial in the winter, when snow and cold could quickly ravage an uncovered soldiery. This was especially true for troops who did not possess good uniforms or blankets. The Continentals frequently lacked both items.

Camp building and administration represented some of the army's most important undertakings. Although commonly referred to as "winter quarters," these camps were typically used from December through June. The complex activities involved in selecting and maintaining camps kept officers and men busy from midautumn through late spring. During the second half of the war, most Continental troops likely spent far more time in camp in New Jersey or the Hudson Highlands than they ever did on the battlefield. Camps were central to the experience of the war, and well-maintained winter camps were crucial to the welfare of the soldiers.

Just as in traditional cities, a large concentration of human bodies and animals eroded hygiene and spread disease. Military camps hosted a range of ailments, such as dysentery, typhus, and smallpox. The larger the army and the longer it occupied the same ground, the greater the risk of infection. In the War of Independence, disease killed far more soldiers than did firearms. To ensure the survival of the army, and with it the revolutionary cause, the Continentals needed to acquire good quarters and keep them clean and healthy.

Despite the importance of encampments, historians have not examined them in depth. Scholars have studied the health of Continental soldiers, and therefore camps, in passing as part of broader social and medical histories of early America.[4] While several have noted military camps as common sites of infection, none have centered their works on camp spaces. Conversely, historians who have written about quarters have done so from a political perspective. They have largely focused on the British Army in North America prior to the Revolution.[5] This scholarship has devoted little attention to the period after 1775 and has not seriously studied quarters' basic function as military shelter.

The 1777–78 winter quarters at Valley Forge stand out as the most famous military camp of the War of Independence. Valley Forge is remembered as the site where Baron Friedrich Wilhelm von Steuben trained the army to fight the British on equal terms and where officers and men alike suffered through winter weather and near-famine conditions.[6] More recent scholarship has complicated and even contradicted the popular narrative. Historians have shown the Continentals to have been adept soldiers prior to their arrival at Valley Forge. The army might have been short on provisions but was rarely in danger of dissolution. Further, the weather was not so bad as legend has it. Valley Forge is now better understood as the center of a complex military campaign that continued unabated through the winter. Washington's men protected the inhabitants from enemy incursions, intimidated the disaffected, and secured provisions while denying them to the Redcoats. Whatever drama cabals, drills, and famines elicited, this winter campaign was the most important result of Valley Forge. Nevertheless, even recent works have commented little on the huts that made up the physical form of the camp. The sanitary problems the army encountered in the spring of 1778 continue to go overlooked.[7]

Beyond Valley Forge, Continental quarters have seen little study. Winter cantonments at Middlebrook and Morristown in New Jersey, West Point and New Windsor in New York, and Redding in Connecticut have received only a few treatments from historians.[8] Aside from the brutal winter at Morristown in early 1780 and the mutinies that occurred there the following year, general histories of the war largely skip over these camps.[9] Such elisions speak to a wider gap in military history. The traditional focus on battles, sieges, and maneuvers has subsumed the seemingly mundane tasks of building and maintaining shelter. Historians have produced voluminous work on how soldiers were recruited, supplied, and led and discussed their weapons, uniforms, and training. Armies' housing has, by contrast, received little attention. Shelter stands among the most basic of human needs, and yet an army's time in camp has been recognized only as a prelude to battles. Retirements to winter quarters serve as convenient ends to chapters rather than the foundation of the story.

While contemporary scholars have overlooked the historical importance of quarters, eighteenth-century military experts recognized the importance of camps and quartering to the overall art of war. They used the term "castrametation" to denote the study of military camps. One 1778 work defined the term as "the art of measuring, arranging, and ordering camps." While military theorists most often focused on the details of camp placement and tent arrangement, castrametation could also refer to broader aspects of military encampments, including their administration and strategic role. A more extensive meaning includes "all the views and designs of a general in the choice of his camps."[10] An 1806 staff officers' manual implored students to familiarize themselves with castrametation's "more general and unlimited acceptation, as extended to and connected with the principal operations of the field or campaign." These included camp positions, security of transportation and stores, use of geography and fortifications for camp defense, and protection of lines of retreat.[11] Essentially, generalship as a whole could not be separated from castrametation.

This book shares with military enlightenment writers the conviction that sheltering armies stood as one of the most important problems generals faced. Housing, far from representing a dull aspect of military minutiae, comprised a critical component of making war. Military housing especially played an important role in the conduct of the Patriots' Continental Army.[12] The Continentals' experiences reveal that decisions on where and how to shelter carried logistical, strategic, and administrative consequences. A lack of adequate quartering infrastructure undermined the Continental Army's ability to fight the British on equal terms in 1775 and 1776. Attempts to implement European housing methods, centering on barracks and billets, proved unsustainable given the material conditions and political attitudes prevailing in the thirteen colonies. These problems forced the Continental Army to develop new sheltering methods. The resulting form of housing, log-hut cities such as the one at Jockey Hollow that caught Ebenezer Fitch's eye, represented an innovation in castrametation and one of the great achievements of Washington's army during the war.[13]

The log-hut city eventually formed the backbone of the Patriots' Fabian strategy and positional warfare in the Middle States. Maintaining the army close to enemy-held cities, yet within defensible hilly terrain, enabled Washington to husband his strength while pursuing a cautious strategy against a stronger enemy. Mathew H. Spring, a leading historian of the British Army in the American Revolution, has succinctly summarized the importance encampments assumed in Continental strategy: "Prudent rebel commanders shunned major confrontations on any but the most advantageous terms by ensconcing their armies in inaccessible and/or virtually impregnable fortified camps in the interior (like Washington at Valley Forge in Pennsylvania or Morristown in New Jersey)."[14]

Spring's statement rings true, but how and why these camps came to be is a complicated story. Developing the log-hut city into a viable quartering method proceeded slowly. Keeping camps of any size and duration required attentive officers and disciplined soldiers who adhered to basic rules of camp hygiene. Maintaining cleanliness was particularly difficult yet important for an army staying in semipermanent structures like huts and barracks. Only in the war's second half did officers and men fully address these concerns and render their camps clean and healthy.

Likewise, ensuring camps were safe from attack and well supplied took several years to perfect. Washington eventually came to place his cantonments in locales protected by geography. Streams, swamps, and ridgelines promised to inhibit British raids, compensating for declining manpower during the war's latter years. Yet geography also frequently proved a hindrance as much as a help. Provisioning a concentrated and stationary army required accessible road networks and ideally navigable rivers. Campsites themselves needed access to timber for both construction and fuel, as well as fresh water and dry ground to keep men healthy. Balancing these criteria frequently frustrated Continental commanders during the middle years of the conflict. The geography of strategy, emphasizing defensibility in the form of rough terrain, often stood at loggerheads with the geography of logistics, in which flat ground and pastures facilitated the movement of supplies. The geography of castrametation rarely aligned with the other two. Not until late in the war did Continental generals fully discern what locations could easily supply, defend, and house their men.

Experience in housing armies from earlier wars of the eighteenth century prepared commanders poorly for the War of Independence. Future Patriot leaders such as George Washington learned their craft as junior officers in the Seven Years' War, augmented by the study of a limited number of military enlightenment texts. Yet Washington and his subordinates struggled through the War of Independence's first years to find good quarters for their men and keep them healthy. At Valley Forge in late 1777, they instituted the log-hut city for the first time. Nevertheless, it took several more years to refine this method into a viable way of sheltering troops. By the war's final winters, however, the better-led, well-trained, and more experienced Continentals finally enjoyed sound lodgings.

The commander in chief had honed his doctrine for winter cantonments over the course of the war. In a December 1780 letter to Connecticut governor Jonathan Trumbull, Washington outlined his criteria for arranging winter posts. He emphasized security of posts, coverage of the country, and the health and comfort of the troops.[15] These criteria make for a useful framework for studying the Revolutionaries' quarters. What follows is an administrative and operational history of the Continental Army in the War of Independence. It eschews narratives of battles and maneuvers to instead examine the stationary periods between campaigns. Correspondence, official documents, orderly books, diaries, and archaeological studies provide abundant material with which to explore the army's decisions regarding shelter. Weaving together an environmental, operational, and administrative history yields a more complete understanding of the army's cantonments.[16]

This book focuses primarily on the Main Army, also referred to as the Grand Army. This force represented the primary concentration of Patriot strength serving under George Washington's direct command throughout the war. Most of the Main Army's service came in the Middle States, and its large size placed the greatest burden on housing, food, and other supplies. The United States also deployed sizeable contingents to the Northern Theater between 1775 and 1777 as well as to the Southern Theater after 1778, but the housing problems faced in those regions remain beyond the scope of this work. The Main Army presented the most persistent demands for shelter, and the most important innovations in castrametation originated from the brigades serving directly under Washington.

In the following pages, Continental Army officers and soldiers stand out as the primary actors driving developments in castrametation, logistics, and strategy. Their presence in this story befits this book's focus on the army's institutional development. To present a tightly focused narrative, several topics related to the Patriots' struggle for adequate shelter receive little attention here. The opinions of civilian leaders toward military housing and the development of quartering laws by state legislatures after 1775 are important stories in need of more in-depth study than space allows for here. From the army's perspective, military needs outweighed civilian concerns, and Washington and his subordinates frequently ignored civilian complaints when making decisions about where and how to quarter their troops.

Similarly, while in camp, officers, soldiers, and civilian camp followers spent much of their time engaged in activities beyond the tasks of camp administration studied below. Generals hosted grand balls, line officers frolicked with local belles, and common soldiers drank, gambled, and occasionally rioted. This social history of Continental quarters deserves further exploration as well. I hope that the work presented here might serve as a foundation for further studies of these important sites of early American military history.

Overall, this book aims to show that improvements in shelter building and placement, as well as related developments to camp hygiene, proved as important to the Patriots' eventual victory as reforms to drill and tactics. Without proper cover and healthy lodgings, Continental troops could never have stayed in the field for eight years to eventually wear down their foe. George Washington's war-winning strategy has been described variously as Fabian, positional, or opportunistic. Regardless of definition, his strategy could not have been implemented without well-placed, well-built, and well-supplied cantonments from which to operate. To better understand the war then, we must study Continental Army camps. Above all, this is the story of the origins, adoption, and impact of the American log-hut city.

CHAPTER 1

"NOT BETTER THAN A SINGLE CLAPBOARD, OR SHINGLE"

Armies throughout history have needed shelter. During war in Europe's medieval period, troops sought refuge in castles, billeted in towns and villages, or camped in the field. Typically, these forces were small and disbanded after a single campaign, making housing only a temporary burden among generals' responsibilities. Soldiers' shelter arose as a distinct problem for European authorities with the advent of standing armies during the seventeenth and eighteenth centuries. As part of what historians term the Military Revolution, European states began to raise larger forces of long-term troops who stayed under arms permanently. Consequently, sovereigns from the seventeenth century onward had to address the problems of health and housing for their men year-round.[1]

In the early days of standing armies, leaders relied on billeting soldiers in public and private buildings, a method supplanted by temporary camps. During the early seventeenth century, civilians had most commonly borne the burden of providing housing for armies at home and on campaign. Between battles, troops most frequently lodged in homes, barns, and public buildings in the towns and villages as they traveled, easily doubling the area's population. This scenario usually created difficulties, as the increased concentration of human bodies spread disease, undermined soldiers' discipline, antagonized civilians, and overburdened housing stock.[2]

During the eighteenth century, officers reined in their soldiers and mitigated their impact on civilian populations. The widespread implementation of drill and a rising proportion of officers to men made armies more disciplined and therefore less prone to violence and plunder against noncombatants. Shifting cultural values that began emphasizing restraint and order also helped to curtail depredations as rulers instituted codes of conduct for their men while newly created military courts punished violators. The decline of religious motivations in warfare reduced antagonisms between soldiers and inhabitants, even when armies occupied enemy territory. Finally, as commanders wanted to maintain discipline and effectiveness, they sought to reduce prolonged contact with civilian populations.[3]

Therefore, fewer soldiers found themselves billeted in towns during the eighteenth century. As soldiers' numbers increased and enlistment terms lengthened, governments sought alternatives. During the late seventeenth century and through the eighteenth century, European states embarked on expensive programs of barracks construction. France, Prussia, and Austria all erected permanent structures to lodge soldiers on home soil. During wartime, these same structures housed soldiers and their supplies as they marshaled to depart for active theaters. France erected barracks and fortresses along its western frontier and used them as jumping-off points for campaigns in Germany and the Low Countries. Barracks and forts in Prussian and Austrian territory fulfilled a similar purpose for those states, although there were fewer of them than in France. Thus, developments in military housing contributed to new infrastructure that increasingly undergirded regular armies' operations in the eighteenth century.[4]

In the field, more active central governments made their greatest impact on shelter by supplying armies with larger numbers of tents.[5] Prior to the eighteenth century, tents remained too few in number to cover sizeable armies on campaign. During and immediately after the Thirty Years' War (1618–1648) in France, when billets in towns were unavailable, soldiers commonly sheltered each night in hastily built brush huts. While these huts presented no financial burden to army or state, they suffered from leaks and drafts and depended on locally available supplies. The steadily growing standing armies of the later seventeenth and eighteenth centuries sought more reliable campaign housing. Consequently, through the latter years of Louis XIV's reign, French troops discontinued the use of huts as their preferred temporary lodging and opted instead for tents. Provided by suppliers under contract from the French government, tents took less time to erect, were less prone to leaks, and were more comfortable for soldiers than shanties.[6] Europe's other armies generally followed suit. Frederick the Great of Prussia furnished his hard-marching bluecoats with tents featuring canvas-covered floors, providing an added layer of protection from the elements.[7] Soldiers in a well-supplied army of the eighteenth century could hope to spend their nights covered by tents, even when campaigning at a distance from barracks or large towns.

Despite the spread of tents and barracks, however, a plurality of soldiers continued to take residence in civilian homes during this period. If the baggage train fell behind the infantry or if rainy weather threatened to ruin an army's tents, nearby civilians bore the brunt of the troops' housing needs. On the march, soldiers could expect to find shelter among civilians even for the briefest of respites. Notwithstanding Prussian battalions' fine tents, these units typically marched from village to village and spent their nights on straw beds laid down in barns, houses, and public buildings.[8]

The rise of regular armies also led to the development of winter quarters as an issue distinct from campaign shelter during the seventeenth century. In earlier eras, armies in the field typically disbanded at the close of the spring-to-fall campaign season. In contrast, the increasingly large and long-term forces raised during the late sixteenth and early seventeenth centuries required year-round shelter. Since tents made for poor cover in cold and snowy conditions, most commanders resorted to billeting and barracking their men come winter. For comfort and ease of subsistence, this generally entailed a withdrawal back to home territory.

Over time, leaders came to realize that decisions regarding operations and winter quarters affected one another. During the Thirty Years' War, French generals in southern Germany seized towns east of the Rhine late in the year to provide winter billets for their troops while denying such cover to their opponents. This move allowed French forces to stay in their theater of operations rather than withdraw back to their home territory and abandon any gains they made that year. Marshal Henri de La Tour d'Auvergne, Vicomte de Turenne, one of France's most successful generals of the Thirty Years' War, articulated the benefits of winter quarters: "You can gain command of a tract of territory in which you have all the winter to refresh and remake your army."[9] During subsequent decades, most generals came to follow Turenne's advice and dispersed their armies into nearby towns during the winter. In the Low Countries during the War of Spanish Succession, soldiers also constructed small wooden barracks with straw and plaster coverings, followed by kitchens, stables, and even bridges. As such construction consumed much material, time, and effort, armies only adopted this practice sporadically.[10]

Billeting in towns persisted as the preferred option for winter shelter, as homes and buildings provided the most comfortable and abundant accommodations. To find satisfactory billets, armies typically spread themselves far and wide for the winter, with detachments quartering in friendly, neutral, or captured enemy towns, barracks, or fortresses depending on the theater of operations. In early 1758, the French army of the Comte de Clermont, operating in western Germany, occupied a chain of cantonments stretching seventy miles in length and fifty in width from Cologne to Cleves between the Rhine and Meuse Rivers.[11] Farther east, commanders spread their forces across entire provinces and packed troops into the larger towns. For example, during Frederick's wars with Austria after 1740, he frequently distributed his army in winter billets among Silesian, Saxon, or Bohemian towns, depending on where his forces closed the campaign season, with his headquarters placed in the most significant town in the area.[12] In the French Army, winter quartering in towns and villages remained the official practice through the 1760s.[13]

Aside from skirmishes between outposts, retirement to winter quarters typically entailed a cessation of operations. Widely spread units could not conduct large-scale actions or even institute strict training programs. Instead, armies took this time to repair damaged equipment, leaving men to rest in what contemporaries termed "quarters of refreshment." Officers returned home on furloughs or participated in the social scene that prevailed where they were quartered. In the French Army of the late eighteenth century, only one-third of infantry officers and one-quarter of cavalry officers stayed with their units during the winter. The rest departed for Paris or their home estates.[14] Armies concentrated in spring and gathered in large tent encampments. Here, raw recruits and veterans alike could be trained, supplies gathered, and new equipment issued before the start of a new campaign. While winter quarters rarely witnessed the drama of the campaign season, they nevertheless provided armies with the crucial opportunity to rest men and repair equipment. An army that emerged from winter quarters healthy and well rested could face the next campaign with an optimistic outlook.[15]

Regardless of how a general quartered his men, disease persistently threatened eighteenth-century armies. Armies' steady growth outpaced the abilities of nascent medical staffs to care for them. Billets and tent encampments presented a special problem for medical staffs due to the crowded conditions that allowed for the easy transmission of illnesses between soldiers that were frequently passed on to nearby civilians as well. Ailments such as dysentery most frequently spread in camp through contaminated drinking water. Armies that failed to keep their privies separated from their wells incurred bouts of dysentery. A force on the move faced a minimal threat as it would likely find new water sources. Conversely, long-duration camps carried a greater risk of infection. A soldier who chose to relieve himself in a conveniently close stream rather than a distant latrine could cause the infection of his comrades. Beyond the illnesses deriving from bodily functions, accumulations of animal carcasses and garbage also contributed to sicknesses such as typhus. The youngest soldiers proved most susceptible since many had never been exposed to such diseases prior to their arrival in camp. Up to a quarter of disease-related military deaths occurred during soldiers' first year of service.[16]

Eighteenth-century medical services struggled in combating disease. Even as growing bureaucratic strength, administrative skill, and officer professionalization streamlined the conduct of war in recruitment, training, and logistics, military medicine continued to lag. While ill soldiers in camp or garrison did not often require the era's rudimentary surgical services that treated battlefield casualties, they could hope for little more than a blanket and hospital bed. During stationary periods, commanders could also establish more permanent hospitals in nearby houses and buildings. Developing extensive military infrastructure could thereby alleviate soldiers' sufferings by providing comfortable beds and sturdy roofs. Nevertheless, French, Prussian, and Russian hospitals garnered a reputation for corruption and bureaucratic neglect; one French hospital during the Seven Years' War recorded a 40 percent death rate among its patients.[17]

Therefore, officers could best prevent the spread of disease by enforcing strict regimens of cleanliness and striving for sanitary conditions in camp. Particularly at the regimental level, officers devoted their attention to the placement of camp privies and the selection of good water sources. Orders frequently reprimanded soldiers for using any but the designated latrine sites. Men could face fines, confinement, or even corporal punishment for violating the rules. Commanders also addressed bodily cleanliness by mandating the frequent washing of clothes and regular bathing. In addition, they ordered the sweeping and cleaning of camps, barracks, and billets and the burning of garbage. In an era of rudimentary medical care, health relied on attentive officers and disciplined soldiers.[18]

Eighteenth-century commanders recognized that the selection of proper quarters for their armies, whether they took cover in towns, fortresses, or tent encampments, produced important consequences for both the health and discipline of the troops and the potential outcome of an engagement. Prudent generals also realized that camps could become battlefields and must therefore be placed in locales that rendered them easily defended. During the Seven Years' War, Frederick the Great reflected on his Austrian opponents' employment of encampments protected by numerous artillery pieces "and their ability to make better use than has been made before of natural obstacles in arranging the disposition of their troops."[19] The Austrians, it seemed to Frederick, always placed their camps in the most advantageous positions, using "ravines, cliffs, swamps, rivers, or towns," and choosing, wherever possible, to wage their campaigns "only in rugged or forested country." The Prussian king himself entrenched his army in a fortified tent encampment at Bunzelwitz in 1761 that stymied Austrian efforts to penetrate into Silesia. The following year, both the Prussian and Austrian armies waged a war of posts from their entrenched camps, largely eschewing major clashes. In response to his opponents' predilection for making strong fortified camps, Frederick wrote a work on the subject, *Elements des Castrametrie et de Tactique*, in which he listed castrametation, alongside more renowned aspects of the military arts, tactics, and artillery, as topics his generals must study. In the next conflict between the two Germanic powers in 1778, both sides marked time in entrenched camps in Bohemia. The War of Bavarian Succession, as the conflict was known, did not yield a single significant battle.[20]

The fact that Europe's foremost soldier recognized the importance of castrametation underscored the developments in military shelter that had taken place over the course of the preceding century. By the time of the Seven Years' War, commanders faced numerous decisions regarding housing. As Frederick alluded to in his work, the placement of camps affected operations. A campsite in a vulnerable location could invite a stinging defeat, while a well-placed camp could provide a tactical advantage in the event of an enemy attack. Within camp, orderly arrangements of troops required officers' attention, otherwise indiscipline and poor sanitation could undermine an army's effectiveness. A network of barracks, fortresses, villages, and camps contained not only shelter but also supply magazines and hospitals. This infrastructure undergirded eighteenth-century campaigns, giving commanders reliable and well-supplied quarters to which they could retire in the winter and a foundation from which to launch operations during the active season. Castrametation thus required an officer's attention to strategic as well as administrative concerns.

The future commanders of the Continental Army learned of European castrametation practices via the texts of the military enlightenment. Throughout the eighteenth century, military scholars from famed commanders such as Frederick the Great to less-renowned officers such as Britain's Col. Humphrey Bland produced various treatises, manuals, and guidebooks to instruct officers on military subjects. For Continental officers, most of them bereft of experience on European battlefields, printed works provided education in the art of war. During the War of Independence, the Hessian captain Johann von Ewald recorded that whenever his men captured Patriot baggage, he discovered his opponents' knapsacks "filled up with military books." Ewald listed some of the titles commonly owned by Rebel officers, including Frederick the Great's *Instructions to His Generals*, Johann Gottlieb Thielke's *Field Engineer*, and Thomas Auguste Le Roy de Grandmaison's *La Petit Guerre*.

Historian Sandra L. Powers has explicated Ewald's observation into a study of what military enlightenment works were known to North American readers at the time of the Revolution. She has found that Continental leaders proved to be eager consumers of European military texts, documenting more than sixty texts that were known to Patriot officers before or during the War of

Independence. These ranged from translations of such classics as Julius Caesar's *Commentaries* to recently printed theoretical works like Campbell Dalrymple's *A Military Essay.* Prior to the establishment of formal military academies, these books served as the best means for aspiring officers to learn about their craft.[21]

The majority of the works known to Continental officers addressed the most salient military topics of the day: infantry drill and tactics, artillery ballistics, and the construction of fortifications. Most eighteenth-century writers devoted less attention to castrametation. Nevertheless, instructions for how to quarter troops, the best practices for maintaining camp sanitation, and recommendations for camp security and fortification did feature in a minority of military enlightenment texts. Of the pre-1775 works known to have been read by Continental officers, Humphrey Bland's *Treatise on Military Discipline,* Frederick the Great's *Instructions,* Bennett Cuthbertson's *For the Complete Interior Management and Economy of a Battalion of Infantry,* Maurice de Saxe's *Mes Revieres,* and Lancelot, Comte Turpin de Crissé's *Essay on the Art of War* all engaged with the placement, construction, or administration of military camps. This small body of literature comprised the intellectual underpinnings for the Continental Army's approach to quartering.

For generals, the works of Turpin de Crissé, Frederick the Great, and de Saxe provided insights into castrametation as a strategic problem. De Crissé's text, purchased by George Washington early in his career in the French and Indian War, included a section on the strategic selection of quarters.[22] The French writer emphasized the benefits gained by a commander who was aware of the strengths and weaknesses of his opponent's placement of winter quarters.[23] To prevent a catastrophe from befalling one's own men, de Crissé implored his readers to attentively study local geography when selecting sites for winter quarters. Commanders were to inspect nearby roads, valleys, forests, and heights to make themselves aware of any potential avenue of attack toward their quarters. By knowing the terrain, a commander could also spare his men the burden of extensive patrols and guard posts, thereby using geography to compensate for manpower.[24]

Frederick the Great's *Military Instructions, Written by the King of Prussia, for the Generals of His Army* largely paralleled de Crissé's recommendations, particularly regarding camp security. Unlike Frederick's *Éléments de Castramétrie et Tactique,* which received only limited circulation, *Instructions* garnered a wide audience, including Continental officers in North America. To secure winter quarters, the Prussian king recommended the placement of a chain of troops, taking advantage of terrain features such as a river, a mountain, or a line of fortified towns. Employing examples from his personal experience, Frederick related how he had arranged his army behind the barrier of the Elbe River in Bohemia during the winter of 1741–42 early in the First Silesian War. Frederick declared that rivers served as the least reliable type of defensive barrier because they were prone to freezing, as the Continental Army was to discover during the 1779–80 winter in New Jersey. For the winter of 1744–45, Frederick instead relied upon the Bohemian mountains to safeguard his quarters. Like Turpin de Crissé, Frederick cautioned his generals to always remain wary of potential enemy attacks. In particular, he implored them to wait until they were certain their opponents had parceled out their armies into winter quarters before doing so themselves lest they be surprised by a still-active opponent. Frederick cited the historical example of the French marshal Turenne, who had defeated the Elector of Brandenburg, Frederick William I, in the Alsace in 1675 by launching a surprise maneuver after imperial troops had retired early to winter quarters.[25] Washington was to make a Hessian brigade pay for the failure of its commander Col. Johann Rall to heed such sound advice at Trenton in 1776. Later, fears of an enemy attack would delay Washington's decision to enter winter quarters in both 1778 and 1779.

Frederick's contemporary Maurice de Saxe also covered quartering issues in his broad study of war making. His work, which proved popular with Continental generals including Nathanael Greene and Anthony Wayne, included a section on erecting tents and making camps. He gave advice on winter quarters and strategy, recommending commanders stay in their cantonments until well into summer. Doing so would afford a commander time to train and provision his men, leaving them prepared to attack the enemy in autumn, when opponents "must infallibly be ruined."[26] The French marshal devoted much of his attention to coverings for cavalry, however, which is an unhelpful focus considering the small role that arm played in North America's wars.[27] More usefully, de Saxe also outlined the basics of provisioning an army by actively foraging, building up magazines, and establishing wagon trains.[28]

While general works like Frederick's and Turpin de Crissé's placed castrametation within the broad context of the military arts, manuals more focused on unit management including Humphrey Bland's *Treatise on Military Discipline* and Bennett Cuthbertson's *For the Complete Interior Management and Economy of a Battalion of Infantry* examined military camps as specifically administrative problems. Bland's text outlined the various duties of regimental officers in arranging quarters for their men, with regimental quartermasters riding ahead of their units and selecting suitable sites, barracks, or villages for shelter. Commanders were to strive to maintain unit cohesion and avoid parceling their troops out into overly distended positions.[29]

Along with strategy and discipline, military enlightenment writers recognized camp sanitation as a crucial aspect of castrametation. Cuthbertson's instructions for battalion commanders paid special attention to cleanliness in quarters, with a focus on hygiene in tent encampments and barracks. When camped in one locale more than one night, soldiers were to dig drainage trenches around their tents to prevent the inundation of the interiors during periods of rain. To further ensure that quarters stayed dry, which was believed to deter infestation by vermin, Cuthbertson also instructed officers to have their men air out their blankets each day and strike their tents for two hours at noon to allow straw floors to dry.[30] While in barracks, soldiers could expect to sweep floors clean twice a week and were "never permitted to urinate" inside their rooms. Commanders were also to provide each barracks room with hand towels to dissuade soldiers from the habit of wiping their hands on bed sheets. By enacting these measures, Cuthbertson's readers could expect that a barrack "will always be sweet and healthy."[31]

Bland similarly emphasized cleanliness and hygiene in camp but put the onus for maintaining clean quarters on an appointed sanitary staff, known as color-men. Following the regimental quartermaster to the campsite, color-men were to mark out their unit's boundaries before digging "necessary houses," or latrines. Upon the regiment's arrival, color-men were to keep the camp "sweet and clean" while camp guards were to enforce strict discipline to maintain sanitation. Sentries were to make sure not to "suffer anyone to ease himself" anywhere besides the designated privies. Covering the full range of camp inhabitants, Bland declared to commanders that any "soldier, servant, or sutler" violating sanitation rules should be "severely punished." During prolonged encampments, new privies were to be dug at least once a week.[32]

While Frederick did not dwell on camp sanitation in his *Instructions*, the Prussian monarch included one crucial recommendation, that camps be placed conveniently close to sources of wood and water. Access to the former would provide men with an abundant supply of fuel, while fresh water would facilitate hydration and cleanliness.[33] Turpin de Crissé likewise emphasized the presence of wood along with forage and "some villages" as considerations for a commander when selecting a campsite.[34] For Continental officers, North American landscapes would frequently provide abundant wood for armies seeking campsites, but finding a suitable combination of timber, fresh water, and ground suitable for erecting shelter would present a frequent problem.

On the whole, the works addressing military shelter available in North America before the War of Independence fell well short of comprehensive coverage of the topic. While soldier-scholars Turpin de Crissé and Frederick the Great did offer insights into how to best quarter an army, neither author made these matters central to his work. Frederick's chapter on winter quarters comprised only three out of more than one hundred pages in his *Instructions*.

Likewise, Bland and Cuthbertson subsumed camp administration under their more extensive coverage of drill. Works written and published in North America before the conflict largely ignored camp administration. American authors Timothy Pickering and Lewis Nicola focused exclusively on drill and battlefield maneuver in their publications.[35]

In contrast, a number of enlightenment works, most of them in French and German, addressed castrametation in depth but apparently went unknown in North America. In France, Guillaume Le Blond's *Essai sur la Castramétation* (1748) and Joseph de Fallois's *Traitè de la Castramétation* (1771) both provided book-length treatments of the subject of building and arranging military camps. Beneton de Perrin's *Dissertation sur les Tentes ou Pavillions de Guerre* (1735) likewise offered a complete history of the use of tents in war, with examples ranging from antiquity to contemporary conflicts. These French writers featured wider-ranging coverage of shelter and included many more historical examples than the works read in North America. Perrin's *Dissertation* began with a lament that his peers focused too much on battles and sieges rather than camps.[36] Le Blond similarly depicted castrametation as an important aspect of the military arts that had been largely ignored by his contemporaries and looked back to the Roman writer Vegetius as the last military scholar to adequately address the topic.[37] To remedy this lack of recent work, Le Blond studied France's wars of the sixteenth and seventeenth centuries, explaining the different methods French armies had used for shelter, and cited specific examples of men quartered in towns, tents, and huts. Fallois's later work emphasized the benefits of tent encampments or timber-built field shelters known as *barraques de toile*, compared to billets in villages, as camps that could be arranged for easy assembly for drill or in case of attack.[38] In addition to their historical examples and theoretical models, each of these French authors included detailed, hand-colored plates showing ideal camp layouts, dispositions for camps to take advantage of terrain, and drawings of different types of tents. Fallois also included detailed plans for the arrangement of tents in camps depending on an army's size.

By the late eighteenth century, studies of castrametation flourished beyond France. Frederick produced his aforementioned study of the subject in response to the growing proliferation of field camps toward the end of the Seven Years' War. Other Prussian writers addressed castrametation during the 1770s. In 1778, Johann Dietrich Karl Pirscher published *Von der Castrametation*, a work of similar length and coverage as those by his French peers, with equally detailed plates illustrating various camp layouts.[39] Another Prussian author, Friderick von Miller, produced in 1776 a work simply titled *Castrametation*, exhibiting a series of drawings depicting hypothetical camp placements with an emphasis on advantageous locations atop hills or anchored by bodies of water.[40] An anonymous Prussian, likely of the same era, wrote a similar work, *Castrametatio*, which included extensive tables stipulating the dimensions and frontages to be occupied by armies of different sizes and compositions.[41] Farther afield, a Portuguese writer published in 1792 *Pequeno Resumo de Castrametaçao*, also including a similar milieu of diagrams of camp layouts.[42] Together, these works reveal the increasing complexity of military camps during this era, as well as the greater attention to detail required of officers in arranging their men's shelter.

Lewis Lochée's 1778 *Essay on Castrametation* was the first published book-length study in English of camp making. Lochée's work highlighted the neglected yet crucial topic and provided detailed insights into the distributions and depths of camp arrangements for infantry, cavalry, and artillery, as well as an explication of the camp duties of officers.[43] Invaluably, Lochée also composed a series of maxims gleaned from the foremost European authorities on the art of war, including Turpin de Crissé, Jacques François de Chastenet Puységur, and François de La Valière. While these authors addressed the subject of camps and quarters only in passing, when their ideas were taken together, they formed an expansive corpus of castrametation knowledge.[44] Additionally, Lochée included illustrations of tents, camp arrangements, and dispositions. In particular, his warnings regarding the pitfalls of using huts as winter shelter would have proven especially useful for Continental officers. Unfortunately for Patriot readers, Lochée's work was published only after the Valley Forge encampment, and there is no record of it reaching an audience across the Atlantic. Nor was Frederick's work on castrametation nor Le Blond's nor Fallois's available in North America for officers who were literate in only English and French. Continental Army commanders therefore remained ignorant of the most advanced writings on castrametation at the time of the War of Independence.

As a whole, the writings of the military enlightenment codified in print a new science of castrametation encapsulating the practical experience gained during recent conflicts and observations of Europe's foremost military minds. Treatises and guidebooks articulated a clear taxonomy of different housing options available to commanders and stipulated the roles and responsibilities of officers in placing and erecting encampments. Manuals prescribed proper camp layouts for the placement of shelters, streets, parade grounds, and fortifications, bringing a degree of order to camp environments befitting the improved discipline of standing armies. Finally, writers recognized the importance of maintaining healthy camps and established clear procedures for minimizing the spread of disease. Those who read Frederick II and Turpin de Crissé would also stand ready to defend their encampments and array their quarters in strategically advantageous postures.

Nevertheless, European castrametation texts provided the Continental Army's future leaders with a narrow overview of quartering practices that would prove an insufficient guide when it came time to shelter Patriot soldiers during the War of Independence. Texts targeted at both general and field officers devoted the majority of their space to the problems an army encountered when billeting in towns, with a secondary focus turned toward barracks. Much of North America lacked both the barracks and the numerous towns in which European writers expected armies to quarter. De Crissé, Frederick, and Bland offered few insights into how to best arrange tent encampments, while Cuthbertson provided the only brief overview of rudimentary shelters like huts. Aside from Frederick and Turpin de Crissé's short treatments of the subject, no authors seriously addressed winter shelter as a separate problem, and European soldier-scholars mostly associated winter quarters with the retirement to a chain of billets in towns and cities well removed from the enemy. Had any of the works that were specifically dedicated to castrametation been available to Continental officers in 1775, they would have entered the conflict equipped with plans and diagrams for camp layouts, extensive historical references, and the recognition of castrametation as a distinct subfield of the study of war. Instead, this knowledge lay scattered in abridged form throughout works focused on matters of drill and maneuver.

Further, while military enlightenment writings did cover camp sanitation, they provided few insights into the prevention of epidemic diseases. Sir John Pringle's *Observations on the Diseases of the Army, in Camp and in Garrison,* first published in 1754, represented the most widely read work on military medicine.[45] Pringle had served as British surgeon general in the War of Austrian Succession, where he had noted the frequency of sickness in British camps during that conflict. Pringle and the later medical writers Sir Richard Brocklesby and Donald Monroe emphasized good food and bedding for ill soldiers as the best remedy for their ailments. The latter authors called for good climate-appropriate uniforms.[46] In their focus on cleanliness, cover, and comfort, these works largely reinforced the emphasis on camp hygiene found in Bland and Cuthbertson.

Medical authors recognized smallpox as one of many ailments that threatened soldiers and civilians about camp. From a European perspective, however, that disease presented less of a threat than it would to North American troops. In urbanized western Europe, far more soldiers had picked up immunity than the overwhelmingly rural colonists had. Some had also inherited limited resistance from their mothers. Europeans also viewed inoculation, the deliberate infection of a patient with smallpox, with less suspicion. The British Army encountered few difficulties in inoculating its vulnerable troops whenever an outbreak appeared. For the Continental Army, comprised largely of a population lacking smallpox immunity, the concentration of soldiers in close quarters during the first years of the War of Independence gave rise to a smallpox epidemic that threatened to ruin the army's effectiveness. Continental commanders faced this crisis with little input from European experts.[47]

Beyond printed works, practical experience in North America's eighteenth-century wars provided future Continentals with firsthand knowledge of military housing problems. British North America's early military experience had brought little need for long-term military housing. While European states in the seventeenth century raised increasingly large standing armies, the colonies relied on short-term militias to wage war against Native Americans, abrogating the need for substantial shelter. Most colonial forces operating during the early conflicts established only limited infrastructure, such as the small fortified posts and blockhouses guarding the New England frontier. Many militiamen served close to their homes and could commonly shelter with friendly communities, if not in their own houses. Small units operating in northeastern forests typically relied on simple structures built of timber and brush. Overall, early colonial wars did not present the housing problems of the scale or duration encountered in Europe.[48]

A large regular-army presence in the North American colonies did not arise until the outbreak of the Seven Years' War in the 1750s. Then, the influx of Redcoats after 1754 brought a lodging crisis in British North America. The soldiers' arrival precipitated a legal as well as logistical predicament for colonial governments. As historian John Gilbert McCurdy has ably demonstrated, local leaders in the colonies grappled with where and how British soldiers were to be quartered between 1754 and 1757. Placing soldiers in private homes upset civilians, but legislatures initially proved too parsimonious to appropriate funds necessary to build new lodging. After much debate, most colonies embarked on a barracks-building program. By 1757, permanent structures for soldiers' housing could be found in eastern towns from Charleston to Boston. These buildings hosted newly arrived regiments before they deployed to combat zones on the frontier.[49]

More pressing than political wrangling, the small size of colonial towns, the dispersal of settlements, and the lack of preexisting quartering infrastructure meant that British officers commonly faced greater difficulty in securing suitable shelter for their men in North America than they did in continental Europe. Disease, especially smallpox, deterred commanders from quartering their men in towns, especially if their contingents included vulnerable provincials. The varied terrain, harsh climate, recalcitrant locals, and lack of standing quarters all clashed with European expectations of military shelter. Soldiers often found that even their tent encampments were unhealthy and uncomfortable. British colonel Henry Bouquet's complaint that he would rather "make two campaigns than settle the quarters of any of our American towns" summed up the difficulty officers encountered when attempting to arrange shelter for their men under North American conditions.[50]

Fortunately for colonial legislatures and their constituents, much of the fighting in the French and Indian War occurred in areas far to the north or west of the more densely settled coast. In these distant regions, British and provincial regiments did not face the complaints of homeowners about billeting or wait for local governments to build barracks. Instead, the Crown's armies struggled to adapt their castrametation practices to fit local conditions since they found few settlements capable of sheltering large forces. Disease proved a greater problem than politics. British regiments, composed mainly of urban-recruited troops, made potent vehicles of disease transmission. While troops may have often held immunities, colonists living in nearby settlements did not. Smallpox and influenza epidemics consequently followed behind the army in the course of its operations in western Pennsylvania and beyond. Even for immune soldiers, isolated camps and forts often proved deadly breeding grounds for dysentery and typhus. The former spread through bad water, the latter through lice that infested dirty bodies. Diets lacking in fresh fruit and vegetables exacerbated health problems.[51]

Campaigns on the Virginia and Pennsylvania frontiers provided young George Washington with his first exposure to the problems of providing soldiers with shelter. While serving under Brig. Gen. John Forbes in April 1758, Colonel Washington of the Virginia Regiment informed his superior that his men suffered a "great want of tents" at newly built Fort Loudoun. The installation had no barracks, and nearby civilian houses could not accommodate his regiment.[52] Two months later, the regiment returned to Fort Cumberland in Maryland, but the colonel continued to despair the absence of good covering for his men, a problem compounded by their shabby uniforms. A fresh shipment of tents supplied by Philadelphia contractors arrived only at the end of July.[53] In late September of that year, Washington faced the problem of winter quarters for his poorly clad regiment. He wrote Virginia governor Francis Fauquier that he did not see how "men half-naked can live in tents much longer."[54] This conscientious outlook toward his men characterized Washington's correspondence throughout the fall of 1758. He expressed great relief at the fall of Fort Duquesne at the end of November, abrogating the continuation of the campaign into the winter. Washington nevertheless spent the last months of 1758 haranguing Virginia's governor for new uniforms and other supplies to cover the men expected to remain at frontier garrisons.[55]

Washington's time as a regimental colonel also afforded him lessons in maintaining camp cleanliness. In 1756 at Fort Cumberland he instructed his Virginia Regiment to sweep the streets between barracks, clean latrines, and carry off "all filth and garbage" near the fort.[56] In June 1758, Washington ordered a subordinate to see to it that the garrison of Fort Loudoun kept that post "clean and wholesome."[57] At a camp in September of that year, the colonel admonished his men for easing themselves outside the proper latrines and declared violators should "be severely punished." Men were also to keep the camp "swept very clean and constantly kept so."[58] Washington owned a copy of Humphrey Bland's *Treatise*, and if his orders to troops in camp are any indication, he read and understood the book well.

While Washington and his Virginia Regiment campaigned on the western frontier, the largest concentrations of British and colonial troops fought in the war's Northern Theater in northern New York and Canada. Redcoats and provincials marched against French positions along Lake Champlain and the Saint Lawrence River between 1757 and 1760. These armies, numbering up to 15,000 men, brought a heavy demand for housing to a region lacking military infrastructure. British commanders held on to traditional methods, emphasizing tents in the field. Near Fort Edward in June 1757, the Earl of Loudoun banned his men from building rustic huts.[59] A proper army campaigned in tents, not shanties. The Earl changed his tune come October, however, as he now encouraged his men to build their coverings as temperatures dropped. Any men found damaging or destroying huts would not be allowed to return home come winter.[60] Provincial soldiers improvised to meet North American conditions. A soldier in the 1758 campaign described raising his tent "up above two foot from the ground with timber" in late July, perhaps to protect himself from the wet ground.[61] Despite these improvisations, orthodox methods mostly prevailed. The close of operations in 1758 saw most men return to barracks in Albany or nearby fortresses.[62]

Even when quartered in substantial fortified posts, chaotic camp layouts and poor administration undermined hygiene and health. At Fort William Henry, British lieutenant colonel Ralph Button complained that Massachusetts troops had arranged their privies, kitchens, graves, and slaughterhouses seemingly at random throughout that post. The provincials' officers had likewise failed to keep their men clean and healthy, for Button described the soldiers as "indolent and dirty to a degree [that] the fort stinks enough to cause infection." The poor conditions at the fort left 20 percent of the 2,500-man garrison inactive due to sickness. A similar sick rate prevailed at Fort Edward, another post in New York.[63]

Despite these health issues, retirements to preexisting installations presented the best option for quarters. The armies in New York and Canada lacked the time and resources needed to build new housing along their routes of march sizeable enough to accommodate all troops present before the onset of winter. Sir Jeffery Amherst's army of 15,000 finished the 1759 campaign season at the recently captured French post Fort Saint Frederic, on the shores of Lake Champlain. There they began to erect a series of smaller fortifications to anchor their position. Until permanent structures could be built, however, Amherst's army needed shelter for the cold months of 1759 and 1760. The British general announced a retirement to winter quarters at the end of October. Weather was already turning chilly, and Massachusetts soldier David Holden described "a very tedious time for cold and coughs in camp." Some of Holden's comrades labored on a 120-foot barrack at a new fort under construction. This building would eventually comprise part of the new Fort Crown Point. Working on the new project late in the season proved hard and dangerous. Three men fell from the roof of an in-progress stone barrack, leaving them "greatly bruised." Holden himself never moved into the building, for he and his provincial comrades were dismissed on November 17.[64]

While the barracks remained unfinished, British and provincial troops erected wooden huts. These rudimentary structures supplanted tents in the cold climate but represented a temporary expedient in response to local conditions. They were made possible by the abundance of timber in northern New York. As the army had little experience in constructing such shelters, the Crown Point huts exhibited little uniformity. Amherst described them as "not better than a single clapboard, or shingle," while another officer recorded his hut's dimensions as a scant nine feet by six.[65] Alongside their regular comrades, the remaining provincials failed to meet their British counterparts' orderliness and discipline. New England soldiers' encampments often featured poorly cleared ground littered with stumps and haphazardly placed shelters. The provincials' huts also proved even more unrefined than the British regulars', with colonial soldiers commonly sheltering in wigwams made from bark, brush, and animal skins.[66] This lack of uniformity in dwelling placement and style reflected the colonists' amateurishness in the military arts overall, and castrametation in particular.

Amherst's negative commentary revealed the seasoned general's preference for traditional methods. Likewise, his dismissal of many of the provincials highlighted the limitations infrastructure imposed on the campaign. Rather than have his men struggle to build shelter in the wilderness during the severe winter, the British commander simply sent them home to be re-recruited come spring. For the regulars, Amherst opted for dispersal. At the barracks and huts so laboriously constructed along the banks of Lake Champlain, he left only two regular regiments and two ranger companies. Even with a reduced

Rudimentary shelter in the Champlain Valley. Captain Thomas Davies, "A South View of Crown Point" (1760). Library of Congress, Prints and Photographs Division, Washington, DC.

force, crowded conditions and the North American disease environment led to a smallpox outbreak by spring.[67] The rest of Amherst's army retired to more comfortable lodgings farther south and west. A total of seven battalions and three independent companies took refuge in barracks and billets split between Albany, Schenectady, and Forts Niagara, Stanwix, and Oswego in the Mohawk Valley. Another battalion spent the winter in the comfortable confines of New York City. Amherst himself resided in that city rather than more rustic lodgings closer to the Northern Theater, leaving regimental commanders to administer their troops. The British thereby occupied a few forward posts to hold their gains while sending most of their army to a network of towns and fortresses in the rear. Across the Atlantic, French, Austrian, and Prussian generals followed the same model. While this method afforded troops good shelter, it had operational consequences. Gathering the widespread army together and bringing in a new class of provincials delayed the start of the 1760 campaign until July.[68]

A second British force spent the 1759 winter in the newly captured town of Quebec. These soldiers, under Gen. James Murray, relied on billeting. Despite the shelter French colonial homes afforded, Murray's army faced the Canadian winter ill prepared. The cold temperatures and attendant prodigious fuel requirements caught European-experienced officers off-guard. The British had failed to gather firewood adequate for a seven-thousand-man garrison. Many soldiers consequently passed the winter with cold hearths. Murray had also stockpiled insufficient rations. The freezing of the Saint Lawrence River cut off outside sources of supply, while foraging was impossible in the snow-covered Canadian countryside. Rampant scurvy caused by poor nutrition compounded the miseries of cold, hunger, and minor winter ailments. Spring arrived with 40 percent of Murray's army sick and unfit for duty. The winter at Quebec demonstrated that even experienced regular soldiers with secure shelter could still suffer in winter quarters if they failed to make adequate preparations.[69]

Overall, the French and Indian War brought limited opportunities for future Continentals to garner experience in creating and managing large military camps. The isolated fortified posts built along the Pennsylvania or Virginia frontiers bore more resemblance to earlier colonial methods than to contemporary European practices. Barracks construction in eastern towns alleviated some of the overcrowding brought on by the arrival of armies, but colonial legislatures had proven sluggish at responding to military housing needs. Even the 1759 winter encampment on Lake Champlain indicated that European quartering practices would not suffice unaltered for North American conditions. The small scale of conflict prior to the 1750s left the colonies with little need to develop the expansive quartering infrastructure that undergirded the European military system. North America's comparatively sparse population on the frontier and lack of military housing in coastal areas presented a reduced number of shelter options, even for smaller North American armies. Nowhere in the 1750s or 1760s did British North America appear prepared to quarter a large standing army.

Nevertheless, European methods encapsulated in enlightenment texts and the limited experiences of the Seven Years' War provided the foundation of Continental Army thinking about castrametation techniques at the outbreak of the War of Independence. Fortunately for the revolutionary cause, future commander in chief George Washington had read theory from Turpin de Crissé and Bland and gained practical understanding leading the Virginia Regiment. Washington possessed qualities that would serve him and his soldiers well in the next war, especially his attention to camp cleanliness and discipline, his willingness to pressure civilian leaders for support, and his great concern for his soldiers' well-being. Despite Washington's leadership, the contrast between North American and European conditions would eventually reveal the inadequacy of contemporary techniques and force the Patriots to seek alternative methods of providing shelter and maintaining the health of their army.

CHAPTER 2

"No Tents, and No Houses to Lodge In!"

1775–1776

Militiamen from throughout New England flocked to the Boston area in the weeks after the Battles of Lexington and Concord on April 19, 1775. They quickly encircled British-occupied Boston, beginning a siege that would last nearly eleven months. Rebel leaders soon discovered that armies were effectively small cities in that they brought thousands of people and animals together in dense arrangements. The Patriot force would soon exceed Boston's peacetime population. Unlike the Redcoats in that town, however, the revolutionaries could not rely heavily upon existing public and private buildings for shelter. Like almost all of British North America, the Boston hinterland that first hosted the Patriot army lacked military infrastructure. Beyond the enemy-controlled city, no barracks, fortresses, or magazines stood nearby to support operations. Tents appeared to be the obvious solution, but supplies were initially limited.[1] Even when troops did obtain coverings, the concentration of humans and animals around Boston rapidly spread disease. Although the British garrison made few moves after the bloody Battle of Bunker Hill on June 17, the problems of shelter and sanitation threatened soldiers throughout the siege. One of George Washington's first tasks as commander in chief was to contend with these issues. More than a year later, in late 1776, he would continue to face similar difficulties in and around New York City. Adapting castrametation methods to fit the realities of the new war would prove to be one of the most significant challenges to Washington's generalship.

Housing appeared to be an obvious problem from the war's first weeks. The shelter around Boston was highly varied and mostly inadequate, befitting soldiers used to short-term duty close to home. Some militia units brought tents, while others did not even have blankets. Officers organized their men into makeshift camps, but these bore little resemblance to the well-ordered tent cities prescribed in European writings. Consequently, units moved between whatever available buildings they could find. Massachusetts militiaman Phineas Ingalls spent May 24 in a "town house," but the following night "laid in a barn." In mid-July he moved into a Harvard College building.[2] Lt. Joseph Hodgkins declared that he and a comrade were "much pleased," lodging in a tent outside Cambridge in early June, even as other officers in his militia unit quartered in a "very pleasant chamber" in a nearby building.[3] John Greenwood, a young fifer, recalled quartering in the vacant home of an Episcopal minister who had fled to British lines. Bereft of blankets, he slept in his clothes on the floor: "To call it living is out of the question," he complained in his memoir.[4]

By mid-July, the flood of soldiers into the Boston area had yielded an array of shelter types. Soldiers who had neither tents nor billets experimented with a variety of building materials. While passing through Continental camps, Rev. William Emerson of Concord observed structures made of boards, sailcloth, and combinations of the two, as well as stone and turf, while still others were built of birch and brush. Emerson described a built environment in which many shelters appeared "thrown up in a hurry and look as if they cannot help it." Some soldiers apparently took time to erect structures "curiously wrought with doors and windows done with wreathes and withes in the manner of a basket."[5] Men without good tentage embarked to build something better as soon as possible. Some soldiers put up shanties in a single night and gave these structures the grandiose title of barracks.[6] Other soldiers took refuge in barns and referred to them similarly.[7] These variegated domiciles' individual character and style contrasted with expectations of orderliness and uniformity commonly associated with military life.

This slapdash collection of shelter met George Washington when he arrived to take command of the newly created Continental Army in early July. He immediately noted a "want of tents," which persisted despite the Massachusetts Assembly's campaign to collect sailcloth from nearby port towns.[8] The housing shortage bred operational concerns. Splitting men between houses, public buildings, and tents left the army in isolated and potentially vulnerable detachments. In early July, the commander in chief therefore requested that John Hancock, the president of Congress, send for additional tent cloth from Philadelphia so that the Continentals might be gathered into orderly camps. In the interim, the army had no other option but to remain "much dispersed in quarters" in Cambridge and Roxbury.[9] New tents from the other colonies arrived by the end of the month to alleviate some of quartering problems.[10]

Poor shelter and inattention to camp hygiene promised to undermine soldiers' health. Inadequate housing threatened to accelerate the spread of disease, while exposure to the elements degraded performance and morale. The common soldiers gathered around Boston brought resistant attitudes toward the regimentation of daily life that yielded clean and orderly camps. Massachusetts leaders admitted that their men had not learned "the absolute necessity of cleanliness in their dress, and lodging, continual exercise, and strict temperance, to preserve them from diseases."[11] This neglect of personal hygiene might have derived from reticence toward elite standards for grooming, a manifestation of anxiety over military service, or simply the collective habits of mostly rural young men gathered together for the first time.[12] Regardless of the reason for them, dirty camps caused commanders headaches from the war's first weeks and would continue to do so for years to come.

Maintaining health required a dedicated officer corps and strict disciplinary measures. Senior commanders could issue countless orders mandating proper latrine placement and tidy camp streets. Without alert colonels, majors, and captains, however, individual regiments would falter in keeping their camps salubrious and soldiers healthy. After all, the hygienic measures set forth in Bland's and Cuthbertson's works were intended for field and line officers rather than generals. Unfortunately for the army in 1775, the New England militia officers hardly engendered confidence. Brig. Gen. Nathanael Greene of Rhode Island judged the young army harshly in late June. "Regularity and discipline are much wanting," he wrote to his brother Jacob. "Our people are raw, irregular, and undisciplined," he said of his Rhode Islanders, yet he believed they had so far performed better than the rest of the army. Some officers stood out in their efforts to "exert themselves to bring camp into regulations." Yet many captains and subalterns had neglected their duty, "some through laziness and some through obstinacy." Greene labored hard to bring his camp to order, but this was a tall task indeed without reliable subordinates.[13] Conditions in units under less active leadership were worse.[14]

Recognizing the importance of camp cleanliness to the overall health of the army, Washington quickly laid out guidelines for cleaning company streets, removing offal and carrion from camp environs, and digging new necessaries weekly that aligned with the provisions laid out in Cuthbertson's and Bland's influential works. Reflecting the army's haphazard housing arrangements, Washington acknowledged that enforcing cleanliness regulations remained an officer's duty whether his men found themselves "in barracks, or quarters."[15] Further missives against uncleanliness continued in the following months.[16]

To improve administration and better implement his orders, the commander in chief also rationalized the staffs of the assorted New England regiments he now commanded. He appointed permanent regimental quartermasters who carried the responsibility for distributing rations, clothing, and ammunition, as well as assigning quarters and placing encampments. These officers also selected details of camp color-men who assisted in camp upkeep. This move departed from British practices, in which regimental quartermasters served without permanent appointments. Washington also created higher-level formations, arranging his regiments into six brigades and three divisions. Doing so streamlined administration as well as tactical command and control. By autumn, the young Continental Army consisted of 22,000 men occupying four encampments located at Cambridge, Prospect Hill, Roxbury, and Winter Hill.[17]

For the men encamped outside Boston, exposure to the elements and diseases that spread in dirty camps presented greater health risks than the docile British Army. This first weeks of the war featured fine spring weather that made for comfortable conditions. The arrival of summer, however, exposed soldiers to sun, heat, and the occasional thunderstorm. Thousands of men accustomed to lodging in their own homes at night now had to adapt to enduring the elements with only rudimentary shelter. Men found that even summer rain and wind could make for misery. The rustic housing that supplemented tents improved little upon the latter article. Given these conditions, soldiers' health wore down as the Boston siege continued.[18]

A number of New England soldier-diarists left behind vivid accounts of the life in the newly minted army. Benjamin Craft judged his fellow soldiers to be "all in good health" in June, but the summer sun exhausted men on guard and outpost duty. A "very hot day" on June 18 left his comrades "much fatigued." Two days later, Craft reported that some of his company were unwell. The lieutenant himself developed a fever on July 11. Poor shelter offered little respite from the rain. Unsurprisingly, in early August, Craft related, "Our men complain very much." During an August rainstorm, Craft found it was "with difficulty [that I] could keep myself from being wet." His lodgings received the blame, for "our house is like Jack Straw's, much the best in dry weather."[19] Phineas Ingalls's Andover unit similarly fared poorly in early August, with four of the diarist's comrades falling ill. Tents presented a poor substitute for proper hospitals. The Massachusetts men improvised by moving the sick into unoccupied houses.[20] Conditions had improved somewhat by late August, when the regiment endured "a night to be remembered for thunder and lightning" with little difficulty. Within their new shelter they were "protected from the rain, and passed the night comfortably."[21]

The deteriorating health of the army revealed the disastrous impact of ineffective shelter and poor camp hygiene. In August 1775, one observer found that some men suffered from camp diseases, several had died, and "a great many" in the country were sick.[22] A turn toward rainy weather beginning in late August soured Benjamin Craft's health; he suffered from a sore throat and "bad cold" in early September.[23] This sickness worsened as he stayed on duty, developing "extreme pain from head to feet" on September 9. A doctor attended to him on September 10, and Craft kept to light work during the following days.[24] Benjamin Boardman, a chaplain, described his worsening health in mid-August. Likely suffering from dysentery, he wrote, "Have had the camp disorder 2 or 3 days; discharged much blood." Boardman was fortunate to move out of his tent and into a house. He was not alone in his illness, for he noted the death of a soldier after "a long distressing turn of camp sickness" on August 17. The environment had shown itself to be a more dangerous foe than the Redcoats, confounding soldiers' expectations of war. At the end of the month, Boardman totaled nine of his regiment who had died of sickness, versus only six to enemy action. The number climbed to twelve by late September.[25] James Stevens, a New England militiaman and carpenter, spent much of early August attending to sick comrades in an overcrowded hospital. Perhaps as a result of his presence around his unwell mates, he fell ill at the end of the month.[26] Samuel Richards of Connecticut recalled, "As the autumn advanced a considerable number of our men fell sick of dysentery, that scourge of camps."[27]

Soldiers struggled to perform their duties when campaigning in the elements. Thomas Cushman spent the summer and fall of 1775 manning an alarm post. He found shelter in a local house amid a bad storm on the night of September 12. On the twentieth he got wet during another storm, apparently unable to find cover this time. Throughout September and October, Cushman admitted to staying in quarters when weather threatened: "It rained all night and I did not go to the alarm post" became a common refrain in his diary.[28] Other men similarly put off duties when inconvenienced by the weather. James Stevens and his comrades did not work on army construction projects whenever rain or snow intervened in autumn and winter.[29] Maryland riflemen likewise eschewed patrols and spent a rainy day on August 29 in their quarters, which consisted of abandoned homes near Cambridge.[30]

Some troops took advantage of the proximity of their homes to the front lines and rested with their families. John Greenwood obtained a furlough to visit his aunt, who lived twenty miles from his billet in Cambridge.[31] Nathaniel Morgan of Connecticut fell ill August 11 and departed camp five days later for a two-week furlough.[32] Benjamin Craft returned to his Manchester home from September 15 to 21 during his bout with camp illness.[33] Several of Thomas Cushman's comrades went home sick on October 25.[34] While most common soldiers around Boston hailed from New England, those from farther south struggled to adapt to the local climate. Daniel McCurtin of Maryland complained in late September, "Oh my! The piercing coldness of this night."[35]

Not long into his post, Washington recognized that deficient shelter portended a significant problem come winter. He highlighted potential shortages in clothing, fuel, and winter housing in an August 4 letter to President Hancock. The general pointed out that "if the army, or any considerable part of it is to remain embodied" as a standing army, that would necessarily complicate the difficulties of making war through the winter.[36] On August 15, Washington ordered the Continental Army's quartermaster general, Col. Thomas Mifflin, to begin an examination of the housing situation of every regiment around Boston. Those units still quartering in civilian homes were to be provided with tents or boards necessary to build proper military shelters.[37]

In early September, the commander in chief wrote his subordinates to discuss winter quarters. This established a pattern that would hold through the end of the war in which Washington sought input from senior officers in determining where, when, and how to dispose the army for the winter. In this instance, he sent a circular to his general officers, soliciting their opinions on two points: whether the army should attack Boston before winter and what the army should do for shelter if the campaign continued through the winter. Recognizing that the approaching cold season would necessitate more substantial shelter, Washington wished for "warm, comfortable barracks" that would ensure "the security of the troops against the inclemency of the winter." He realized, however, that maintaining the blockade through the winter promised to strain the local environment. To supply the army with wood for both construction and fuel, Washington believed the Continentals would deplete the region's "fences, woods, orchards, and even houses themselves." The housing shortage also threatened a recruitment shortfall. Soldiers would be less likely to enlist and remain in service if they lacked decent shelter during the winter.[38]

So pressing was the shelter problem that Washington listed it as a justification for a potential attack on Boston at a September 11 council of war. A successful assault on the city would abrogate the need to keep the army embodied through the winter and therefore remove the expense of building and fueling barracks. Nevertheless, the unlikelihood of success in such an endeavor led Washington and his subordinates to unanimously reject the idea. Consequently, the army would have to confront the problem of building suitable winter shelter with limited resources.[39]

The threat of a health crisis made acquiring or building proper winter shelter more vital. Yet the Continentals could not feasibly imitate the typical European method of occupying quarters in towns and cities. The only urban site containing enough housing for a large army was Boston, which was firmly under British control. The surrounding Massachusetts towns were too small to accommodate most of Washington's men. Patriot leaders also sought to minimize civilian antagonisms in this early stage of the conflict. Barracks presented an alternative. Purpose-built, permanent structures had sufficed to cover soldiers in forts and towns during the Seven Years' War. In 1775, they once again appeared to be the army's best option. Several regiments had already constructed buildings referred to as "barracks" in the late summer, although these were likely small and rustic compared to what had been erected in the last war. For the winter, Rebel officers believed they needed proper barracks. In late September, President Hancock promised congressional support for construction.[40] In early October, Washington ordered Quartermaster General Mifflin to study the potential expenses involved in building winter housing sufficient for the 12,000 men expected to remain around Boston into early 1776. This established a trend, to continue throughout the war, of Washington delegating to his quartermasters general the responsibility for arranging the Patriots' lodgings.

Mifflin responded with a proposal for the army's first designated shelter type of the war. The barracks he suggested would be wooden buildings with dimensions of ninety-six feet by sixteen feet, divided into six rooms. Each structure would accommodate a company of one hundred officers and men. The army would need substantial building materials to complete this project, including boards, joists, frame timbers, shingles, nails, and bricks. Including the extra wages Mifflin expected to pay to soldiers employed in construction, the total cost of a single barracks approached £100. With more than ten thousand men expected to remain with the army through the winter, the quartermaster planned for ninety barracks at Cambridge and another thirty at Roxbury. The army would also need to pay for skilled laborers from outside the ranks to assist in barracks construction. The total costs incurred in building these dwellings and providing them with firewood for six months reached £20,000 in Mifflin's estimation. A contemporary report by Commissary General Joseph Trumbull on feeding Washington's army for the next six months estimated a total cost of £200,000. Thus, housing the Continental Army would be only 10 percent of the budget for food expenses.[41]

Notwithstanding the costs involved, the Continentals stationed around Boston made their first attempt to produce adequate winter quarters throughout late 1775 and early 1776. Although Washington had organized the army into six brigades, the burden of overseeing construction fell overwhelmingly to each regiment's colonel or acting commander. The quartermaster general provided only limited overall direction. This led to inadequate organization and oversight, and building proceeded haphazardly, with fortifications, storehouses, shanties, and barracks competing for materials and labor that were poorly apportioned.

Barracks construction represented the Continentals' most significant undertaking during fall and winter, and several diarists recorded the difficulties involved. James Stevens labored on barracks throughout the autumn of 1775. A carpenter by trade, he represented the skilled workers in the ranks whom the army hoped to rely upon to erect infrastructure around Boston. In early October he briefly worked on a floating battery, but on the ninth joined his comrades in constructing a barrack in Harvard Yard. He recorded in his journal that he was tending to the barrack every day for the following week. A shortage of tools led him to purchase a set of chisels on his own. After one week, the men had completed a single frame and begun on another. Construction carried with it dangers, especially for unskilled men; one of Stevens's comrades "fell off the frame and hurt himself very bad."[42]

The assorted orders Stevens received for different construction projects exhibited the mismanagement of the building initiative. On October 17, new orders directed Stevens to "fix an old barn for provincial use." Rainy weather that continued through much of the autumn impeded Stevens's work for the next several days. Only on October 26 did he return to toiling on the barracks. At the start of November, Stevens worked for a week on a hospital, only going back to carpentry on the ninth. He labored on the Cambridge barrack every day through November 22, weather permitting. The "windy and cold" conditions he described in his journal likely spurred on his work, but intermittent rains throughout November slowed progress. Building these substantial structures proved a complicated task. Stevens had to travel to nearby Inman's Point to "cut ribs" on the morning of November 13, and then he worked on frames back at Cambridge through the afternoon. On November 19, Stevens described laying out sills for a new barrack, "one hundred eight feet long," and joining them together. Three days later, two inches of snow fell, providing further impetus to finish the shelter. Nevertheless, the following day found him diverted to other projects: erecting a guardhouse at Cobble Hill and mending another barn. He did not resume construction on the Harvard barrack until November 29 and continued through December 10. His tasks then included cutting shingles, raising frames, and leveling sills. On December 11, Stevens was dismissed and spent the next week and a half idle in camp. He departed for his home on December 20 for a brief rest.[43]

When Stevens returned in early January, his comrades had turned to smaller and easier-to-construct buildings. The Andover carpenter's journal ceased mention of barracks. Instead, on January 14, Stevens recorded collecting "boards to build us a house." The following day he "worked on a little hut at Prospect Hill." Officers maintained their commitment to the larger domiciles, however, and Washington banned the construction of more rustic housing.

Stevens tacitly admitted to partaking in unsanctioned construction, for orders quickly arrived that "forbid us working any longer." For an army short on building materials, officers wished to conserve whatever timber and tools they had on hand.[44]

The experience of Simeon Lymon, a militiaman serving in a company from New London, Connecticut, corroborates the difficulties James Stevens encountered. Lymon's company arrived at Roxbury on September 27 as part of a levy of New England militia that bolstered the Continental Army's numbers during the autumn. Lymon received boards to augment his tent on October 4.[45] Two weeks later, officers ordered the militiaman to "tend mason," to build chimneys for under-construction barracks. This service absolved him of all other duties until his work party finished the chimney. He also gained an extra gill of rum per day as an added incentive.[46] A day later, however, officers dismissed the New London soldier on the grounds that the militia, due to depart in December, was unlikely to stay in barracks more than a few days. Throughout October and November, the Connecticut man found himself instead posted to picket duty, foraging, and cooking in camp.[47] Rain continued intermittently throughout the month, and the soldiers were likely grateful to receive another shipment of boards to cover their tents on October 26. On November 17, amid dropping temperatures and the first snows of the season, Lymon's comrades exchanged their tents for a barn. The soldiers departed the camp on December 10, having spent their entire three-month tenure without having seen the inside of a completed barrack.[48]

Throughout fall and early winter, both military and civilian authorities proved overly expectant in assessing when the army would finish building its winter quarters. The difficulties of building barracks confounded observers, who proved wildly optimistic in predicting when these structures would stand complete. In early November, Congressman James Warren informed John Adams that barracks construction continued outside Boston and he hoped they would be finished by the end of the month.[49] They were not. In a mid-November letter to William Ramsay, Washington admitted that the army's time had "been much taken up in building barracks," and he did not believe his men would complete the task for another twelve days.[50] Even this prediction was an underestimation, as Washington admitted to his aide-de-camp, Col. Joseph Reed, on December 25 that barracks were "not yet done." He included the want of shelter alongside other shortages in such crucial articles as wood, blankets, and powder.[51] Similarly, at Prospect Hill, Brig. Gen. Nathanael Greene reported on December 18 that the barracks there were incomplete.[52] One month later, another general order reiterated that "barracks are to be finished as speedily as possible." Washington expected that militia regiments scheduled to arrive in camp would not find adequate housing in the incomplete barracks and would therefore have to "look out in time for other quarters."[53] Dr. James Thacher's Massachusetts Regiment found alternative quarters in late February, appropriating the mansion formerly owned by colonial governor William Shirley in Roxbury.[54] Samuel Richards and his Connecticut comrades occupied "a line of slight barracks" only in February after spending two months in abandoned homes. So poorly sited were the new structures that they came under nightly fire from British lines.[55]

When Washington's troops managed to finish any barracks, they used them chaotically, with regiments occupying several different types of shelter. An anonymous account of the state of military lodging in January 1776 reveals the sloppy manner in which the army went about building these quarters, as well as the continued prevalence of other housing types. For Col. Jedediah Huntington's Eighth Connecticut Regiment at Roxbury, field and staff officers resided in a civilian house while company commanders and their staffs occupied four rooms in different houses, a "small barrack," and eight rooms in two other barracks not yet finished. The rank and file boarded in five rooms in civilian homes, three holding twenty men each and two, presumably smaller, holding twelve apiece. The six rooms of a completed barracks held 120 privates, while 110 were left to shelter in huts. At Prospect Hill, another regiment had only two barracks, sufficient for 240 men, forcing two whole companies to winter in nearby barns. More than 1,500 men remained in buildings belonging to Harvard College, while those still assigned to private houses in Cambridge went unrecorded. Daniel McCurtin and his Maryland comrades boarded in college buildings during January, despite having labored on barracks intermittently since October.[56]

The insufficiency of winter shelter forced the army to keep its tents in service even as cold weather arrived. Tents unsurprisingly provided unsatisfactory protection from the elements. Lt. Joseph Hodgkins at Prospect Hill complained that his tent "grows cold" in early October and was subsequently buffeted by an autumnal rainstorm.[57] Heavy rains left interiors cold and damp, as rain falling through the chimney put out the fire. Hodgkins's men fortunately transitioned to a newly built barrack in early January; however, a separate room for officers was not finished until February 12.[58]

Using tents through the winter also threatened to wear them out when they were needed for shelter during the active campaign season. In November, Washington directed his units to return their scarce tents to the quartermaster general's department upon completing their barracks. The returned tents were to be washed, repaired, and preserved for the upcoming campaign.[59] Nevertheless, the inexperienced army outside Boston failed in some instances to

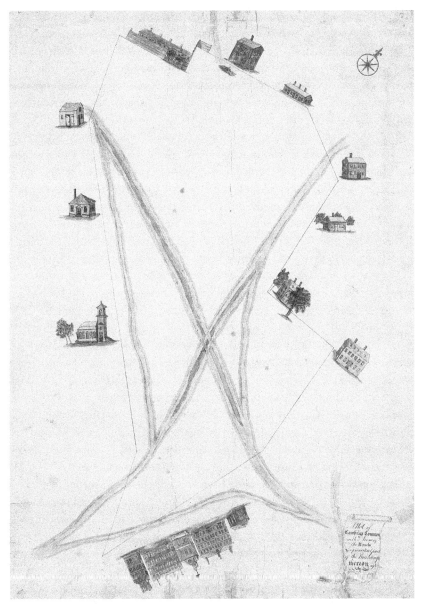

A sketch of the buildings in Cambridge from 1781. The structure in the upper left appears to be a timber barrack, possibly constructed in 1775–76. Joshua Green, "A Plot of Cambridge Common with a View of the Roads & a Principal Part of the Buildings Thereon" (ca. 1781). HUV 2181 (Folder 3), olvwork400303, Harvard University Archives.

properly look after these vital articles. In early January, Washington expressed dismay at seeing tents vacated by a unit that had moved into a barrack "standing uninhabited, and in a disgraceful, ruinous situation" rather than returned for storage.[60] Washington continued to express his concern over tents throughout early 1776. He implored President Hancock for greater congressional support, and lamented to Lt. Col. Joseph Reed, his aide-de-camp, that he feared a lack of tents would inhibit the coming campaign.[61]

The general's complaints spurred the national government to act. A January 30 resolution in Congress ordered the purchase of all available tent cloth in Philadelphia and New York, which was to be forwarded to Washington's army around Boston before the arrival of spring.[62] In a follow-up message to Reed in February, Washington recognized that "in all my letters I fail not the mention of tents" and appreciated that his persistence had come to fruition in the form of the Congressional resolve of January 30. Reed agreed, replying, "What our army is expected to do without them I cannot conceive."[63]

Congress's growing authority over tent procurement demonstrates the positive impact the national government could have on improving the army's military housing situation. Yet neither Congress nor the army showed itself to be capable of overcoming the shortages in building materials or the lack of skilled labor that inhibited barracks construction around Boston, some of which remained unfinished as late as February. Beginning with Washington's orders to regimental carpenters on October 1, 1775, the Continental Army spent at least four full months working to construct permanent shelters. By February, little remained of the inactive winter season in which the barracks would have been most useful. Indeed, the British evacuated Boston only eight weeks after the general order of January 24, 1776. Given these lengthy delays, the 1775–76 barracks-building program outside Boston stands out as a failure.

The blame for the army's inability to erect adequate winter shelter in 1775–76 could be appertained to several factors. Foremost was the shortage of building materials. In August, Washington had appealed to the Massachusetts government for aid in gathering timber for firewood and construction.[64] The Massachusetts House of Representatives responded by approving £2,000 for purchasing cut wood and timberland in the vicinity of Boston.[65] Yet this supply barely fulfilled the army's need for fuel and would fall well short of the material required for building 120 barracks. At the end of December, Nathanael Greene blamed the lack of timber, stating, "We have suffered prodigiously for want of wood," because of which "the barracks have been greatly delayed."[66] With few sources available, Greene's men had expended all fences and trees within a one-mile radius of camp. The local environment contributed to this shortage, as the area in close proximity to Boston had been one of continuous settlement for 150 years; therefore, few extensive forests remained.[67] The strategic necessity of encamping the Continental Army so close to the British-held city thus carried negative consequences for the Patriots' means of shelter building. Future Continental quarters would benefit from placements in more remote locales.

In addition to wood shortages, fault lay with the overambitious nature of the barracks. Erecting structures large enough to house one hundred men lay beyond the young army's administrative and technical capabilities in 1775 and early 1776. Housing up to an entire company in a single structure would have greatly streamlined the Patriots' arrangement around Boston. Washington envisioned whole brigades "quartered as compactly as the barracks will admit of."[68] The time and resources needed to build such large structures meant that they could not be relied upon for winter quarters. Although the commander in chief had ordered men from each regiment with carpentry experience, like James Stevens, to spearhead construction, building barracks of such size and complexity required skilled workers, building materials, and tools beyond what were available locally. Neither the Patriots' army nor the Continental Congress could provide any of this in 1775 in Massachusetts. In subsequent winters, Washington's men would demonstrate the practicality of smaller, less ambitious structures.

Regardless of the types of shelter soldiers used, keeping so many bodies close together exacerbated the spread of disease. Patriot troops hailed from overwhelmingly rural backgrounds, as the rebelling colonies contained only a handful of towns of more than five thousand souls. Most men had had few encounters with dense urban environments prior to the war. They had thus not been exposed to the variety of ailments that spread rapidly within condensed populations. Consequently, even in barracks, tents, and billets, the Rebel army lay vulnerable to diseases such as smallpox and various camp fevers.[69]

A potential smallpox outbreak, caused by the *variola* virus, posed a particular danger.[70] Indicative of the fear with which rural colonists regarded the disease, a Connecticut soldier commented at the end of July, 1775, "We heard today that . . . one man got the smallpox though I hope that it is not true."[71] Before Washington's arrival outside Boston, Maj. Gen. Artemas Ward had established a smallpox hospital far removed from the main camps to quarantine those infected. To prevent that disease's spread, Washington forbade soldiers in early July from visiting freshwater ponds in that particular hospital's vicinity.[72] Toward the end of that month, he expressed confidence that such measures had prevented smallpox from spreading to the army.[73] In early December, however, civilian refugees fleeing Boston introduced the disease to the Massachusetts countryside.[74] David Avery, a chaplain serving with the Connecticut troops, logged in his diary in late December that three hundred men had died of smallpox at Roxbury and Cambridge since the start of the Boston siege. On January 6, 1776, Avery noted that his regiment had experienced an "extraordinary dying week," with up to fourteen soldiers having died in the past seven days.[75]

The European texts that had informed the Continental Army's organization and administration remained mostly silent on the topic of managing smallpox. Inoculation, the deliberate infecting of at-risk individuals with mild strains smallpox, rendered subjects immune, provided they survived their bout with the illness. Europeans viewed inoculation, also known as variolation, with less suspicion than North Americans and demonstrated greater willingness to implement measures to prevent the disease's spread. Redcoats stationed in Boston underwent inoculation, and throughout the conflict, smallpox did not impact British operations to the same extent as it did the Patriots'.[76]

By contrast, most of Washington's soldiers had not undergone inoculation. Colonial communities had developed their own methods for coping with outbreaks during the eighteenth century, relying on the quarantining of the infected. The possibility of death from even a mild case of the disease and the difficulty in limiting the illness's spread made inoculation an unpopular practice at the time of the Revolution.[77] Given the constant coming and going of soldiers among the camps around Boston, attempts to quarantine infected civilians from the army met with only limited success, though Washington managed to avoid a serious outbreak until the following year.[78]

Beyond *variola*, blights such as garbage, animal carcasses, and human waste all posed serious health concerns for the immobile army. Despite Washington's efforts to procure tents and barracks and his frequent injunctions against uncleanliness, dysentery and other camp fevers continued to spread among the undisciplined troops. In November 1775, James Thacher recorded that hospitals in camp were "crowded with sick soldiers" suffering from camp illnesses.[79] While early strength returns (the monthly reports of the army's manpower) indicated 13 percent of the army lay unready due to illness during 1775, this number increased sharply to 16 percent in early 1776.[80] The turnover in assembled forces after January 1 and the docility of the Boston garrison mitigated diseases' impact on Continental operations, but the increase in smallpox and dysentery cases in camp indicated the potential hazard illnesses posed to a stationary army. This threat would become more apparent in late 1776.

Washington avoided a larger scope of a housing and health crisis outside Boston due to the short terms of his soldiers' enlistments. The majority of the men who had served through summer and fall departed at the beginning of December 1775. This forced the commander in chief to call out five thousand New England militiamen to cover his lines, but most of these men stayed only until the new year. Even those who nominally remained under arms around Boston frequently spent nights at home.[81] The militiamen's departure left only 5,600 men fit for duty in January. A month later, Patriot manpower remained under 10,000.[82] The Rebels therefore lacked the numbers to adequately man the siege lines encircling Boston, much less fill their camps. The static nature of the Boston siege meant the Continentals, some of whom had been in place since May 1775, enjoyed ample time to erect shelters, haphazard and rudimentary as they may have been.[83] The Main Army did not face the test of sheltering its men during a mobile campaign or providing winter quarters for many long-service troops. It also faced few challenges in feeding soldiers. By controlling the abundant agricultural hinterland around Boston, the Continentals secured adequate supplies. The transportation, monetary, and administrative problems that would characterize Rebel logistics later in the conflict barely manifested themselves in the war's first winter. Having an essentially part-time army that came close to disbanding in midwinter eased provisioning, even if it did cause the commander in chief operational headaches. Washington and his men would face a tougher test later in 1776.

The British evacuated Boston in March 1776, leaving the revolutionaries victorious in the war's opening act. The Continental commander in chief then shifted his forces southward to New York City, where the conflict's next campaign was to unfold that summer. New York offered better prospects for quartering Patriot forces than the Massachusetts countryside had. The city held prewar barracks and fortifications, as well as four thousand houses in which to billet soldiers. Some officers doubted, however, whether the extant infrastructure would be enough to quarter the large army Washington intended to bring to the area.[84] Across the East River, sparsely inhabited Long Island possessed too few houses to accommodate the troops stationed there. The open terrain would make for good campgrounds if tents were available.[85]

To support the coming campaign in a new theater, Washington took preemptive measures to ensure that the army marching for New York would enjoy adequate shelter upon its arrival around the city. On March 24, 1776, the commander in chief directed Quartermaster General Mifflin to go to New York and make arrangements for barracks construction, fuel, and forage, as well as to secure houses for general officers' quarters, hospitals, and horses.[86] In the interim, until adequate barracks could be built or tents could arrive in New York, the Continentals resorted to lodging in civilian homes and the few military structures standing in the city.[87] Mifflin began on April 25 to lay out tent encampments on Long Island. Camping in that island's countryside presented few possibilities for antagonizing the inhabitants and a better environment in which to instill discipline on the still-raw army. On April 29, the Patriots prepared to march into their new sites carrying their tents, straw, firewood, and other camp equipage. The bulk of the army made do with tents and temporary structures. Only the artillerists stayed in the city, lodged in prewar barracks on Manhattan.[88]

Throughout the summer, the Patriot buildup continued around New York City. Militiamen swelled Washington's numbers to nearly 20,000 by the end of June. Their arrival strained the region's quartering infrastructure. The commander in chief beseeched Congress in early June to "have all the tents and cloth proper for making 'em that can be procured" sent to camp immediately.[89] In the absence of tents, soldiers found quarters in a mix of barracks, civilian homes, public buildings, and newly built rudimentary structures.

Many men had no option but to quarter in New York City itself, despite the problems of urban billeting. Philip Vickers Fithian, a chaplain serving with the New Jersey militia, described his company as being crowded into houses on Crown Street. He and his comrades slept on floors with only blankets for comfort. "Lodging you will say hard enough. I think so too," he recorded in his journal. Fithian found his berth uncomfortable, but he saw his company "in health and tolerable good spirits."[90] Infantrymen who camped on Long Island in spring likewise returned to Manhattan in the summer months to find cover. In early July, Col. Loammi Baldwin of the Twenty-Sixth Continental Regiment stored his baggage and boarded in a civilian home next to his men's camp within sight of the Hudson River. Baldwin described the army from his vantage point as being "in very good health."[91] Neither Fithian's nor Baldwin's good physical condition was to last.

As the occupation of stationary camps in the summer heat continued, sanitation deteriorated, and with it, soldiers' health. There were several reasons for the summer decline in health. The army around New York was more permanent than the previous year's force near Boston. Most men did not intermittently go home and therefore kept quarters crowded. Order and discipline also compared poorly with 1775. New arrivals showed an acute aversion to camp routine. Soldiers continued to relieve themselves in ditches and fortifications rather than specified latrines. Regimental officers did a poor job of enforcing sanitation rules, particularly in militia units. The ill-disciplined army around New York thereby rendered its surroundings polluted and putrid. The sick rate in the Main Army surged from less than 10 percent in June to more than 30 percent by September.[92]

Soldiers in camp noted the army's waning health with growing concern. In late July, Massachusetts soldier Solomon Nash reported, "I was taken not very well." On July 26, he complained, "It is very sickly in our army here at New York."[93] In early August, Edward Morgan, a Continental captain from Connecticut, informed his wife, Hannah, that he was "now in a good house." Notwithstanding the sound quarters in which he found himself, some of his comrades were "sick with camp distemper."[94] Another Connecticut soldier similarly described conditions as "a good deal sickly in the camps."[95] One veteran recalled after the war that "the only sickness which I have ever had in my life" occurred while stationed in New York in August 1776.[96] Philip Vickers Fithian perceived, "The vile water sickens us all. I am very sick." The Jerseyman suffered from "a confirmed flux" that left him bedridden on July 19. He had contracted dysentery.[97]

Shelter deficiencies also afflicted Washington's opponents at the start of the campaign. Much of the Redcoats' camp equipment had been in poor shape when the war started in 1775. Therefore, the British undertook a complete re-equipping of tents and other camp items at the start of 1776. Although Gen. William Howe's army landed on Staten Island in early July, the British commander had to wait for adequate tentage until shipments arrived from England at the end of the month. The cautious Howe refused to undertake a campaign until his men had access to suitable shelter.[98]

Compared to the dispersed, undisciplined, and dirty camps the Continentals erected, the British force embodied the order and cohesion expected of a regular army's castrametation practices. After the tents arrived, Howe's men set about building neat and orderly encampments to shelter the large expeditionary force. The long-service Redcoat and Hessian soldiers had the experience and discipline needed to maintain an orderly camp, while their officers knew the core tenets of castrametation well. Participants highlighted the Staten Island camps' sanitary conditions, clean water supply, and even pleasant smell.[99]

Beset by the illness and indiscipline produced in camp, the weakened Patriot army faced Howe's advance at a disadvantage. Less than half of Washington's nominal strength of 20,000 men stood ready to confront the Redcoats and Hessians in late August. The rest remained in Manhattan and outlying posts or were sick. Solomon Nash described the frightful conditions prevailing in camp on August 19: "It is very sickly in our army yet and a great many dies every day."[100] The Rebels consequently suffered a crushing defeat at the Battle of Long Island on August 27.

That debacle set into a motion a disastrous campaign season that saw the Patriots lose much of the ground and quartering infrastructure they had occupied around New York since March. Continental officers struggled through frequent retreats to adapt their quartering methods to a mobile campaign. On August 30, the Patriots evacuated Brooklyn. With the army freshly concentrated on Manhattan, Washington ordered his men to lodge in houses within the city. Recent rainstorms had left the army's entire complement of tents wet and unsuitable for habitation.[101] Any hopes of using the city's houses for shelter were quickly dashed. On September 15, Howe's forces landed at Kips Bay, north of the city, forcing Washington to abandon the urban area at the southern tip of Manhattan.

The Patriots now found themselves in a strategic situation resembling the previous campaign at Boston, with a large Rebel army operating outside a British-held port. Even before the evacuation of New York, Washington envisioned a strategy similar to that of the past winter by maintaining a fixed position close the enemy-controlled city. Following a September 7 council of war, the commander in chief laid out plans to establish posts in upper Manhattan and Kingsbridge, just north of that island. He hoped defenses at Fort Washington on Manhattan and Fort Lee across the Hudson River in New Jersey would secure that waterway. The Main Army could then establish winter quarters at Kingsbridge. Fortifications on the Heights of Harlem, four miles south of Kingsbridge, would provide a forward defense. By holding these posts, the Patriots could keep Howe's army confined to New York City itself.[102]

Washington recognized that his new strategy would require permanent shelter for his men. The recent retreats had deprived more than a third of the army of its tents, while the rigors of the campaign left the remaining ones in worn condition. The approaching winter would not, in Washington's estimation, "admit of continuing in them long." Furthermore, the army's complement of clothes, shoes, and blankets were intended, like the tents, for a summer campaign. These items would likewise provide insufficient protection from the winter's cold.[103] On September 9, Washington's aide-de-camp, Lt. Col. Tench Tilghman, described the situation to Col. Stephen Moylan, who had replaced Thomas Mifflin as the Main Army's quartermaster general in early June: "The season advances fast, when it would be impossible for the troops to lay in camp, even if they were all supplied with tents and had a sufficient stock of blankets and other clothing." Therefore, Tilghman recognized, the army "must then depend upon barracks for shelter."

Experience at Boston had demonstrated how a lack of building materials would retard construction and delay getting the army covered. To avoid such pitfalls in 1776, Washington sought out lumber supplies from several sources from mid-September onward. In contrast to Boston, New York's environment promised more abundant natural resources to sustain barracks construction. Tilghman directed Moylan to procure quantities of wood, plus brick or stone, along with lime, to build chimneys and ovens.[104] Meanwhile, Washington appealed to the Northern Department, requesting that white-pine boards cut in northern New York be shipped down the Hudson to Kingsbridge. Maj. Gen. Philip Schuyler, the departmental commander, responded that he hoped to send 40,000 boards and additional rafters while the New York government might provide another 20,000.[105] The abundant forests of upstate New York afforded the Continentals plenty of wood, while the Hudson River made for a straightforward supply route. Nevertheless, boards did not arrive in sufficient quantity to begin construction until October 9.[106]

With building materials en route, Washington turned his attention to the optimal placement of barracks in northern Manhattan and Kingsbridge. Following a skirmish at Harlem Heights on September 16, the Patriot position stabilized. On September 21, Washington directed Maj. Gen. Israel Putnam and Brig. Gen. Joseph Spencer to examine the ground around Kingsbridge to find suitable sites for winter camps. Applying proper castrametation practice, the Continentals sought dry, level ground with access to fresh water. When suitable spots were found, Quartermaster General Moylan was then to mark out sites for barracks and assemble building materials as quickly as possible.[107] Meanwhile, deputy quartermaster general Col. Hugh Hughes hired ninety carpenters in three teams to facilitate construction.[108]

While the Rebels attempted to build substantial housing on proper ground, they began to consider winter quarters other than barracks for the first time. Washington's orders of September 21 prescribed huts as a suitable alternative, recognizing the difficulty the army would likely encounter in building larger structures.[109] He had likewise suggested rudimentary huts to cover Col. John Glover's brigade stationed at Throggs Neck, six miles east of Washington's headquarters in upper Manhattan. Glover's men suffered from the army's chronic lack of tents and had few civilian structures available for quartering beyond barns, which were already occupied by the sick. Washington argued that huts could provide practical late-season shelter "until proper barracks can be erected."[110] Rustic huts also provided shelter at Fort Constitution in New Jersey, where a lack of nearby buildings forced officers to lodge several miles from the camp.[111] While the barracks required the use of boards and stone, the huts that were to supplement them could be built of straw, rails, and sod, essentially whatever building materials could be acquired cheaply and quickly nearby.[112] Some men in the field improvised. Soldiers along the lines around Harlem made "tents of boughs" that Philip Vickers Fithian found to "keep off a shower well."[113]

Proper winter quarters appeared imperative in autumn 1776 as the Continentals' current shoddy lodgings undermined morale.[114] Capt. Edward Rogers, of Col. Fisher Gray's regiment of Connecticut state troops, informed his wife on September 17 that he had lost all of his shirts and stockings, his regimental coat, and his watch in the confused retreat from Brooklyn and lower Manhattan. He described his regiment to be "in a broken state," with its colonel captured, its major ill, and only three captains fit for duty.[115] The Twenty-Sixth Continental Regiment similarly lost most of its baggage in the withdrawal up Manhattan.

Col. Loammi Baldwin was fortunate in that his possessions made it onto a raft sent up the Hudson to Fort Constitution (soon to be renamed Fort Lee) in New Jersey, where he was reunited with his marquee and clothing.[116]

On September 20, Washington reckoned half his army lay "greatly distressed" without cover while the other half stood "comfortably supplied." The commander in chief implored officers in regiments that still possessed tents to "store their men thicker" to free up space for the less fortunate. Doing so could, of course, exacerbate the spread of camp fevers, but this presented the only alternative to leaving men exposed to the elements. Five days later, Main Army brigade commanders met with the quartermaster general to divide up whatever tents were on hand.[117] Such arrangements, however, did little to lift the army's spirits. In a letter to President Hancock, Washington complained that new arrivals in camp, ignorant of military life, "particularly in lodging," quickly became ill, homesick, and undisciplined.[118] So poor was the quality of the army's few tents that soldiers took boards intended as flooring to reinforce the structures' walls. This "practice peculiar to this army," in Washington's words, indicated that the rank and file preferred to lie in the mud rather than endure the wind and rain coming through their drafty cloth shelters. Washington nevertheless banned the practice. The general realized that given the army's poor attire and the unsanitary conditions prevailing in camp, uncovered tent floors would likely exacerbate the spread of illness. Due to these uncomfortable conditions, morale and order broke down. Soldiers increasingly plundered nearby farms even as they carelessly allowed beef provisions to rot in company streets.[119]

Conversely, the small number of soldiers who still had access to intact tents enjoyed better health. Zaccheus Towne, a Massachusetts private, "faired very well" in late September while covered by a good tent on the New Jersey side of the Hudson.[120] On Manhattan, Philip Vickers Fithian noted men in his regiment "appear hearty" after withdrawing from the front lines and having an "opportunity of drying their arms—and themselves." He was fortunate to receive a large tent and "slept sweetly in our new marquee" on September 18.[121]

For the most part, though, bad weather, insufficient shelter, and poor camp hygiene continued to sap men's physical and mental health. The unfortunate Captain Rogers contracted a camp disease in late September. On October 2, he wrote to his wife from his sickbed and declared, "Lodging at present uncomfortable makes the soldiers grow feeble."[122] Colonel Baldwin admitted on October 1 to being "not as strong and hearty as I used to be."[123] Amid the dirty conditions at Fort Constitution, Baldwin soon contracted a "camp disorder," dysentery.[124] By October 9, he lay unable to carry out his duties, telling his wife the disease "weakened me considerable."[125] He had no rest as Washington brought the Twenty-Sixth Regiment across the Hudson to reinforce defenses at

Throggs Neck on Long Island Sound. Toward the end of the month, the still-suffering colonel gave his wife a detailed description of the disease's effects on his body. After four weeks with "the flux," he continued to suffer "with blood with a very bad sickness at my stomach." The ailment also led to weakness in the joints and limbs, leaving him "unfit for the present extraordinary fatigues of the campaign" that had seen his regiment move its camp seven times in the past week.[126] His condition changed little by the end of the month. Baldwin realized his prospects would improve if he could secure bedrest lodging in houses, but he settled for a night's sleep on a homeowner's floor.[127]

Other men met even worse outcomes. Philip Vickers Fithian chronicled the declining state of health in his militia regiment in late September. Much like Loammi Baldwin, he complained of the frequent striking and pitching of tents that the mobile campaign entailed. "We are here Pilgrims, roving from spot to spot," he wrote on September 18. Four days later, he admitted, "Many of our battalion [are] disordered at present. I suppose it is brought on by the damp and hard laying in tents without boards on the ground." Like Washington, he saw that this practice would likely lead to sickness. Fithian was one of its victims. He fell ill on September 23 and made no further entries in his journal. He died on October 8.[128]

Despite the army's declining condition, fortifications took precedence over housing. Unlike the previous year, the British army now stood poised for further offensives, forcing the Patriot army's primary concern to be defensive works. While Washington emphasized regularity in hut arrangement in his general orders of October 9, he placed shelter construction as secondary to building trenches and redoubts. Lt. James McMichael of the Pennsylvania line confirmed on that date near Fort Washington on Manhattan, "Our lines [are] advantageous and well-fortified, both by nature and art," but his regiment remained covered only by tents.[129]

Despite the resources and effort expended, however, the Rebels never completed the barracks, huts, and fortifications at Harlem and Kingsbridge. The Continentals' plan for a protracted defense of upper Manhattan came undone when, on October 12, Howe's army landed at Pelham Bay in Westchester County, threatening to cut off Washington's force from the rest of the state. Within a week, the bulk of the Rebel army abandoned the few structures it had built along the Harlem River and withdrew northward to a line covering New Rochelle.[130] The barracks available at Peekskill, north of White Plains, were set aside to shelter ill soldiers, while the rest of the army resorted to what was left of its tattered tent supply, the bulk of which had been deposited at the now isolated at Fort Washington.[131] Officers and men lodged in houses, barns, shacks, huts, and a diminishing stock of tents during the chaotic final weeks of October.[132]

Henceforth, Washington's men suffered with little cover in the field. James McMichael's men spent the beginning of November "very uncomfortable," camped in a forest near White Plains without tents, the "cold and frost very severe."[133] The toll two months of mobile warfare with little cover had taken on the army is evident in a letter from Colonel Baldwin penned on November 15 from North Castle, New York. He described his Twenty-Sixth Continental Regiment having "pitched and decamped" nine times in the past week. His men had mostly moved their meager baggage without any assistance from wagons. After a skirmish at Pell's Point the Twenty-Sixth marched two miles during the night to evacuate its position despite the fatigue of a day's fighting. Baldwin claimed his spirits remained high, despite contending with a bout of dysentery that had lasted seven weeks.

Shelter represented an important component to maintaining health, with permanent structures holding a clear advantage over tents and shanties. Baldwin expressed his preference for houses, barns, or other places that kept his "body from the damp of the ground." The exigencies of the current campaign forced the colonel to instead lodge in "a common tent, other times on a bare floor or the soft side of a board without blanket." A night's rest in a "good feather bed" had eluded Baldwin for much of the past month. The loss of equipment in the fall of New York and disruptions to the extant baggage trains meant that some evenings several regiments huddled together without any tents. Even on nights when he secured decent quarters, fear of a sudden enemy movement kept the Twenty-Sixth's commanding officer awake. In such conditions, personal cleanliness deteriorated along with morale. Baldwin had his surely filthy clothes off only three times in two weeks. In bold script he concluded: "*Thus a soldier lives sometimes better, but never worse.*"[134]

Unfortunately for the bedraggled colonel, conditions did not improve during the following weeks. Fort Washington represented the Rebels' only post in Manhattan, and it fell into British hands on November 16. A month earlier, General Greene had recommended that the barracks standing at the fort should be torn down to prevent the enemy's use of them for winter quarters. Greene's recommendation went unheeded, and the barracks, as well as much of the Rebels' tent supply, was lost to Howe's army. The British then crossed the Hudson and commenced their invasion of New Jersey with the seizure of Fort Constitution, recently re-named Fort Lee.[135]

Housing considerations played a significant role in Howe's shift of the campaign into New Jersey, as well as his dispatch of Lt. Gen. Henry Clinton's force to Rhode Island.[136] Continental officers had recognized that denying shelter to the enemy could weaken their opponents' morale and health. In September, both Nathanael Greene and Charles Lee suggested setting fire to

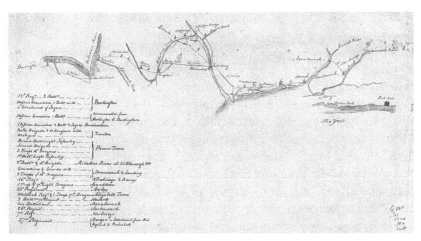

The British Army dispersed for winter quarters in New Jersey, following typical eighteenth-century practice. "Map of British Outposts between Burlington and New Bridge, New Jersey" (December 1776). Library of Congress, Geography and Map Division, Washington, DC.

New York to deny its housing to the British and Hessians. While Washington agreed with his subordinates, Congress denied him permission to torch the city. Nevertheless, a terrible fire broke out on September 21, destroying more than six hundred houses and leaving many others unsuitable for habitation.[137] The city's remaining homes could not meet the large Crown force's quartering needs. Across the Hudson River, New Jersey's Seven Years' War–era barracks in Burlington, Trenton, New Brunswick, Perth Amboy, and Elizabethtown beckoned to shelter Howe's men. In addition to those barracks, the good-size towns along New Jersey's heavily populated central corridor could provide billets for British and Hessian troops. In keeping with proper European practice, Howe sought to disperse his regiments into towns throughout the region for comfortable winter quarters.

Washington likewise fixed his attention on the shelter available in New Jersey's population centers. As the commander in chief had done prior to the New York campaign, he took steps to prepare adequate lodging for his men as the scene of fighting shifted. On November 7, he ordered Nathanael Greene to prepare for the defense of the state. That included readying the barracks in New Brunswick for occupation and establishing a magazine in that town.[138] Similarly, Washington requested that Gov. William Livingston arrange for repairs to the barracks at Elizabethtown and Perth Amboy.[139] The rapid Patriot retreat through the state, however, rendered these preparations futile. Through late November and early December, Rebel troops alternately camped in woods or lodged in the larger towns along their line of march, including Newark, Elizabethtown, New Brunswick, and Princeton, but fell back any time the enemy approached.[140] One artillerist in Washington's column despaired, "The privations and sufferings we endured is beyond description—no tent to cover us at night—exposed to cold and rains day and night."[141]

By December, the only area of northern New Jersey free of British occupation lay west of the Watchung Mountains and north of the Raritan River. In late November, Continental forces under Maj. Gen. Charles Lee moved from New York into this region. Lee commanded seven thousand men above White Plains on the Hudson's east bank. Washington ordered Lee to march southward to join the main body while keeping "between the enemy and the mountains."[142] Lee dithered in departing New York, however, worrying in part over where his poorly clad men would find shelter as they marched into the mostly uninhabited mountains along New York's border with New Jersey.[143]

Like Washington's force, Lee's contingent endured the onset of winter weather with only tattered tents and shanties for cover. Loammi Baldwin's detailed account of the difficulties encountered on the march from North Castle reveals how morale eroded in the absence of clean and comfortable living conditions. On the night of December 3, the little army of 3,000 men and 120 wagons crossed into New Jersey, where it camped in tents at the foot of the Ramapo Mountains. Baldwin lamented the absence of houses for billets, leaving him to lie on the "very cold ground." Rainfall intensified during the night, and "the flood came down the mountains and ran in torrents among and through our tents and almost washed them away." Baldwin had only a small blanket to shield him. Rhode Island sergeant John Smith, also serving in Lee's task force, observed of conditions in the Ramapos, "Water was scarce and mud plenty."[144]

Exposure to the elements forced Lee to halt his march at midday on December 4 to give his exhausted men time to rest. The Patriot soldiers found little sympathy from the Loyalist-leaning population in the region; Smith related that "the inhabitants abused us calling us damned rebels and would not sell us anything for money." The weather improved on December 5, and the army made good progress through Pompton and Chatham, reaching Morristown, "a place pretty thickly settled," in Smith's words, on December 10. Whig refugees fleeing the British onslaught crowded the town, forcing the Continentals to again camp in the woods and swamps.[145]

Bad weather and uncomfortable accommodations continued to wear down the column as it proceeded across the Garden State. Charles Lee spent the night of December 13 at Basking Ridge, where British cavalry captured him. The next day, the army resumed its march westward under Maj. Gen. John Sullivan's command. They continued to lodge in worn tents that provided little comfort.

Baldwin "slept none" that night, suffering from hemorrhoids that were caus-
ing him "excruciating pain." Good food and lodging brightened men's spirits
on the rare occasion they were available. On December 14, the soldiers dined
on salt pork, what Baldwin judged to be the first good meal since departing
North Castle. On December 16, the army enjoyed its first real relaxation since
embarking on the campaign at Easton, Pennsylvania. Baldwin spent the day
in a house where he "got a hot breakfast," which he highlighted as "the first
drop of victuals or drop of drink" he had taken in any house since December
2. He had not lodged in any house nor had "a mouthful of any kind of sauce"
since the same date. He emphasized that he had spent two weeks subsisting on
unsalted beef and dry flour, without even camp kettles for preparation. "I know
at this time" he admitted, "what sacrifice and hardship in conjunction are."

After a one-day furlough, Baldwin rejoined the Patriot column and spent all
day on December 19 marching. He was fortunate to secure a house for lodging
after that busy day. Baldwin closed his long letter on December 20, writing
from the broad hall of a town meetinghouse "on meeting day" in Buckingham,
Pennsylvania. The tired and sore officer pointed out that he now lay four hundred miles from his wife. In three December weeks he had covered 150 miles in
a roundabout journey from the Hudson to the Delaware and spent only a few
nights with a solid roof over his head.[146] The experience broke Baldwin's health,
and he left the service at the end of 1776.

Even as the Patriots abandoned much of New Jersey in November and
December, the British and Germans discovered that New Jersey's towns were
often too small to accommodate their considerable numbers. On the eve of the
Patriot counterattack at Trenton, the Hessian regiment sent to garrison nearby
Bordentown found that the village possessed too few houses and buildings for
its men and therefore had to camp on the open ground outside of town.[147] Evidently, neither army operating around New York encountered circumstances
that would enable it to quarter using methods customary in Europe. Howe's
troops, at least, enjoyed better access to suitable clothing, blankets, and most of
the region's public and private buildings.

In contrast, Washington's army, now outside Trenton in Pennsylvania,
found itself in an area devoid of military infrastructure. The commander in
chief instructed his subordinates "to quarter their brigades in houses or huts as
compactly as possible."[148] Maj. Gen. William Alexander, Lord Stirling, reported
that three regiments under his command lay "compact & well-covered with
boards."[149] Hastily built shanties, however, proved vulnerable to conflagra-
tion. Sgt. Thomas McCarty recorded on the night of December 13 that his "hut
burned and most everything I had." The Virginia rifleman lost his breeches,
shirt, and socks and soon fell ill.[150] In such conditions, soldiers understandably

sought billets in private homes in Bucks County.[151] When a Loyalist tavern keeper refused to billet troops in exchange for Continental money, Gen. Israel Putnam ordered his property plundered.[152] Nevertheless, many men spent the end of December without cover. One soldier recorded being "without tents or blankets" before Washington's crossing of the Delaware.[153] Lt. James McMichael's unfortunate Pennsylvanians bivouacked in the woods, "having neither blankets or tents." On December 29, as the Continentals rested between the first and second Battles of Trenton, McMichael lamented that his men posted at Yardley's Ferry had "no tents, and no houses to lodge in!"[154]

By late December, William Howe judged the campaign to be effectively over and retired his forces to inactive winter quarters. Washington famously chose to keep his army in the field and launched a counteroffensive on December 26. Popular accounts of the crossing of the Delaware and the subsequent campaign have long characterized Washington as a maverick who shocked his enemies by waging an unorthodox winter campaign. When viewed in light of eighteenth-century castrametation texts, however, he had essentially adhered to the maxims of Frederick and Turpin de Crissé. These writers had warned generals not to retire from the field without first ensuring that their opponents had done so. Howe had failed to heed this advice. As a consequence, Washington destroyed a Hessian brigade in its quarters at Trenton and routed a Crown contingent at Princeton on January 3. The lack of housing in Pennsylvania might have also inspired Washington's decision to attack. The alternative, retirement toward Philadelphia, would have likely surrendered more of the countryside to the British and hastened the disbandment of his army.[155]

The rank and file Continentals deserved credit for continuing to march and fight despite having spent the last three months on the move and battered by the elements without proper housing. The army's worn-out condition further explains Washington's decision not to pursue the campaign after the Princeton battle. After twelve weeks without cover or rest, the men had reached their physical and mental limits.

The troubles around Boston and New York highlighted an unpleasant truth: the Patriots entered the War of Independence unprepared to house the newly formed Continental Army. European forces typically had the option of quartering in large towns and barracks. While Rebel military leaders sought to emulate their contemporaries, providing barracks and even tents exceeded the nascent United States' resources. Officers and men alike failed to adapt to the environmental and strategic conditions governing quartering in North America. The low morale and poor health brought on by inadequate cover led to increased desertion rates and hindered recruiting efforts. Fortunately for the

Patriots, short-term enlistments mitigated the problem of housing and feeding an army through the winter.

As 1777 dawned, the Rebels faced significant changes in their army. Many of the previous year's Continentals would soon see their terms of service expire; few men would stay on through the winter. Many of the incoming class of recruits would hold little experience in camp life and discipline. Congressional approval of long-term enlistments and the boost of morale that the victories at Trenton and Princeton garnered meant that the new force raised for 1777 would exceed its predecessors in size and permanence. Consequently, Washington and his officers embarked on new efforts to house and keep the men healthy on an unprecedented scale.

CHAPTER 3

"FIT FOR SOME
IMPORTANT PURPOSE"

1776–1777

During 1777, the Continental Army underwent significant changes to its composition. As a result of a Congressional resolution of late 1776, new recruits now enlisted for "three-years or the war." Unlike the levies assembled around Boston or straggling from Princeton in January 1777, the army gathering in the spring would not disperse at year's end. The new army also promised to be the largest Continental force yet assembled. Congress had authorized the states to raise eighty-eight battalions and then approved additional regiments to bring the total force to more than one hundred battalions. At full strength, this would give Gen. George Washington some 80,000 men. While actual recruitment fell well short of this number, the 1777 reforms put the army on a more stable footing. This new force would place even greater strains on military quartering methods that had already proven inadequate.[1]

Through the first half of 1777, Washington contended with the continuing difficulties of waging war without sufficient shelter for his men or the means of keeping them healthy in their quarters. While in 1775 and 1776 he had sought barracks for his troops, in the new year he resorted to another traditional European method, billeting. This afforded the Patriots solid cover at minimal expense, but it carried negative consequences. Dispersing the army to various towns rendered it impossible to oversee drill and discipline. Small-scale fighting continued through the winter, further wearing out exhausted soldiers. Men crowded into billets spread diseases rapidly. Smallpox, which had torn apart the Northern Army under similar conditions the previous year, began to pass among Washington's men. Finally, come spring, Continental officers could expect a new crop of undisciplined recruits who might again pollute their camps. Congress might have approved of a new, more regular army, but

Washington and his subordinates faced considerable hurdles in putting the
new force on a solid footing before the active campaign season began.

For the war's second winter, the Patriots again faced the prospect of making
quarters in a region largely devoid of military infrastructure. Entering the new
year of 1777 on the heels of a victory at Princeton, the Continentals marched
northward on January 3. They headed toward New Jersey's northwestern
region that had escaped British occupation. The region's military geography
bears analysis as it hosted Patriot troops through the remainder of the war. In
northeastern New Jersey, the Passaic and Hackensack Rivers watered a mix of
farmland and marshes in Essex and Bergen Counties. Hackensack, Newark,
and Elizabethtown comprised the principal towns along these streams. Each
would host Rebel troops, but the towns lay too close to British-held New York
to make quartering more than small outposts viable. Moving west, the Watchung Mountains, two parallel lines of eight-hundred-foot-high hills, ran from
the northeast to the southwest, terminating near a bend in the Raritan River in
northern Somerset County. Although not high, the ridges impeded east–west
travel and had only one gap, near Chatham. West of the Watchungs rose a line
of rocky, broken ground labeled the New Jersey Highlands. These hills hosted
the village of Morristown but otherwise featured mostly small farms and forges
interspersed with woodlots and swamps.[2]

Terrain ignored political boundaries. The same boulder-strewn hills and
narrow valleys that defined the New Jersey Highlands around Morristown
continued northwestward along the Ramapos and across the border with New
York. Here, they were identified by the more widely recognized name, the Hudson Highlands. For fifteen miles the Hudson River ran through these jagged
hills that narrowed its course and hastened its flow. Any British attempt to
sail up the Hudson and cut off communication between New England and the
Middle States would have to pass through the Hudson Highlands, marking it
as a vital geographic feature.[3]

Overall, the region north of the Raritan and west of the Watchungs was
difficult to access from the east and made for an ideal position from which to
strike from the rear any army marching from New York to Philadelphia. Roads
passing through the area made for secure lines of communication. Charles Lee
had recognized this strategic potential in late 1776 before his capture. In 1777
and afterward, the Rebel army under Washington would attempt to utilize
northwestern New Jersey and the Hudson Highlands' geographic advantages,
which would require maintaining a large army in a region ill-suited to such
purposes. Yet New Jersey had been among British North America's least

urbanized areas in the eighteenth century, contrasting greatly with the densely populated provinces that typically billeted European armies through the winter. As a result, the Patriots would need to create the infrastructure for war.

This process had already begun in the Hudson Highlands during the previous campaign. Throughout the summer of 1776, Continentals and New York militiamen had worked on forts and barracks to guard the Hudson's passage through the mountains. The soldiers in the Hudson Highlands encountered delays, however, since the Main Army in Manhattan siphoned away most of the skilled labor, boards, and nails available in the region. Even after adopting a less ambitious model for barracks compared to those at Boston in 1775, the structures in the Hudson Highlands stood incomplete in the last months of 1776.[4] In the interim, the Continentals resorted to rudimentary huts.[5] Washington officially approved such methods on November 12, recommending to the local commander, Maj. Gen. William Heath, to have his men build "the cheapest kind of barracks," made from logs rather than cut boards.[6] Despite the new sanction, rocky ground and tool shortages impeded progress and yielded poorly made structures. It would still take several years for the Continentals to erect shelter to accommodate the garrison needed to defend the Highlands.[7]

The Patriots faced a different situation in New Jersey. No barracks existed in the northwestern part of the state, and early January was far too late into the winter to begin construction. Even huts were beyond the exhausted army's capabilities. Soldiers had spent the final marches from Princeton to Morristown largely without any cover at all. January 4 found the Rebels at Pluckemin, at the southwestern terminus of the Watchung Mountains, twenty miles from Morristown. Here Capt. Thomas Rodney of Delaware recorded in his journal, "The army in this situation was obliged to encamp on the bleak mountains whose tops were covered with snow, without even blankets to cover them." Rodney, covered in only his greatcoat, lodged in a nearby house where he "fared comfortably well."[8] Pennsylvania lieutenant James McMichael's men rested only on "large stones, which served us as pillows."[9] Capt. John Chilton of the Third Virginia Regiment spent "four or five days on the side of a mountain without tents. Ground covered in snow."[10] Without shelter, uniforms quickly deteriorated, along with morale and health. Brig. Gen. John Cadwalader of the Pennsylvania militia wrote his state's government from Pluckemin, begging for new shoes, shirts, blankets, and jackets. Without these items, he feared his troops would return home.[11]

Washington recognized the pitfalls of waging an extended winter campaign with his poorly clothed army. The conscientious streak that dated back to planning winter quarters on the Virginia frontier manifested as Washington resolved on January 5 to put his troops "under the best cover I can."[12] The following day, he arrived in Morristown and quickly surmised that the town offered a position "best calculated of any in this quarter, to accommodate and refresh" his men. After resting the army, Washington hoped to relocate, though the general offered no indication of where he intended to move his army after Morristown. He admitted, "I do not know how we shall procure covering for our men elsewhere."[13] Ultimately, the commander in chief would make his headquarters in Morristown for the following five months.

Operating in a region devoid of barracks or fortresses, the Patriot army resorted to billeting. The concerns over civilian animosity and eroding discipline gave way to practicality. Morristown contained a prewar population of about 250 people inhabiting some 50 houses. Washington's army, despite stragglers and expiring enlistments, still numbered more than four thousand men. To billet these soldiers, Patriot officers crowded their men into civilian houses. Thomas Rodney's Delaware infantry took over the "very large house" of Jacob Ford, a prominent resident of Morristown and colonel in the militia. Ford's family of six shared their living space with Rodney and thirty-five of his men during early January.[14] Elsewhere in town, John Read, a Pennsylvania militiaman, complained on January 8 of being "forced to write on my knee as the house is exceedingly crowded."[15] A week later, he was still "surrounded by a roomful of people."[16] In Hanover, a few miles north of Morristown, Rev. Jacob Green's house provided billets for ten officers and two servants in addition to the family of nine.[17] John Chilton of the Third Virginia spent two weeks quartered in a home two miles outside Morristown before moving into the town itself, where he stayed through early February.[18] Despite the congested conditions, Rebel troops found the substantial coverings to their liking. After weeks spent under the open sky, Lt. James McMichael recorded on January 7 having "secured good quarters, where I lived happily while we remained in Morristown, with very agreeable people."[19]

By ending a campaign with the billeting of an army in the theater's towns, Washington seemed to be following the European model of winter quarters. Unlike typical eighteenth-century practices, however, the Rebel commander in chief did not use winter billets as quarters of refreshment. Instead, throughout the following months, he dispersed his forces across northern New Jersey and used these detachments to wage a partisan campaign. British troops continued to hold Perth Amboy and New Brunswick, as well as New York City and its environs. Washington distributed his men to hem Sir William Howe's forces into those towns and deny them access to the New Jersey countryside. Patriot detachments holding Washington's right stretched from the Sourland Mountains around Princeton in the south up to Bound Brook at the foot of the Watchung Mountains in the center. Troops at Chatham guarded the approaches to Morristown, while smaller contingents continued the line through Bergen County and up to the Hudson Highlands around Peekskill. The rebels did not stay confined to their garrisons, but kept up active patrols in the vicinities of Newark, Elizabethtown, New Brunswick, and Perth Amboy.[20]

Dispersing the army to wage this partisan fight eased the task of finding billets. While stationed in Chatham, Lieutenant McMichael recorded obtaining "very agreeable quarters" in the "suburbs" of that town.[21] From their post at Chatham, McMichael's men spent the third week of January patrolling the New Jersey countryside below the mountains, resting on successive nights in Westfield, Springfield, and Quibbletown.[22] A week later, another sweep took McMichael's unit closer to British lines as it marched through Elizabethtown, Connecticut Farms, and Springfield before returning to their comfortable quarters at Chatham.[23] The latter town made for a popular destination for billets given its location at the edge of the Watchungs, close to the zone of Continental forage sweeps. Sgt. Thomas McCarty's Virginia comrades followed McMichael's Pennsylvanians in a similar sweep through Westfield, Scotch Plains, Quibbletown, and Chatham at the end of January.[24] Massachusetts sergeant Joseph White later garrisoned in Chatham and described his unit staying in a small schoolhouse that held forty men, with "not room enough for all to lay down."[25]

Despite the cover billets afforded, days spent on patrol in the depths of winter wore down Washington's largely militia army. Pvt. Zacchaeus Towne and his comrades in a foraging party spent most of January 18 in Springfield but marched southwestward to Westfield in the evening in response to an alarm. They arrived at the latter town at two in the morning, "extra cold." January 19 saw Towne lying in a wood a mile from British posts near New Brunswick. He spent the night in houses in nearby Woodbridge. The following day Towne's party headed west to Boundbrook, where they helped capture twenty-five British wagons and one hundred horses. Barns and campfires provided the only protection from the elements that night. Towne spent the following week marching between Metuchen and Woodbridge in search of enemy foraging parties. On January 23, the Patriots encountered five hundred of the enemy outside New Brunswick, leading to a sharp skirmish. Further reconnaissance failed to detect any enemy units during the following days. "A mountain traveled and brought forth a mouse," Towne complained on January 27. He and his comrades returned to the Patriot base at Chatham at the end of the month. The diarist's enlistment expired in mid-February. Despite the last weeks of his service spent agreeably, Towne returned home to Massachusetts.[26]

Scattering the army across the region eroded order and discipline. Brigade and regimental officers tried to keep up camp routine and drill. For example, a brigade of Massachusetts militia under Nathaniel Warner posted to Bridgewater, near Bound Brook, turned out daily at 10 A.M. for assembly and exercise during late January.[27] Nevertheless, it proved difficult to maintain discipline while camped so far from Washington's oversight. Orderly sergeants attempted to pass off their duties to privates, while captains neglected taking roll daily. Men frequently loaded and fired their weapons against orders.[28] Officers also addressed concerns over health and cleanliness, which were crucial with soldiers confined to crowded billets. A subaltern in each regiment near Bound Brook was made responsible for inspecting soldiers' quarters, ensuring that they were kept clean and that food was properly prepared. Failure to adhere to this order, however, led to its reissue two weeks later. Like much of the force in New Jersey earlier in the year, Warner's contingent went home at the end of their service obligation, departing at the outset of March.[29]

Similar problems afflicted Patriot soldiers in the Hudson Highlands. There, Maj. Gen. William Heath led a contingent composed largely of militia with the goal of seizing forage in Westchester County and denying it to the British.[30] While garrisoning in the Highlands, Heath's soldiers benefited from cover in the huts and recently finished barracks at Peekskill. When on active operations, however, they, too, relied on billets and temporary shelter. While besieging a Hessian-manned fort at Kingsbridge in early February, Heath's men had no option but to scatter their camps over an eight-mile radius since no suitable accommodations could be had closer to hand. A heavy rainstorm drove four regiments from poorly built shanties, while an enemy sally then ejected the Rebels from their siege lines. Heath judged the gentlemen leading his militia troops unequal to the task of winter campaigning, writing, "A diffidence & uneasiness were discovered in even the bravest officers." Poor shelter undermined morale, as his men exuded "a universal desire to get more advantageously quartered."[31] Billets could support small foraging patrols and outposts, but substantial operations such as sieges would have to wait for better weather and better coverings.

Overall, this partisan warfare proved an innovative but temporary solution to the army's housing problem. To his credit, Washington used his mix of Continentals and short-service militia to secure much of New Jersey. By recovering much of the state, the Patriots denied most towns and barracks to their opponents. To maintain a foothold in the state, Howe kept more than ten thousand troops at New Brunswick, Perth Amboy, and nearby villages. Combined, these locales contained too few buildings to cover such a large force. New Brunswick's four hundred houses hosted four battalions of British and Hessian grenadiers, as well as two full infantry brigades, artillery, and a dragoon regiment. Light infantry erected shanties in the countryside outside of town that proved uncomfortable and unhealthy. Reinforcements arriving from

Rhode Island had no option but to stay on their transport ships anchored in Raritan Bay. Through the first months of 1777, the Crown's soldiers suffered the ill effects of inadequate shelter much as the Patriots had during the previous year. Disease spread rapidly among the troops packed into towns and aboard ship while morale eroded.[32] One British officer described having spent "a very disagreeable winter" in New Brunswick.[33] Another condemned the "miserable cantonments" in Brunswick and Amboy, with up to seven officers and their servants "obliged to lay upon the floor in the same room for want of quarters."[34] Thus, the New Jersey campaign led to a reversal of fortune in the two opponents' respective quartering situations. The Patriots, who in late December had suffered in the open along the banks of the Delaware, by late January had secured decent billets for themselves. While Howe's men languished along the Raritan, the Rebels gained the chance to recuperate in relative comfort.

Nevertheless, the winter campaign carried several detriments. It wore out soldiers and equipment and set back training. It relied on short-service militia who could not be expected to perform well in larger combat. Behind the thin screen of posts along the Watchungs, Washington had almost no army. Writing to Maj. Gen. Philip Schuyler in late February, the commander in chief admitted, "I do not apprehend however that this *Petit Guerre* will be continued long. I think matters will be transacted upon a larger scale."[35] Such transactions would begin in the spring. Waging this expected conventional campaign would require assembling the new long-service enlistees who were then undergoing recruitment.

Even with a small force dispersed into billets, disease again threated to decimate Rebel ranks. During the early months of 1777, smallpox, rather than Hessians and Redcoats, posed the greatest threat to the Rebel army. The pestilence presented a particular threat to the army whenever it remained stationary for long periods. In winter camps and billets, smallpox spread quickly amid frequently crowded and unsanitary conditions. The close quarters Patriot troops kept while billeted helped to spread *variola*. A new influx of recruits from unexposed rural areas also led to a rise in sicknesses.

Washington's limited measures of quarantining ill soldiers and refugees had prevented a major outbreak in 1775. The case was not the same for the Northern Army. The Patriot force that invaded Canada during the 1775–76 winter found quarters within Montreal itself. In crowded urban conditions, smallpox rapidly spread through Continental ranks. The arrival in camp of infected refugees from Quebec City exacerbated the outbreak, as did the frightened Continentals' practice of unregulated self-inoculation. With smallpox ravishing the Northern Army, the Patriot invasion of Canada collapsed, and the disease-ridden Continentals withdrew back to New York during the spring of 1776.[36] In dire need of manpower after the defeats around New York, Washington had drawn reinforcements from the Northern Army, which was still reeling from disease. The arrival of these northern troops, as well as others levies who had passed through urban locales such as Philadelphia on their way to New Jersey, further contributed to *variola*'s spread within the camp.[37] Finally, the poor weather and lack of shelter that had exposed many men to unhealthy conditions during November and December 1776 left the Rebels especially vulnerable to sickness. Consequently, the number of rank and file reported sick peaked at 34 percent in December 1776, largely due to smallpox.[38]

By January 1777, with an increasingly ill force quartered upon a rural civilian population who lacked any immunity, smallpox reached a crisis level.[39] Fearing the "unhappy situation of our Northern Army last year," in late January Washington pressed his subordinates to assist him in crafting a response to the disease.[40] In spite of congressional sanction and expert advice from army physicians, however, Washington hesitated to enact inoculation wholesale. He feared that to do so would leave him with too few healthy soldiers. With his men occupying close quarters alongside civilians, it would be difficult to maintain a system of quarantine. Nevertheless, the commander in chief continued to place his faith in isolating the disease.[41]

The ongoing recruitment of new soldiers throughout the colonies, and their subsequent movement to the front lines in New Jersey, ultimately forced Washington to reconsider his stance. So, too, did the spread of the disease to the army's civilian hosts in New Jersey. While quarantine and rerouting might have allowed some soldiers to avoid contracting smallpox in Philadelphia, these measures promised to do little to alleviate the plight of the soldiers garrisoning in New Jersey's towns. Smallpox was also spreading among recruits in New England.[42] An exasperated Washington admitted to Maj. Gen. Horatio Gates on February 5, "I am much at a loss what step to take to prevent the spreading of the smallpox." The following day, he informed Gates that he had decided to implement inoculation wholesale. Washington declared, "This is the only effectual method of putting a period to the disorder."[43] He resolved to inoculate all troops at Morristown and all new levies arriving at Philadelphia.[44]

Washington also saw that the new army levying throughout the states would require protection form smallpox. The Patriots consequently established smallpox hospitals in Connecticut; at Trenton in New Jersey; at Fishkill, the Hudson Highlands, and Fort Ticonderoga in New York; at Bethlehem, Newtown, and Philadelphia in Pennsylvania; and at Alexandria, Colchester, Dumfries, and Georgetown in Virginia.[45] Thus, inoculation took place wherever significant army concentrations already existed and wherever recruits gathered before marching to active theaters. The Continental Congress Medical Committee expressed its approval for these measures on February 13, acknowledging that "smallpox may greatly endanger the lives of our fellow citizens who compose the army."[46]

Implementing a nationwide inoculation system standardized practices that would prevent smallpox from afflicting the army in quarters. Throughout spring, variolations proceeded successfully in northern New Jersey under the supervision of army doctors. Eleven of the twelve Continentals quartered in Rev. Jacob Green's house endured the procedure, the only exception being an Irish-born waiter who had already contracted the disease. Green's family was also inoculated and experienced particularly mild cases of the illness.[47] Capt. John Chilton and the Third Virginia Regiment underwent inoculation in Hanover in late February. He recorded, "We had the smallpox very lightly generally."[48] Not all soldiers were so fortunate. Brig. Gen. Samuel Holden Parsons lost twenty of his Connecticut recruits to the disease, while the remainder of his men delayed their march to join Washington. Smallpox had, in Parsons's words, "been very heavy on them."[49]

While inoculation promised a long-term solution to the smallpox problem, in the interim it left the Rebels without an army. The imperative of treating men before they marched for New Jersey meant that reinforcements for Morristown would suffer significant delays and arrive piecemeal. Washington impressed upon his subordinates the importance of proceeding with inoculation rapidly wherever recruits for the new army assembled. Washington wrote to Col. George Baylor in Virginia, insisting he inoculate his men "as fast as they are enlisted" and send them on to camp even if they were not yet equipped with weapons.[50] A late-March memorandum to the generals in charge of recruitment in Connecticut, Rhode Island, and New Hampshire similarly urged commanders to send their regiments toward the front lines, in fragments if need be, but to let nothing interfere with inoculation.[51]

Treating new levies invariably upset plans for organizing and training recruits. Brig. Gen. James Varnum had to divide his class of levies in Rhode Island, sending 150 men who had already had the disease westward at the beginning of April but retaining the remainder in the hospital until they had recovered from intentional infection.[52] Varnum had delayed setting up smallpox hospitals in Rhode Island, placing that state behind its peers in the recruitment process and earning him Washington's ire.[53] The brigadier general attempted to excuse his delay on a communications error.[54]

The commander in chief's worries over the weakness of his force derived from his awareness that the new campaign season was about to begin. As an astute reader of military enlightenment texts, Washington realized the potential danger of being caught in winter quarters unprepared by a more alert enemy. In a letter to Col. Samuel Blachley Webb dated April 7, the general railed against his recruiting officers for remaining in their homes in comfort and delaying their departure for the front. Realizing that inoculation meant that unit cohesion would be lost, he settled for having his men sent forward in penny packets, "even by twenties," with disciplinary infractions ignored, all in the name of bringing recruits to Morristown. Until they arrived, Washington complained, he was left to "take the field with little more than my family," meaning his headquarters staff. The Continental commander recognized the importance of having a concentrated force to begin operations and worried that due to recruitment delays he would lose the opportunity to gain a strategic advantage at the outset of a campaign. With the active season "on the very eve of opening," he feared a "decisive blow at the beginning" that could potentially leave his force crippled for the remainder of the year.[55]

Civilian observers shared the general's apprehension. Reports of the arrival of British reinforcements in New York in late February led Robert Morris and George Clymer of the Executive Committee of Congress to fear a renewed thrust against Philadelphia while inoculation rendered Washington's army ineffective. Inoculations, with their concomitant impact on the army's size, worried the two lawmakers more than "any other thing as it makes us weak and will keep us so for sometime."[56]

By early March, variolation, coupled with expiring enlistments and the departure of most of the militia, left Washington with fewer than a thousand Virginian Continentals in five understrength regiments and the remnants of three other battalions. Pennsylvania and New Jersey militias augmented this meager force, but in Washington's dim view, "They come and go when they please." Shielded behind the Watchung Mountains, the Patriots' tiny force enjoyed safety only through British ignorance. Otherwise, the commander in chief believed his opponents "would never suffer us to remain unmolested." So weak was Washington's army that he felt it imprudent to admit its situation on paper for fear of revealing its true strength to his enemy.[57] Returns submitted on March 15 indicated the Patriots had only 2,543 regulars and 976 militia manning positions stretching from Princeton to Chatham.[58] Fortunately for the Rebels, the screen of militia troops east of the Watchungs, and British quiescence, kept the army safe from enemy attack throughout late winter and early spring.

On April 26, Thomas Davis, an ensign in the Fifteenth Virginia Regiment at Morristown, angrily questioned what had caused "the delay of the Southern troops. Her Virginia follows into lethargy, her brave ones all asleep?"[59] Although the officer did not realize it, disease and the complications wrought by preventative measures, rather than lethargy, bore responsibility for hindering the deployment of fresh troops. In Connecticut, Jonathan Trumbull lamented the "strange delay of raising and completing the standing Continental Army" imposed by the combination of enlistment expirations and inoculation. He hoped that the measure would "prove effectual."[60] It did. By late spring, the smallpox crisis had passed. On June 17, Washington reported to Brigadier General Parsons in Connecticut that in northern New Jersey there remained "but one woman in the whole army who has it [smallpox] and she will be removed."[61] The same day he similarly informed Maj. Gen. Israel Putnam that "the camp is thought to be entirely clear of infection and the country pretty much so."[62] While the recruitment delays had caused much consternation, the new army of three-year enlistees promised to be healthier than the levies of 1775 and 1776.

During the spring of 1777, the arrival of freshly inoculated troops induced further improvements to Continental quartering methods. These men, enlisted for "three years, or the war," presaged the transformation of the Continental Army into a fully permanent, regular force. The haphazard mustering of recruits resulting from inoculation, however, produced a poorly disciplined, disorganized army. As these new regiments gathered in northern New Jersey, Patriot leaders sought to organize their men into orderly, disciplined, and sanitary camps that surpassed in size and concentration any witnessed previously in the war. Since many of these men had been rushed forward to New Jersey piecemeal, the spring camps in that state would provide recruits with their first opportunity for proper discipline and drill.

The swelling of Continental numbers coincided with the arrival of warmer weather. This allowed Washington's men to exchange their billets for tent encampments in the neighboring countryside.[63] Continental officers immediately addressed sanitation in the new camps. Washington warned his men that the consequences of an unsanitary camp near town "may be fatal, as well to the soldiery, as the inhabitants." Throughout April, he directed camp-wide cleaning that removed "garbage and filth" as well as "dead horses, dogs, or any kind of carrion in and about the town."[64]

With the army still spread throughout northern New Jersey, detached units had to address order and hygiene on their own. Farther from the commander in chief's gaze, local commanders assumed responsibility for implementing these measures. Virginia officers operating near Bound Brook chided men who made a habit of "lying or sitting on the ground, often on such as is wet or cold." In the Third Virginia, Col. Daniel Morgan impressed upon his officers "that they will take care that their men in like manner for the future appear decent & clean on the parade as nothing attends so much to the health of soldiers as cleanliness."[65] Nevertheless, the dispersal of Continental camps made facilitating discipline and order difficult.[66] Continentals frequently returned from sentry duty drunk, leading to the flogging of "three or four men every day," according to Rhode Island sergeant Jeremiah Greenman.[67]

During April and May, recruits flowed into the region, increasing the Continentals' numbers substantially. On May 20, Washington reported a total strength of 8,188.[68] Two days later, he arranged these units in eight brigades from Virginia, Pennsylvania, Maryland, and New Jersey. Major Generals Nathanael Greene, Adam Stephen, John Sullivan, Benjamin Lincoln, and Lord Stirling served as division commanders, directing two brigades each. Henry Knox commanded the field artillery.[69] The commander in chief once more had an army large enough to contend with the British. The newly minted Rebel brigades nevertheless required further training before they could undertake active operations.

Washington sought to gather these troops into a single camp, at which he could streamline their instruction. Given the presence of Howe's force in New York, the commander in chief also wanted to establish a forward base from which to operate during the opening of the coming campaign. For a campsite, he selected Middlebrook, fifteen miles south of Morristown. Nestled between the southwestern slopes of the Watchungs, the area had briefly hosted both Rebel and Crown forces over the previous winter. While not as remote as Morristown, Middlebrook nevertheless enjoyed a strategic flanking position along the roads linking New York and Philadelphia, but more important, there was security afforded by the nearby hills.[70]

Events along the Hudson had demonstrated the crucial importance of camp security in the spring of 1777. While Washington marshaled his brigades in New Jersey, New England recruits had concentrated in the Hudson Highlands. In March, the commander in chief had surmised that "very commodious" barracks at Peekskill would help house the eight new Massachusetts regiments then marching to New York.[71] Unfortunately for the Patriots, British troops sailed up the Hudson on March 23, burning the Peekskill barracks and destroying significant quantities of food and equipment.[72] The Rebels therefore had to send for tents stored in Boston to be forwarded to the Hudson Highlands.[73] By June, four brigades had concentrated near Peekskill under Maj. Gen. Israel Putnam, with a strength of nearly five thousand men. With the barracks damaged, an inadequate mix of tents, shanties, and barracks at nearby posts housed this contingent.[74]

Secure at Middlebrook, Washington could confidently expect to avoid a similar embarrassment. With levies arriving in northern New Jersey throughout the spring of 1777, Continental officers again turned their attention to shelter, sanitation, discipline, and strategy. As the army's first task, officers needed to find ground suitable for encamping more than eight thousand men. Washington assigned his trusted subordinate, Maj. Gen. Nathanael Greene, along with deputy quartermaster Col. Clement Biddle, to Middlebrook on May 24 to inspect the ground and begin laying out the camp. The Watchungs' foothills provided an ideal setting for good campgrounds, and Greene and Biddle rapidly selected a locale suitable for the army's tent arrangements. Greene showed a strong ability to read the terrain for suitable camp geography. Middlebrook was to make for a more convenient and healthier locale for the Continentals' tent city than the sites Thomas Mifflin had selected in New York a year before. Mifflin himself was absent from camp in Philadelphia.[75]

At the camp's opening in late May, it first appeared as if tent shortages would again present a problem. A British raid on Danbury, Connecticut, in April destroyed a significant stock of Continental camp equipage that had been earmarked for the coming campaign. Greene informed Washington on May 25 of a "great want of tents" among several of the brigades that had arrived in camp.[76] This proved only a temporary inconvenience, as Congress procured new tents from North American and foreign sources. Quartermaster General Mifflin noted on May 27 that he had gathered 4,035 tents for operations in the Middle States, with an additional 500 on hand in Philadelphia. Another 500 were due to arrive from France. The only shortfall was the marquees, only 35 in number, which was too few for all of the army's officers.[77] The quartermaster's efforts ameliorated the shortage that Greene had decried on May 25. At the end of the month, Washington recorded the arrival of 2,306 tents, more than needed. In this one item, at least, the chronically undersupplied force under Washington enjoyed an adequate stock.[78]

This bounty of tents came at the price of shortchanging the Northern Army. This second sizeable Continental contingent of the war's early years also confronted a shelter crisis during the 1776–77 winter. In northern New York, an absence of civilian settlements, coupled with the region's severe climate, wore out tents and necessitated more substantial cover. After the Patriots' defeat in Canada, the Continentals encamped near Fort Ticonderoga, turning first to the fort's stone barracks, sufficient for four hundred men. Soldiers also built additional barracks on Mount Independence for another eight hundred men. Nevertheless, the hasty construction of these substantial post-and-beam structures yielded unsatisfactory shelter for the northern Continentals. Lt. Ebenezer Elmer from New Jersey described the miserable conditions inside. The barracks, he wrote, featured "a room so open, I could not sleep."[79]

As the Ticonderoga barracks could hold only 1,200 men, the Northern Army sought alternative forms of cover. Turning to the abundant resources of New York's forests, Rebel troops placed boards and bark over their tents to provide protection from the weather, with grass and leaves added for insulation. Some soldiers made further refinements with wood or stone floors or dug their tents into the earth. Organization remained poor. Dimensions, placement of doors, roofing materials, and presence of windows and bunks varied from hut to hut. Whether soldiers used bark, boards, or cut wood, roofs leaked throughout the winter. One soldier returning from a hospital stay found his hut fully occupied, forcing him to take shelter on a piece of bark lying between two huts. These methods reflected similar techniques used in this theater a generation earlier, indicating the persistent castrametation problems that the environmental setting inflicted upon armies operating in that region. So poor was the encampment's condition by May 1777 that Maj. Gen. Horatio Gates, now assigned to the Northern Department, wrote to Washington, imploring his superior for tents to augment the meager cover available at Fort Ticonderoga.[80] These huts, which Gates described as "made of earth and flimsily put together," failed to meet the army's needs. After a winter of use, Gates claimed the buildings were "mostly in ruins."[81]

The major general's request for tents again raised the issue of shelter's impact on Continental strategy. Washington tied the means of cover to the Northern and Main Armies' prospective strategic posture for the coming campaign season. Presuming the northern force would keep stationary through the summer, Washington argued that they could rely on fixed structures. By contrast, the expected mobile campaign in the Middle Department meant "nothing but tents can serve us." Overestimating the capacity of the Ticonderoga barracks, as well as the Northern Army's construction abilities, the commander in chief claimed that Fort Ticonderoga could accommodate up to four thousand men, provided Gates ordered the barracks' expansion or augmented them with huts.[82] Ultimately Congress intervened to alleviate Gates's shelter shortage, sending one thousand tents to the Northern Army at the end of May.[83] In June, with the Champlain Valley now "well supplied" with tents, Congress diverted new tents to Washington's force in New Jersey.[84]

With their men properly sheltered, Continental officers at Middlebrook turned to the second crucial aspect of castrametation: maintaining soldiers' health in camp. By late spring, inoculation had successfully diminished smallpox's prevalence among the newly raised forces making their way to New Jersey. However, illnesses resulting from poor camp hygiene and improper food preservation, such as dysentery and typhus, presented new threats during May and June 1777. The newly rebuilt army remained unskilled at upholding sanitary conditions within camp, further contributing to illness and reinforcing the need for discipline. Consequently, Nathanael Greene observed on May 25 that "the camp fever begins to prevail among some of the troops." Unless the troops were brought to order soon, health problems similar to those witnessed outside New York in 1776 would return.

With the past year's experience, Greene perceived that camp fevers represented a significant threat to the army's operational capabilities at the outset of the active campaign season. He implored Washington to take measures to reduce illness in camp. For Greene, health stood as "an object of great importance," for a sick army was "a burden to themselves and the state that employed them." Just as smallpox had threatened the army during the winter, springtime illness promised to rob the country "of many useful inhabitants and the army of many brave soldiers." The Rhode Islander linked some of the troops' sickness to the presence of rancid meat, a result of poor preservation practices.[85]

For a remedy, Greene drew on European castrametation knowledge gleaned from military enlightenment texts. Informed by Maurice de Saxe's *Mes Rêveries*, Greene suggested the widespread use of vinegar to ensure better preservation of meat.[86] Apparently swayed by this argument, Washington ordered Greene's recommendations put into practice on May 30, directing the commissary general to procure a supply of vinegar for the army at Middlebrook.[87] To further improve soldiers' health within camp, the Continentals also used the local environment to augment their rations. Noting that the surrounding New Jersey countryside offered an abundance of vegetables such as French sorrel, lamb's-quarter, and watercress, Washington recommended soldiers gather these items, all "very conducive to health," and use them to make an "agreeable salad." This would prevent scurvy as well as "all putrid disorders."[88]

In addition to safe food supplies, the Rebels also needed fresh water. Here, Humphrey Bland's *Treatise of Military Discipline* informed the steps Continentals took to prevent the spread of waterborne illness. Washington ordered his brigadiers to appoint guards to watch over springs to prevent men from contaminating them by using them to wash their utensils. Men were also to remove all animal carcasses from camp and bury them deeply.[89] In addition, Washington issued detailed instructions for the placement of the camp slaughterhouse, as well as for maintaining latrines. By following these steps, Washington expected that the Continentals could keep the Middlebrook camp "in all respects clean, and free from everything noxious, or offensive."[90] Brigade and regimental orders reinforced Washington's injunctions, imparting to soldiers the importance of sweeping camp streets and keeping tents, uniforms, and bodies clean.[91] Through the army's adaptation to the local environment, and officers' employment of military wisdom, the Continentals began to produce a healthier camp.

As the Middlebrook camp took shape in mid-June, Washington directed his attention to improving the administration of hospitals near Middlebrook. He made the highest-ranking officer in the vicinity of army hospitals, with an assisting officer, responsible for the "good government" of medical facilities. Their duties included maintaining order among convalescing soldiers, stationing guards, and reporting cases of neglect and abuse to superior officers.[92] To augment the staffs at army hospitals at nearby Mendham and Black River, Washington increased the administrative staffs and nurses.[93] Through this combination of inoculation, food preservation, and stringent camp sanitation practices, the growing Continental Army at Middlebrook minimized the spread of illness.

Beyond health, Continental commanders also used the concentration the encampment afforded to improve order and discipline. During the first days of the Middlebrook camp, Greene exercised direct command while Washington stayed at his headquarters in Morristown. Greene's brief time leading the army in camp demonstrated a clear awareness of the administrative attention needed to manage a large, concentrated regular army. He implemented a strict regimentation of daily life in camp and established routines for camp guards, pickets, and patrols.[94]

Washington officially transferred his headquarters from Morristown to Middlebrook on May 29 and issued a series of general orders building on Greene's earlier directives. With many new units drawn together for the first time, the commander in chief expected "punctual regard" to be paid to all orders.[95] All new officers present in camp, if not attending to specific duties, were to study veterans and hone their craft. Regiments were to parade each day following a roll call, with absentees punished. While assembled on parade, the new levies were to "behave well in their ranks," and stay "*silent, steady,* and *orderly.*" Once a day, the men were to take part in drill exercises informed by their brigadier's chosen manual, with an emphasis on marching and forming. While this process ensured that all units experienced similar levels of training, the absence of a single manual shared by all units limited the effectiveness of drill.[96] Regiments appointed officers "best acquainted with maneuvers" to oversee drill.[97] This problem would not be rectified until the adoption of Friedrich Wilhelm von Steuben's *Regulations for the Order and Discipline of the Troops of the United States* in 1779.

Soldiers in camp faced strict regulation of their schedules. To ensure a prompt turnout at morning reveille, all lights in camp were to be put out by 9 p.m. Washington assigned a provost marshal to patrol the camp and surrounding area and round up disorderly persons, curtail sutlers from selling liquor, and enforce all other camp rules.[98] Company musicians, whose playing Washington criticized as "being in general very bad," were to redouble their efforts to improve. New orders on June 4 detailed specific instructions for drummers for the beating of morning reveille and evening retreat.[99] Regimental officers were directed to keep an account of ammunition held by their men, while company captains were told to keep a list of their subordinates' clothes and inspect their uniforms every Sunday.[100]

Washington also stepped up camp security. He ordered each unit stationed along the boundary of the encampment to post guards at every entrance to the complex. These guards combated desertion, a growing problem for the army. On May 31 courts-martial held eleven trials for desertion and another for quitting a post without permission. Guards also prevented unauthorized civilians from entering camp out of fears of espionage and undermining camp discipline. Anyone in camp unable to provide a satisfactory explanation for their presence was, as per general orders, "to be confined and reported to the nearest brigadier." Both officers and men suffered reprimands from Washington for the "unsoldierly practice of straggling from camp." Anyone found more than a mile outside the lines would be charged for disobedience of orders.[101]

Overall, the series of orders Greene and Washington issued during late May and early June established new standards for routine activity in camp and thereby began to instill regularity into an army containing many recent levies. The Patriots thus overcame the disorganization that had reigned during the period of inoculation and recruitment in March. The steady stream of orders and regulations also fostered a greater sense of regularization among officers and men. This would help make the lackadaisical habits of the largely militia army of 1775 and 1776 a relic of the past.

The army at Middlebrook received its first test in mid-June, as Howe concentrated 18,000 men at New Brunswick and threatened an overland march through the heart of the state. Washington and his commanders responded by further refining their defensive strategy, relying on the rough terrain of the Watchungs to anchor their position. Here, as Washington explained to Brig. Gen. Benedict Arnold, "Our position is strong, and with a little labor will be rendered much more so."[102] The Watchung Mountains to the north and east effectively blocked any potential British advance in that direction, while Middlebrook's strong natural position deterred an enemy attack on the camp. A British participant commented that the Rebels were "very strongly situated amongst the blue [Watchung] mountains."[103] Maj. Gen. John Sullivan's detachment in the Sourland Mountains promised to slow any British advance to the south and allow the Main Army at Middlebrook to fall on Howe's rear.[104]

The Continental Army leveraged its well-defended camp, central location, rough terrain, and militia support into a careful strategy that stymied Howe's thrust without risking a general engagement. The Austrians and Prussians would have recognized this strategy from their own experiences in the latter years of the Seven Years' War. A commander as cautious as Howe was unlikely to risk his small and hard-to-replace army in a direct assault on a well-defended camp perched in the hills.

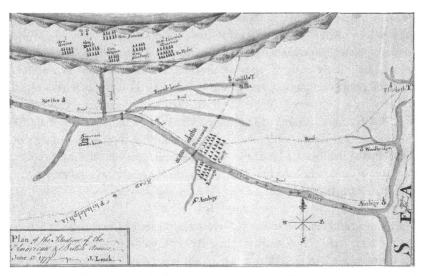

This map from June 1777 reveals the natural strength of the Continental encampments' position between the ridges of the Watchung Mountains. J. Leach, "Plan of the Situation of the American & British Armies" (June 15, 1777). Mount Vernon Ladies' Association. Gift of Richard H. Brown and Mary Jo Otsea.

Ultimately, Howe restricted his attack to a limited push down the Raritan Valley. The Patriots responded to a British advance on June 11 by keeping their regulars concentrated at Middlebrook and harassing Howe's flanks with light troops and militia.[105] Unable to draw the Continentals into an engagement, the Redcoats pulled back on June 19, evacuating New Brunswick and withdrawing to Perth Amboy. Six days later, they made another foray into New Jersey toward Westfield before returning to Staten Island. Throughout this offensive, the main body of the Continental Army kept aloof from its opponent, moving only as far as Quibbletown before returning to the Middlebrook camp. When Washington described the extended affair to his brother, he remarked that he largely spent his time "in my tent, about five weeks."[106]

With New Jersey secure, the Continental Army stood prepared to counter threats in other areas. With the army inoculated, concentrated, increasingly disciplined, and tested by the initial sparring in a new campaign season, Washington ordered his men to strike their tents and evacuate Middlebrook on July 2, 1777.[107] Initially the Patriots headed northwestward toward the Hudson Highlands before countermarching to the Delaware to contest Howe's advance on Philadelphia.[108]

While it had lasted only five weeks, the May–June 1777 encampment at Middlebrook, coming as it did after the adoption of three-year enlistments, signaled progress in the army's development. As General Greene boasted to John Adams in late May, "Our army is now encamped, and I hope will be very soon completely organized, fit for some important purpose."[109] Washington penned a similarly positive report, claiming, "The army is now on a permanent and honorable footing, and as the general has the credit of it very much at heart, he expects every officer" to lend "their aid to support the character of it."[110] Observers considered Howe's withdrawal as a signal achievement for the Continental Army. John Hancock exclaimed that should the British "be compelled to finally abandon the Jerseys," it would represent "the most explicit declaration to the whole world, that the conquest of America is not only a very distant, but unattainable object."[111]

Washington and his men learned several valuable lessons in early 1777. Selecting the New Jersey Highlands for their strategic value and defensive terrain, the army once again faced a shortage of adequate shelter and reverted to the traditional methods in billeting. Dispersing troops across northern and central New Jersey flanked Howe's army and reduced the enemy's access to forage and shelter while lessening the burden of housing every soldier in one area. Yet the spread of the army rendered it impossible to oversee drill and discipline. In addition, the small-scale fighting continued through the winter, further wearing out exhausted soldiers.

Billeting also spread diseases rapidly, forcing the implementation of an army-wide inoculation program for all soldiers, including new recruits. With the onset of a new campaign season, Washington and his subordinates concentrated the army in a large encampment in Middlebrook and streamlined training and administration. The Middlebrook encampment thereby represented a brief but important step on the Continental Army's path toward establishing itself as a viable regular force, the "respectable army" of Washington's vision. In the coming months, it would face a new challenge: how to take the castrametation lessons learned in early 1777 and apply them to winter quarters for a long-service army.

CHAPTER 4

"It Looks in Camp like Some Grand City"

1777–1778

The Middlebrook encampment provided an initial proving ground for new Continental officers and enlisted men. The next campaign soon tested them. In the summer of 1777, the scene of fighting shifted from northern New Jersey to southeastern Pennsylvania. Sir William Howe sailed up the Chesapeake Bay and landed at Head of Elk, Maryland, in late August. From there, he planned to seize Philadelphia. Unlike in previous years, the pursuing Continentals did not stumble through the summer and fall ill-covered and unclean. Tents proved effective in sheltering Washington's men on campaign. Frequent moves and improved camp maintenance alleviated the worst problems of fouled water and camp fevers.

Improvements to order and discipline set the Continentals on the path to a better showing on the battlefield. Nevertheless, Washington's army suffered several reversals in Pennsylvania. The army deployed to defend the Patriots' de facto capital but met with defeat at the Battle of Brandywine on September 11. On September 26, the British captured Philadelphia. For the next two months, Howe fought to clear his lines of communication along the Delaware River while Washington maneuvered to retake the Quaker City. The Redcoats repulsed a Patriot attack on Germantown, northwest of Philadelphia, on October 4. Washington then withdrew northward to Whitemarsh, Pennsylvania, where he remained through early December.[1]

The Rebels then found themselves in a familiar situation. The British held the region's largest city, with the Patriots expelled to the countryside. Winter approached. Washington's men would again need to secure protection from the cold in an area lacking traditional military housing infrastructure. In a departure from previous years, however, the Rebel army would not dissolve and have to be recruited from scratch. Instead, more than ten thousand troops would need winter quarters. They could not resort to waging partisan warfare with small detachments billeted in dispersed posts, as had been the case in northern New Jersey earlier in 1777. The Continental Army now strongly resembled its European counterparts. For the first time it faced the question of how to establish winter quarters with a long-service army after fighting a conventional campaign. The 1777–78 winter would soon test the Continentals' ingenuity in devising methods of housing a regular army in North America.

At Whitemarsh, Washington pondered his options for winter quarters. As he had outside Boston, he solicited input from his subordinates. On November 30, he questioned his generals as to where and how the army should spend the coming winter months. The responses he received offered three options. The first, which bore the strongest influence of contemporary European practice, suggested that the army retire from the field to a line of Pennsylvania towns stretching from Bethlehem to Lancaster, with soldiers billeted in civilian homes. This would place the Patriots' positions roughly fifty miles from Howe's men. The second option he proposed was keeping the army in the field and maintaining a camp close to Philadelphia in the Schuylkill Valley. With no significant towns present there for shelter, soldiers would remain in tents until linen could be supplanted by timber-built huts. The third option, similar to the first, recommended the army withdraw to Wilmington, Delaware, where it would billet in and around the town, with huts accommodating those soldiers who could find no space in homes and public buildings.[2]

These three seemingly simple solutions obscured what was actually a complicated problem. Should the army retire to winter quarters, which would mean putting an end to large-scale operations for the year, or should it remain in the field to continue the campaign to recover Philadelphia? As was understood at the time, retiring to winter quarters meant drawing away to towns and villages in the hinterland, while continuing active operations meant a more concentrated encampment closer to Philadelphia. If the army retired, could it find sufficient space to lodge in the region's towns? Were these towns so scattered as to hinder the concentration of the army the following year, to say nothing of maintaining discipline and training over the winter? If the towns lacked enough housing, would huts offer a satisfactory substitute? If the army stayed concentrated, what form should its shelter take, and where should it locate its encampment?

The debate over where and how to spend the winter of 1777–78 has captured several historians' attention. Benjamin Newcomb has argued that Washington balanced his generals' concerns, and through a rational selection process determined to keep the army in the field close to Philadelphia. This decision resulted in the building of an encampment along the western bank of the Schuylkill at

Valley Forge.[3] Wayne K. Bodle has complicated Newcomb's interpretation by emphasizing the role Pennsylvania politicians played in inducing Washington to place his winter camp closer to Philadelphia than he might have done otherwise.[4] Both of these interpretations distinguish between the perceived military benefits of retiring to winter quarters to rest troops and repair equipment as opposed to the political need to keep the army in the field near Philadelphia.

Operational and political interests played major roles in influencing the army's quartering decision, but so, too, did practical concerns over shelter. Most Continental generals sought to replicate European methods. Nathanael Greene, the Marquis de Lafayette, John Armstrong, William Smallwood, Anthony Wayne, Charles Scott, and Louis Duportail favored withdrawing to Wilmington. Generals John Sullivan, Johann de Kalb, William Maxwell, Henry Knox, Enoch Poor, Peter Muhlenberg, James Varnum, George Weedon, and William Woodford preferred a chain of cantonments between Lancaster and Redding. By contrast, Lord Stirling advocated a camp in the field, near Great Valley or Tredyffrin. William Irvine also expressed interest in "hutting in a strong position." Casimir Pulaski wanted to pursue a winter campaign. John Cadwalader did not submit a written response, though his later communications indicate he likely fell in the keep-the-field clique.[5]

Washington's generals did not submit their recommendations without qualification. As Newcomb has pointed out, Continental officers recognized that regardless of where the army wintered, finding suitable accommodations would pose a problem. If the troops were to quarter in the Pennsylvania interior, several generals doubted that the state's towns, even those as large as Bethlehem, Allentown, Reading, and Lancaster, contained enough structures to lodge the army. The flight of Whig refugees from Philadelphia to these locations promised to exacerbate the housing shortage. Likewise, Wilmington's small size meant that it could likely shelter no more than a fraction of the army. Wintering a permanent force of some ten thousand men proved a more substantial challenge than distributing three to four thousand short-service troops into various villages, as the Continentals had done in New Jersey in early 1777. Thus, most commanders recognized that even if the army opted to quarter in towns, it would need to supplement its billets with huts.[6]

Throughout the December 1777 debate, the officers appealed to European castrametation works, military history, and recent experience to support and clarify their plans for winter shelter. Joseph Reed, Washington's former adjutant who was now serving as a Pennsylvania delegate to Congress, cautioned against the drain a winter campaign could have on the resources of even a well-equipped army. Reed cited as an example Duke Ferdinand of Brunswick's winter 1759 campaign against the French in the Seven Years' War. While the duke's operations succeeded, they "almost destroyed the allied army by keeping the field till towards spring." Consequently, Reed advised against keeping the army concentrated in a hut encampment, since doing so carried the assumption that operations would continue throughout the cold months.[7]

By contrast, Brig. Gen. John Cadwalader of the Pennsylvania militia pressed Washington to launch a winter campaign to recover Philadelphia. Cadwalader invoked both the recent memory of Washington's attacks at Trenton and Princeton and the more remote example of Frederick the Great's December 1757 operations that culminated in the victory at Leuthen. Cadwalader believed huts would suffice as shelter for his proposed winter campaign.[8] Nathanael Greene occupied a middle ground between Reed's and Cadwalader's positions. The Rhode Islander claimed that a complete retirement into the towns of the Pennsylvania interior would undermine discipline for soldiers and officers alike and urged Washington to "remember Hannibal's army in Capua." That reference alluded to the encampment the Carthaginians occupied after their victory at Cannae in the Second Punic War, where that army's discipline eroded amid wine and women.[9] Greene expressed hope that the army could strike a balance between the rest offered by retiring to the interior and the discipline and political capital it would cultivate by maintaining a more active winter camp.

Col. Henry Emanuel Lutterloh, a German-born officer who had been serving as the army's de facto quartermaster general, drew on his European experience in formulating his response. He advised a winter retirement described as "refreshing quarters," a phrase common in military enlightenment treatises. Lutterloh justified this method by likening it to contemporary practices in use across the Atlantic.[10] The well-read Henry Knox referenced Frederick the Great's *Instructions*, quoting the King of Prussia's maxim that "the first object in winter quarters is tranquility" to further his argument that the army should not quarter so close to Philadelphia to avoid being subjected to frequent alarms. Like Greene, he hoped for a compromise solution that would not see the army abandon so much of the countryside by withdrawing to Redding or Lancaster. Hutting the army thirty miles northwest of the city near the Schuylkill seemed to Knox to promise such an alternative.[11] John Sullivan, on the other hand, recommended against putting the army into huts. To support his argument, Sullivan drew on the example of the reported "mortality among the Hessians" who had wintered in rudimentary structures at New Brunswick in early 1777.[12]

As the senior officers filed their recommendations, Lt. Col. John Laurens wrote to his father, Henry, the president of the Continental Congress, with an assessment of the army's quartering situation. As one of Washington's aides-de-camp, the young officer was well positioned to evaluate the Continentals' predicament. On December 3, he pointed out, "The season advances in which armies in general are forced to repair to more substantial shelter than tents." The Rebels' shoddy uniforms made improved cover all the more important. The younger Laurens believed retiring to cantonments deep into Pennsylvania would abandon swaths of the countryside to Howe. He expected civilians to change their allegiances out of fear, bribery, or resentment at the perception that the army had abandoned them. The lieutenant colonel therefore appeared in concord with the Pennsylvania politicians and militia generals who lobbied Washington to maintain a post in the field close to the lost capital.

To do so, however, implied the continuance of operations. Laurens warned, "Winter campaigns it is said are ominous to the best appointed and best disciplined armies." The Continentals were neither. In their current state, the troops most needed respite from the rigors of campaigning, an opportunity to drill the troops, and warm cover to make up for poor uniforms. A hard winter would leave the army diminished in numbers and health and would likely discourage enlistments. Caught between the need to rest and heal the soldiery and the imperative of securing the countryside against an aggressive foe, the army stood at an impasse in early December.[13]

Demonstrably, the Continental Army's leadership of 1777 possessed a strong understanding of military history and a solid grasp of the prevailing theories regarding the best practices for sheltering troops. Most had also garnered practical experience at Boston, the Champlain Valley, the Hudson Highlands, and northern New Jersey during the war's first two years. Consequently, they associated placing the army in winter quarters with retiring completely from the field and keeping the army concentrated in an encampment nearer Philadelphia with the intention of keeping up active operations. Most officers favoring a concentrated encampment also voiced support for a winter campaign, while those most supportive of retiring to the backcountry towns opposed late-season operations. Even Lord Stirling, whose proposal for a concentrated campsite near Tredyffrin Township closely aligned with the eventual winter camp at Valley Forge, characterized his recommendation as only a temporary expedient. He recognized that posting the army at Tredyffrin would maximize its ability to cover the countryside, deny forage to the British at Philadelphia, and maintain communications with New Jersey. Such a post remained, however, "still only an encampment." Stirling pointed out that placing the army in such an encampment "is not going into winter quarters, it is not procuring for the officers and men that comfort and opportunity of recruiting which they richly deserve after a long and fatiguing campaign." The New Jersey major general acknowledged, however, that proper winter quarters were "not in our power to give them anywhere" and, therefore, that hutting the army in the Schuylkill Valley ranked as the Patriots' best option.[14]

Ultimately, Washington decided on a compact encampment at Valley Forge. Here the army could continue to pose a threat to the British in Philadelphia and provide a reassuring presence to nearby civilian communities. No extant sources reveal Washington's reasoning behind his decision to encamp the army along the banks of the Schuylkill for the winter. Lieutenant Colonel Laurens, in his December 3 letter to his father, hinted that even at that date the commander in chief might have in mind an alternative between a full winter campaign or a complete retirement to the countryside. Laurens wrote, "We may take a position which will not absolutely expose us to a winter campaign, but furnish us excellent quarters for men at the same time that it leaves us within distance for taking considerable advantages of the enemy, and cover a valuable and extensive country." He did not state any details for fear of the letter being intercepted. Nevertheless, Laurens's message indicated that Washington was considering the possibility of an option that would keep the army near the city while providing sound lodging.[15]

Given the lateness of the season, neither the commander in chief nor his subordinates entertained building barracks as in previous winters. Instead, the Continentals would shelter in huts to be built at Valley Forge itself. By December 15, the commander in chief seems to have settled on huts for quarters, though the final location of the camp remained unsettled for another two days.[16] The form of winter quarters departed significantly from either accepted European practices or previous experiences lodging armies in North America. Had Reading and Lancaster not been flooded with refugees, and had Congress and the Pennsylvania government not pressured Washington to protect the countryside from British depredations, it is likely the Continentals would have retired to the state's interior. Likewise, had Wilmington and the surrounding towns been large enough to accommodate most of the roughly ten thousand Rebel soldiers operating in the region, the army might have cantoned in Delaware. Either option would have aligned well with the maxims of Frederick, Turpin de Crissé, and the whole of European military experience during the eighteenth century.

The Continental Army had emerged as a regular force in 1777; however, it waged a war under different circumstances than those prevailing in Europe. It had to stay mindful of civilian populations possessing fragile yet vital political sentiments. It stood answerable to a representative government. Finally, it operated in an arena lacking either the existing infrastructure for quartering or the support of a powerful fiscal-military bureaucracy as in Europe. Encamping the bulk of the army at Valley Forge carried many positives. Discipline and drill could be better effected than with the Main Army dispersed among towns, and communications could be better maintained with New Jersey and New England. Consequently, Washington chose to camp the majority of this army at Valley Forge, on the southern bank of the Schuylkill River, twenty miles northwest of Philadelphia. Two Maryland brigades under William Smallwood wintered at Wilmington, anchoring the army's right flank. Cavalry under Casimir Pulaski went to Trenton to hold the left. The rest, fourteen brigades, spent the next six months at Valley Forge.

The winter encampment represented a departure from European methods and the beginning of military shelter practices suited to waging war in North America. At the heart of this new method stood humble timber structures, log huts, of which the army would build nearly two thousand in the coming months. The army in Pennsylvania resorted to huts due to the absence of significant towns for billeting in the area where it chose to winter, the proven insufficiency of tents as winter shelter, and the lateness of the season that precluded the construction of more substantial barracks. Huts had, over the first years of the conflict, grown increasingly important to Continental castrametation. Rudimentary timber structures had supplanted more substantial shelter around New York City in 1776 and had afforded the Northern Army the bulk of its housing outside Fort Ticonderoga during the previous winter. Outside the winter months, soldiers had also used huts on campaign when tents were unavailable.

Nevertheless, so far in the war, the army had used huts only to supplement other methods of shelter rather than as its chief means of quartering. Early-war huts had varied in quality and had often been made from bark, brush, and sod. They closely resembled the shanties that European armies had used at various points when lacking tents during the seventeenth and eighteenth centuries. As Continental officers debated winter quarters in December 1777, even advocates of huts recognized that these structures provided less-than-ideal shelter. Only Maj. Gen. John Armstrong of the Pennsylvania militia gave full support to hutting through the winter. Provided the weather remained dry, Armstrong believed huts would be "no means incompatible with health" and described them as "most in character for the Army."[17] Lafayette referred to the opinions of "doctors, and American ones who know the manners and physical constitution of our soldiers," that "nothing is so comfortable as well made huts," but given the method's uncommonness in Europe, he preferred billeting in Lancaster or Wilmington.[18] Officers more familiar with North American operations did not share this optimistic view. Sullivan characterized huts as "exceedingly unhealthy and are at best but a miserable shelter from the inclemency of the weather."[19] Smallwood likewise supposed the method would "impair the men's health."[20] Yet no other option palatable to either military men or political leaders presented itself. No commander questioned how to supply such a concentration through the winter, although this would soon prove one of the army's biggest problems.

The Main Army did not arrive at Valley Forge and begin making quarters until December 17. Washington's general orders of that date drew attention to the fact that huts had hitherto provided less-than-satisfactory winter shelter. Refining these structures into decent housing would thereby require hard work and attention to detail. The commander in chief recognized that the army had no other option and declared that the Continentals "must make ourselves the best shelter in our power. With activity and diligence huts may be erected that will be warm and dry." Whatever problems wintering in huts might bring, Washington hoped the chosen arrangement would protect the countryside from the British and leave the army less vulnerable to a surprise attack than if it were divided into smaller cantonments.[21]

The following day's general orders established the plan by which troops were to build their winter encampment. Previous instances of hutting had proceeded with little direction. At Ticonderoga and Peekskill, men had received little instruction in the size, placement, or composition of their shelters. At Valley Forge, the commander in chief established detailed guidelines outlining the duties of officers and men at all levels. Washington delegated to his subordinates the task of ensuring orderly living arrangements. Division commanders were to appoint a field grade officer in each of their brigades to superintend the laying out of brigade camps. Each regimental commander was in turn to select an officer to oversee hut construction. The brigade superintendents held the authority to mark out where each hut in their respective camps was to be built so "that uniformity and order may be observed." Colonels, with their company captains, were immediately to divide the rank and file into groups of twelve men, termed a "mess." One mess would occupy one hut, which the men would erect themselves.[22]

Washington's general orders of December 18 also specified the huts' dimensions and suggested appropriate building materials. Previously, soldiers had built shanties based on no single model, but the Valley Forge huts were to each stand sixteen feet long, fourteen feet wide, and six feet tall. Logs were to constitute the huts' side walls, with clay sealing the interstices between the timbers. Each hut was to have a fireplace, likewise made of logs and coated in clay. Split-oak slabs were to make the doors, which were to uniformly face company streets. To incentivize men to build their huts quickly, the mess in each regiment completing its hut first and in a "most workmanlike manner" would receive twelve dollars. Washington's officers failed to settle on a method of providing roofing for the huts. Boards made for the best covering, but would likely prove difficult to obtain in the region. Washington therefore offered a $100 cash reward to any soldier or officer who could recommend a roofing substitute that could be made more cheaply and quickly than boards.[23]

With nothing in castrametation texts to offer a blueprint, the Valley Forge plan resembled a well-ordered tent encampment, with every hut to be placed in precise order, aligned to produce streets within each brigade camp. Enlisted men's huts were to lie in lines, with officers' huts to the rear. Brigade staffs, regimental field officers, and regimental staffs were allocated one hut each. Captains, lieutenants, and ensigns of two companies were expected to share a single hut. To house the rest of the army, Washington apportioned one hut for every twelve enlisted men and noncommissioned officers. Generals were allotted one hut each. In practice, most senior officers eventually lodged in nearby houses and inns. They would continue to do so throughout the war.[24]

Washington's general orders of December 17 and 18 provided an outline for the layout of winter camps that would prove worthy of reuse in subsequent winters. Translating the plans into reality, however, presented difficulties for an army whose officers and men alike had never taken part in such an endeavor. As Washington had arrived at his decision for a hut encampment at a late date, neither he nor his subordinates had prepared the materials necessary to build this camp. Most notably, a shortage of axes and other building tools retarded the huts' construction even though timber stood in abundance around Valley Forge. Jonathan Libby, a Massachusetts enlisted man, recalled "building our huts in the best manner we could without tools or any material."[25] Jonathan Todd, a nineteen-year-old Connecticut surgeon, provided a vivid depiction of the difficulties of hut construction. He wrote his father on December 25, optimistically stating that he expected "in a few days to be comfortable" but admitted that his comrades had "nothing convenient to work with." Todd was to share his new home with other regimental staff, including an adjutant, a paymaster, a quartermaster, and two doctors. This group had "but one dull axe" with which to build their shelter, and Todd admitted he knew not when they would finish construction. Despite the young physician's optimistic outlook, the next day he related that a black soldier had died in his tent the night before, the first fatality the Connecticut men had suffered since arriving at Valley Forge.[26]

Todd's letter helps highlight the diversity of the army and its log-hut city. Despite Congressional proscriptions, recruiting officers fulfilled their quotas with black and Native American recruits as well as white. These men had marched and fought throughout the active campaign season and now huddled in the cold alongside their white comrades. Extant sources give no indication that enlisted men segregated their tents or huts by race, and it stands likely that the common soldiers wintered in integrated lodgings.[27]

The log-hut city included female residents as well as male. Every eighteenth-century army featured women camp followers who accompanied troops on campaign. Some were soldiers' wives. Others were unattached but sought the work opportunities the army provided, such as nursing and washing clothes. As Washington's Continentals developed into a more regular force in 1777 and 1778, the number of camp followers increased. With men now serving three-year terms, fewer women could afford to stay home. Thus, Valley Forge must have provided many women with their first experience of winter quarters. Scholars estimate roughly four hundred women and an undetermined number of children stayed at the cantonment on the Schuylkill. Washington's orders did not explain how these camp followers were to be housed. Since tents presented such a poor option, most women and children might have crowded into the huts alongside the men. Alternatively, they might have built more rudimentary structures common to earlier camps.[28]

Administrative foul-ups, inaccessible supplies, and soldiers' own lack of skill exacerbated the tool shortages that impeded hut building. Some units found that their officers had improperly laid out the ground upon which they were to build their huts, delaying construction until officers could determine final locations for construction.[29] Men also had to travel long distances to acquire their building materials. A Massachusetts lieutenant remarked in his diary that his comrades would have completed their huts in under the ten days it actually took them had they not had to travel over a mile for the nearest supplies of stone and timber.[30] Guard duty and snowstorms also disrupted construction. In the interim, some men occupied their huts before they were finished, opting to stretch their tent cloth over the log walls for a modicum of protection.[31] Officers frequently, though not always, waited for their men to complete their huts before beginning their own. For example, Capt. Paul Brigham of Connecticut did not begin his until January 5.[32]

When units selected good hut sites and received the necessary equipment, construction proceeded smoothly. Sgt. Jeremiah Greenman of Rhode Island recorded arriving in "a thick woods" on December 19. He and his comrades began work two days later. They received axes, and Greenman did not complain of any deficiency of this item. The Ocean State troops moved into their new homes at the end of the month. Greenman described the new regiment's encampment as "our huts or little town." Overall, the Rhode Islanders' experience seems to have been the exception rather than the rule.[33]

Occupants of the camp recognized the novelty of an entire army building its winter quarters at the close of a campaign season. A Connecticut surgeon characterized the camp as a "log city, part of which is as regular as Philadelphia."[34] Capt. William Gifford of the Third New Jersey Regiment highlighted the army's late-season construction of winter quarters as "an instance of the kind hardly ever known in any country whatever." The captain nevertheless judged the new shelters to be "pretty comfortable" and compared favorably with the tents in which they had taken cover during their first days at Valley Forge.[35] An ensign from Massachusetts declared, "It looks in camp like some grand city."[36] The rank and file seem to have viewed the new shelters optimistically at the winter's outset. A corporal wrote his brother in late January 1778 that "we have got into huts which I expect we shall remain in till spring, which are very comfortable."[37]

Several observers commented on soldiers' laboring to erect their own shelters. A Hessian serving in Philadelphia, Maj. Carl Leopold Bauermeister, recognized the soldiers who "have been encouraged with cash rewards to build solid huts."[38] Another Hessian officer, Capt. Friedrich von Muenchhausen, remarked on the novelty of Washington's army staying at Valley Forge and building huts for the winter rather than retiring. He described the post as "a very advantageous position."[39] In Rebel lines, Lt. Henry Sewall of Massachusetts noted in his diary in early January that he had arrived in camp to find the "troops in huts of their own building."[40] Rhode Island chaplain Ebenezer David likewise commented, "Each mess builds their own," and pointed out the monetary bonus for the mess responsible for the best-built hut in each regiment. While David believed the army's position at Valley Forge was vulnerable, he recognized that that the presence of refugees in Pennsylvania's unoccupied towns precluded the possibility of billeting the army at those locales.[41]

The novel camp along the Schuylkill elicited negative commentary as well. Sir William Howe reportedly referred to his opponents' winter quarters as "log town" while he resided in the comfortable confines of Philadelphia.[42] Captain Muenchhausen wrote that he had heard that the Rebels "do not like the huts they have built in the hills of Valley Forge." He blamed the bad housing, along with an absence of rum and poor clothing, for an increase in desertion.[43] Thomas Paine likened the soldiers building the camp to a "family of beavers," given the troops' frenzied construction. He described the camp as a "curious collection of buildings, in the true rustic order."[44] New Jersey statesman Elias Boudinot criticized the new shelters as "huts of sod."[45] Lafayette referred to the huts as "little shanties that are scarcely gayer than dungeon cells."[46]

Several officers despaired of the hard labor needed to build the camp at the outset of winter. Capt. Samuel Shaw of the Third Continental Artillery recalled, "It was a considerable exertion for the remnant of an army, exhausted and worn down by the severity of a long and unsuccessful campaign, to sit down in a wood, and in the latter end of December, to build themselves houses."[47] Brig. Gen. Enoch Poor feared his men would take up to five weeks to build their huts out of "hundreds of standing trees," lamenting that they would have to undertake such a task when up to a third of his New Hampshire Brigade lacked proper clothes. "Your heart would ache for them," he wrote on December 17.[48]

Brig. Gen. George Weedon of Virginia contrasted the Valley Forge camp with traditional quarters that afforded an army greater repose. "Our present position subjects us to a winter's campaign," he complained on January 4.[49] Col. Henry Beekman Livingston of the Fourth New York Regiment noted the superior shelter the enemy had obtained in Philadelphia, writing that the British had "played the soldier sufficiently to secure them the best quarters."[50]

Brig. Gen. Jedediah Huntington took a particularly dismissive view of the decision to winter in huts at Valley Forge. Huntington admitted to Connecticut governor Jonathan Trumbull in mid-December that he was "not in the best of humor" due to the army's decision to keep the field through winter rather than retire to back towns. Confining the British to Philadelphia to save "three or four counties, already stripped," did not strike the officer as worth the health, convenience, and refreshment sacrificed by eschewing a retirement to proper winter quarters. Hutting the army struck him as a political expedient done at the behest of Congress. Like several of his comrades, Huntington appealed to military history, pointing out that few armies had ever fought two battles like Brandywine and Germantown, in which the Continentals had held their own despite facing a foe possessing superior discipline and numbers. In such circumstances, in Huntington's opinion, the Continentals now needed a refreshing winter spent away from the enemy, not one spent expending their limited strength chasing down British foraging parties.[51]

A week later, Huntington's mood had soured further. Washington's decision to winter at Valley Forge led the Connecticut brigadier to direct his ire toward his commanding officer. He complained to his brother Joshua on December 20 that "the general seems resolved to keep us together if possible. Whether it is for the best or not time will discover." Huntington believed the army was in need of "great repairs" and declared himself "sorry we have not better quarters." He reiterated his claim that a post at Valley Forge would not deter British foraging operations.[52] That same day, he remarked to his father, "I have gone to build me a house in the woods. What do you think of the army's making two thousand log houses in all the regularity of an encampment?"[53]

Huntington's comments revealed that the Valley Forge encampment had produced a built form for the Continental's winter quarters that differed from those of contemporary armies. Indeed, the Patriot army had adopted a structure largely unseen in European military practice for centuries. Lewis Lochée, a military enlightenment writer whose 1778 *Essay on Castrametation* synthesized various European treatises on the subject, considered log huts to be of only marginal utility. Lochée attributed huts to Roman practice, distinguishing the tent encampments Roman legions used while on summer campaign with the more substantial huts employed during colder months, the *castra hiberna*. Lochée relegated the use of log huts to history, remarking, "The Greeks and Romans once made use of both tents and huts; but as they declined in military spirit, they gradually neglected that practice, and quartered their troops in towns and villages." In contemporary European warfare, armies used huts only while engaged in an active campaign late in the year. Such structures provided more protection than cloth tents, but greater concentration and less permanence than dispersed winter quarters. Lochée described these structures as having thatched roofs made of straw or brush, and when hastily built were often dug into the earth or composed of sod for cover. Armies generally avoided remaining in huts through the winter. Such buildings erected late in the season often featured damp interiors, which were, according to Lochée, "of course, unhealthy for the soldiers." The course of the winter would prove Lochée correct.[54]

By early January, most of Washington's enlisted men had succeeded in erecting their new shelters. On December 30, Col. Timothy Pickering found that "a considerable number" of men enjoyed "warm, comfortable huts," but others had made little progress in construction. Pickering blamed deployments to outposts near Philadelphia and tool shortages for the delay.[55] John Laurens reported on January 1 that the soldiers had nearly finished building their "good huts." The camp structures varied from brigade to brigade, however, with the North Carolina troops in particular being "the most backward in their build-ings," for which the lieutenant colonel blamed a "want of sufficient energy."[56] In contrast, the Connecticut line had apparently built its new homes well. Brig. Gen. Jedidiah Huntington's hard stance against wintering in the field softened by mid-January, when he informed the governor of his home state that "the army are in comfortable quarters of their own making."[57]

Jonathan Todd provided the best extant description of a Valley Forge hut in a January 19 letter to his father. He emphasized the uniformity in construction, "built nearly after the same model as the others." The cabin stood eighteen feet long and sixteen wide. This description departed from the prescribed dimen-sions in general orders. It remains unclear if Todd's mess had built theirs to a different size or if he simply provided inexact measurements in his letter. The hut featured a partition dividing the interior into two rooms. Chimneys and hearths formed walls at either end of the structure. The doorway, partition, and floor were all made of split logs. The young surgeon proudly stated that the whole structure had been built with "one poor axe and no other tools." The lack of equipment meant that no more than three men at a time could work. He admitted, however, that the roof made of wooden slabs covered with turf was "not the best in wet weather."[58]

Most accounts indicate soldiers finished their huts in two weeks or less. Later winter cantonments witnessed similar progress despite a more experienced

The modern-day replica huts at Valley Forge exhibit the structures' rudimentary construction. "Reproduction Soldiers' Hut." Valley Forge National Historical Park, Valley Forge, Pennsylvania. Author's collection.

soldiery and more plentiful tools. It therefore stands to reason that the troops at Valley Forge rushed to put up their huts, and construction quality likely suffered. The roofing issue went unsolved through the winter, with huts exhibiting coverings of turf, wooden planks, or even tent cloth. Whatever the material, roofs commonly leaked. Door and chimney placements within huts varied widely. Many units chose to excavate deep foundations for their huts to add extra insulation from the elements. Doing so left hut interiors vulnerable to flooding and mud seepage during the spring.[59] Indeed, Lt. Samuel Armstrong complained of a mid-February rainstorm that "made it very bad walking" in his hut, where the water level had risen above his shoe tops. Rain seeping in through a leaky roof had put out the fire.[60] Modern experiments with reproduced huts at Valley Forge have, however, found that the structures maintained warm interiors, with indoor temperatures exceeding the outside by up to fifty degrees Fahrenheit during the day and thirty degrees at night. A properly built hut might have leaked in the rain, but as long as timber fueled its hearth, it provided a substantial upgrade over tents.[61]

Few huts were built to exact specifications. Archaeological work has largely confirmed that huts deviated from the dimensions and arrangements

Washington stipulated. Some messes sunk their shelters into the ground while others did not. Hearths varied in placement on different walls and even in corners, with some huts apparently containing none. Hut alignments deviated from the expected straight lines. Within brigade camps, one study found the huts' "overall layout seems without plan or purpose." Material evidence supports what the written record suggests. Soldiers constructed the Valley Forge encampment having made little preparation and holding little experience. Troops rushed to get their dwellings finished at the expense of adhering to Washington's guidelines.[62]

After the men finished their huts, Washington ordered the construction of further infrastructure to support the army at Valley Forge. Most crucial were hospitals. Washington had notified Congress that the army suffered from a lack of medical supplies, leaving it unable to treat mild illnesses without sending sick soldiers to distant hospitals in the Pennsylvania interior. Doing so led to a dearth of manpower at Valley Forge and encouraged desertion.[63] To rectify this inconvenience, on January 9 the commander in chief ordered every brigade to select ground and begin building hospitals as soon as possible. Even these temporary timber structures would improve over carting ill men over snow-covered roads to far-off towns.[64]

The army needed convenient medical care due to the increasing health concerns it faced in camp. Problems began within weeks of the army's arrival. The struggle to build huts amid winter conditions with resources, energy, and uniforms depleted from an exhausting campaign season left the Continentals vulnerable to illness. In late January, Jonathan Todd complained of "the regiment growing more sickly" at a time when the unit's senior physician had departed camp.[65]

Smallpox again menaced, though to a lesser extent than it had in early 1777. While most veteran Continentals had been inoculated, new arrivals presented a risk. The army's presence also threatened uninoculated Pennsylvania civilians. With soldiers concentrated into damp huts and dirty campgrounds, and local inhabitants passing through daily, Valley Forge appeared primed for a significant outbreak. Washington and his officers drew on previous years' experience in combating *variola*. In late December, the general pressed state governors to oversee the inoculation of new levies before their departure for the army.[66] Despite the problems encountered with the disease in early 1777, officers had sent vulnerable soldiers to the Main Army against Washington's orders. Such carelessness laid a newly arrived regiment low with the disease in late December. Overburdened Continental hospitals could ill afford to take on new patients.[67]

Washington nevertheless chose to inoculate vulnerable troops in camp. With the threat of a major outbreak growing, on January 6, the commander in chief ordered regimental surgeons to make returns of all men in their units who had yet to suffer the illness.[68] Within two weeks, inoculations were underway at Valley Forge, busying the already overworked physicians in camp. The new brigade hospital huts at least provided shelter for recovering patients. The army also set up smallpox hospitals in nearby houses.[69] One Massachusetts soldier recalled undergoing inoculation on January 21, after which he "retired into the country and had it very favorable."[70] Capt. Benjamin Farnum likewise recorded "taking physic" during the last days of January in preparation for his inoculation. His fellow officers underwent the procedure on January 23 and 29. Officers and men alike recovered while huddled in their leaky lodgings through February.[71]

Despite the huts' shortcomings, they provided necessary cover for an army chronically short of good uniforms. In late January, one Continental officer described the status of clothing in the New Jersey Brigade as a "truly alarming" situation. With no stocks due to arrive, the men of the brigade grew "more and more naked." No doubt the strenuous efforts to build huts, maintain camp, and wage a vigorous partisan war in the countryside all wore out the soldiers' meager clothes. The brigade lacked coats, jackets, and blankets. Given such conditions, soldiers might have been best served by keeping to their huts.[72]

Clothing shortages represented a small component of the myriad of supply difficulties the Continental Army encountered at Valley Forge. Indeed, the poorly clad, half-starved Patriot soldier shivering through the cold months remains engrained in the public imagination of the 1777–78 winter. Scholars have commonly attributed these conditions to poor administration in the Quartermaster Department coupled with bad weather. Quartermaster General Thomas Mifflin resigned in October 1777, but Congress failed to appoint a replacement. Commissary General Joseph Trumbull had likewise resigned in August. Maj. Gen. Nathanael Greene eventually accepted the head quartermaster post in late March 1778 after much cajoling. Col. Jeremiah Wadsworth took charge of the commissary the following month. In the interim, the army passed most of the winter, especially the crucial months at the encampment's outset, without experienced officers in charge of the departments that kept the army fed. Washington, his subordinates, the Pennsylvania government, and Congress all attempted to rectify supply problems through the winter, but their ill-defined and often overlapping authorities were constantly at odds.[73]

Compounding these administrative issues, the army wintered in a region that had witnessed five months of active campaigning by both the Continentals and the British. The latter had only established a reliable line of communication down the Delaware in November and had therefore largely relied on Pennsylvania farms for their food during the early months of the campaign.

In the words of Jeremiah Wadsworth, the army was doomed to winter in "a starved country."[74]

The placement of the encampment itself also contributed to these shortages. As historian John Shy has pointed out, the inadequacy of North American transportation networks and the shortage of human and animal labor to facilitate transportation likely contributed significantly to supply problems, particularly during the winter months when weather hindered movement over dirt roads. In the rush to put the army under cover in December 1777, logistical considerations played a small role in selecting the encampment site. Placing the troops in a concentrated winter cantonment in an inaccessible locale thereby exacerbated the supply shortages brought on by the administrative problems.[75] Unlike a permanent city, the Valley Forge camp lacked the extensive water and road communications networks that facilitated the flow of food and other supplies needed to sustain a dense population. In contrast to a typical military camp during the campaign season, Washington's army did not move on every few weeks to a new position where it could access new local supply sources. Finally, the camp departed from conventional eighteenth-century practice that would have seen soldiers dispersed to a chain of towns, easing subsistence. The British Army spent the winter occupying New York and Philadelphia and took advantage of both seaborne lines of communication and foraging in these cities' hinterlands. Rhode Island's Brig. Gen. James Mitchell Varnum summed up the location's responsibility for the supply shortages in a February 12 letter to Nathanael Greene, stating, "It is unparalleled in the history of mankind, to establish winter quarters in a country wasted, and without a single magazine. We now only feel some of the effects which reason from the beginning, thought us to expect as inevitable."[76]

Food shortages manifested as soon as the Rebels settled into their winter cantonment. Soldiers had enjoyed decent rations at Whitemarsh, but the shift in supply lines stemming from the move to Valley Forge interrupted the flow of provisions. Bread and flour stocks gave out around Christmas. There was little beef available, and much of that of such poor quality that officers believed it was unfit to eat.[77] Washington wrote to President Laurens on December 23 that unless conditions improved, the army might soon "starve, dissolve, or disperse."[78] Washington's letter hinted at the mismatch between logistical capabilities and the choice of winter quarters. If the army dispersed into the Pennsylvania interior for the winter, its regiments would find themselves in a region that had yet to be scoured by British and Patriot foraging parties. Placing soldiers close to this untapped countryside would have considerably shortened supply lines, thereby reducing forage consumption and wear on wagons and animals. Finally, dispersing would have removed the army from contact with the enemy, giving soldiers a chance to recover their strength free from a winter of exertion. Dissolving the army would have essentially repeated the methods of 1775 and 1776 when short-service soldiers went home and reenlisted come spring. This had eased the provisioning burden in past winters. The third option, starve, indicated Washington's pessimism that the log-hut city could be supplied through the winter.

The commander in chief might have overstated his case. Wayne Bodle has posited that the general might have exaggerated the food situation in his December 23 letter in order to extract greater support from civilian leaders. Bodle has made a convincing case, pointing out that the army had recently enjoyed decent rations and that Washington even entertained a bold attack on Philadelphia in late December, when the Patriot force supposedly stood on the brink of starvation. Washington's conduct later in the war, particularly in late 1780, indicates there is merit to Bodle's claim that the letter to Laurens should be taken seriously, but not quite literally. Of course, the planned attack on Philadelphia also had a precedent in Washington's proposal for an assault on Boston in 1775. Then, too, dissatisfaction with arrangements for winter shelter had motivated plans for an audacious offensive. Whatever Washington's true intentions were in writing the December 23 letter, it provides strong evidence of the stresses commanders experienced in adapting to this new form of winter quarters.[79]

Keeping the Main Army fed through the 1777–78 winter required routing wagons over unfamiliar roads and sending foodstuffs down the sluggish and ice-choked Schuylkill River. The Pennsylvania government pressured civilian wagon owners into service to aid in conveying supplies from York and Lancaster to Valley Forge. Washington's men impressed transportation and food to alleviate supply shortages in January. By the middle of the next month, however, the Continentals had consumed most of the readily available food stocks in the region. Pennsylvania farmers resisted further requisitions by hiding their flour and cattle or outright refusing army demands. Reliance on wagon trains likewise depleted the region's forage. Fields covered in snow and mud could not fuel the horse and ox teams that dragged the Main Army's supplies over inadequate roads. Flooding on the Schuylkill further obstructed the passage of wagon trains. Weather, lack of forage, and mismanagement conspired to leave army on short commons during February.[80]

As Washington had in New Jersey in early 1777, he again sought to feed his army while denying supplies to the British through foraging operations. Using militia and detached light troops, the commander in chief attempted to secure southeastern Pennsylvania's agricultural bounty while denying local foodstuffs to the Redcoats. Foraging sweeps kept numerous Continental units in the field throughout the winter. Although the main body wintered at Valley

Forge, the commander in chief placed detachments in an arc stretching from Wilmington, Delaware, to Trenton, New Jersey. This arrangement covered the southeastern Pennsylvania countryside. Continental patrols intercepted British foraging parties and deterred the Redcoats from venturing far into the interior from Philadelphia. The Patriot outposts also attempted to prevent Pennsylvania civilians from trading with the enemy and gathered intelligence. These *petite guerre* tasks blurred the distinction between winter quarters and campaigns. For the many Continentals involved in outpost duty, skirmishes, and foraging, Valley Forge hardly qualified as quarters of refreshment.[81]

The army's most sizeable winter operations came during the depths of the supply crisis in February. Washington dispatched Nathanael Greene on February 12 to curtail British foraging in the area west of Philadelphia and south of Valley Forge. Greene commanded nearly 1,400 men. Historian Ricardo A. Herrera has judged this detachment from the main body sizeable enough to significantly reduce Washington's combat power at Valley Forge, indicating the importance of such foraging sweeps. Greene's column skirmished with Crown forces along the Schuylkill opposite Philadelphia before moving farther south and west. Lacking enough transport to extract the provender they seized, Greene's men instead opted to destroy foodstuffs along the banks of the Delaware to deny them to the British. Civilians found hiding their stocks or suspected of Loyalist sympathies received no receipts from the army for goods taken. Greene's force returned to Valley Forge on February 21. Although disappointed in the total amount of supplies secured, the major general nevertheless held that the operation had rescued the Main Army from an even worse famine.[82]

A second Continental task force under Anthony Wayne entered New Jersey from Delaware on February 19. Wayne's column drove cattle back to Patriot lines, bolstered support for local Whigs, and burned whatever they could not carry off. British forces from Philadelphia pursued Wayne in southern New Jersey and conducted their own foraging in the region. The two sides skirmished near Haddonfield on March 1, after which the British withdrew back to city. Wayne moved his men northward to Bordentown, a few miles south of Trenton, in mid March. By the end of the month, his force returned to Pennsylvania, having marched, foraged, and skirmished for five weeks and moved entirely around the British position.[83]

Greene's and Wayne's expeditions comprised the largest operations undertaken during the winter. Smaller patrols, Continental as well as militia, strove to limit civilian trade with the Philadelphia garrison. Despite Washington's efforts, however, illicit exchange between Pennsylvanians and the British continued unabated until the enemy's departure in June. Combating illicit trade would remain an ongoing problem for the Continentals during winter through the remainder of the war.[84]

All told, the combination of foraging, impressment, and improvisation staved off logistical calamity at Valley Forge through late winter and early spring. Given the national government's chronic undersupporting of the army, Washington's men rarely enjoyed periods of abundant provisions. Concentrating the Continentals in a remote encampment ill-connected to the region's transportation network exacerbated shortages. Foraging operations siphoned away some of the agricultural bounty that followed existing trade patterns into Philadelphia. Impressment and shipping of goods from distant stockpiles also helped. Nevertheless, the Valley Forge winter established a dubious precedent. For Washington's army, retirement to winter quarters would henceforth attend a provisions crisis brought on in part by the placement and form of the log-hut city.

While Continental commanders grappled with supply problems, recruitment of new soldiers continued throughout the states. The victory at Saratoga and the impending entry of France into the war buoyed spirits and helped officers fulfill their quotas. Raising new troops brought further health complications. At recruitment sites, complacency, insufficient hospital space, and local suspicion of inoculation limited the extent of variolation efforts among new enlistees. Brig. Gen. Thomas Nelson, overseeing the raising of new troops in Virginia, complained that the state's inadequate preparations left him unable to inoculate more than fifty soldiers at a time. He feared the next campaign season would be over before he could field a new regiment, and if the British invaded the state, the Patriot Army would succumb to smallpox in a similar manner to the force sent against Canada in 1775.[85] Nelson might have overstated the case, but the experience of the previous year had shown that inoculating recruits impeded their arrival in camp and promised to delay the start of the new campaign. In 1778 the Patriots benefited from possessing a largely intact army with many veterans who already enjoyed immunity to the disease. Valley Forge did not lie so vulnerable as Morristown had the year before. Nevertheless, with the British occupying both New York and Philadelphia, Washington had less patience when waiting for the arrival of new units in 1778.

Compared to the haphazard performances of the states, Continental doctors in camp proved adept in administering controlled infections among the troops in camp who had yet to have the disease. Regiments made periodic returns of their uninoculated members and implemented immediate treatment throughout February and early March.[86] In mid-March, Elias Boudinot reported that three thousand soldiers were "down with the smallpox" due to inoculation, but none had died. General orders of March 18 informed the men that inoculation had been "happily performed on all the subjects in camp." The army's swelling size meant, however, that the disease continued to pose a threat. Washington pressed his regimental commanders to inquire whether newly arrived recruits and men who had been absent during the winter had had the disease. Those answering in the negative were to be quickly quarantined and immediately inoculated by their regimental surgeons.[87] A month later, the Continental commander reminded his officers to prohibit their men from "taking it in the natural way."[88] So effective were the Main Army's physicians at combating smallpox that the commander in chief resolved to conduct all inoculations at Valley Forge rather than rely on states to undertake the process for recruits.[89] From early April, new levies were to march directly to Pennsylvania and take care not to tarry among civilian communities where they might catch or spread the disease.[90]

Thus, the Valley Forge winter represented a departure from the previous year in how the army coped with illness. Washington demonstrated a clear understanding of the potential for spreading smallpox any time soldiers lay in concentrated quarters near civilians. He and the army at large embraced inoculation as a preventative measure. Transferring the site of inoculation from recruitment centers to winter quarters indicated confidence in physicians and a desire for tighter control of the process. These changes to the inoculation program accelerated the arrival of new levies at Valley Forge. Fresh soldiers marched for the Schuylkill Valley without the delay imposed by variolation at their recruitment sites. Jonathan Britton, a seventeen-year-old from Massachusetts, enlisted in the spring of 1778 and headed directly to Valley Forge. In his pension affidavit, written fifty years later, Britton recalled, "As soon as we arrived there we were inoculated for the smallpox." His experience highlighted why many feared the procedure, for the recruits grew "very sickly," and Britton claimed that he "just escaped with my life."[91]

Lower-ranking officers took initiative to secure their men from complications stemming from variolation. Men of the Second Connecticut learned through their regimental orders on March 14 that recently arrived Massachusetts troops undergoing inoculation had died due to overindulging in food and drink while still recovering from their infections. To prevent such a calamity from occurring in the Second Connecticut, a captain was appointed to look after recently inoculated men. To aid soldiers in their recovery, they were to march twice daily under the captain's supervision. This officer would also see to it that the men received proper amounts of food, drink, and fresh air.[92]

As recruits recovered from their bouts with *variola*, they remained safe from the British. The cantonment along the Schuylkill never faced a direct assault. Any such attack would have likely foundered due to the strong natural and man-made defenses of the campsite. Washington's brigade deployments formed an inner and outer line of defense around Mount Joy. Should Valley

Forge suffer a surprise attack, Patriot troops could have easily roused from their huts and into a line of battle. Artillery emplacements and redoubts eventually reinforced an original dry moat to offer additional cover. Building these fortifications took until April to complete.[93]

Behind these defenses, Washington's men honed their craft. Baron Wilhelm Friedrich von Steuben arrived at Valley Forge in early 1778. In mid-March, Washington appointed the Prussian officer to supervise reforms to drill and discipline. The commander in chief ordered the creation of a model company to train under von Steuben's tutelage while brigade inspectors and subinspectors would superintend the implementation of the new drill to their units. Daily exercises in marching in formation and musket drill began on March 24. After three relatively inactive months spent in huts, springtime drill returned men to activity and helped raise morale. Beyond improvements to order and discipline for the rank and file, Washington and von Steuben also demanded greater professionalism from the army's commissioned and noncommissioned officers. These changes took time to reach fruition, and it can hardly be said that the entire army was reborn in the ten weeks between the initiation of the drill program and the start of the new campaign. Nevertheless, the Continentals had begun to chart a new course toward matching their regular opponents in the field.[94]

The foraging, skirmishing, building, and training that characterized the 1777–78 winter proved that the officers who had cautioned Washington that keeping the army at Valley Forge would not provide a quiet and refreshing season had been correct. None of these improvements could have been effected, however, had the army been dispersed into billets in the interior. By spring, Washington's force evinced the results of its recent labors. Sturdy shelters now dotted the landscape. Food was more abundant than at any point in the winter. Men not detached on outpost duty burnished their martial skill through daily drill. The troops enjoyed better clothing, which had been kept intact since the men enjoyed decent protection from the elements in their huts. Capt. Ezra Seldon, adjutant of the First Connecticut Regiment, reported in mid-May "a very different spirit" in the army compared to when he had departed for a furlough earlier in the year. Seldon concluded his positive letter stating, "The army in general is not very sickly." Despite the cheery outlook, however, he admitted that two regiments beset by illness had moved into hospital tents.[95]

Seldon's remarks revealed the gravest threat to the Continental Army at Valley Forge: camp diseases. At the end of May, Washington reported to Maj. Gen. Horatio Gates that nearly four thousand troops lay ill with "smallpox and other disorders."[96] While smallpox might not have posed a fatal threat to most Continentals in early 1778, the "other disorders" Washington lamented to Gates were another matter. Quartermasters overcame the threat of starvation, and defenses and patrols secured the cantonment from enemy attack, but Patriot officers and men proved less adept at combating bacteria and viruses bred from unhygienic camp conditions. Camp fevers that had periodically appeared at previous quarters spread rampantly in Valley Forge's built environment. The cantonment brought together a larger number of troops than any previous camp and kept them concentrated for a longer duration than ever before. Even if veterans of the 1777 campaign had learned the benefits of keeping camp clean, new levies brought the same ill-disciplined attitudes witnessed in 1775 and 1776. Yet, unlike the Boston siege, soldiers were not spread through miles of New England countryside, with short-service regiments arriving and departing regularly. And unlike the Middlebrook camp of the previous June, the army would not march away after a month. Whatever Washington's talents as a camp administrator, he could not devote his attention to hygiene in the huts for fourteen brigades on top of his other concerns.

An inexpert and untutored officer corps also ignored many of Cuthbertson's and Bland's maxims for maintaining healthy camps. Many officers had departed for furloughs during the winter; others had resigned.[97] Von Steuben's reforms had only begun in March. Thus, soldiers and their junior leaders were ill prepared to combat camp ailments come spring, when it was clear that the prolonged occupation of a single site had produced an accumulation of filth and waste. A few conscientious officers attempted to address unhygienic conditions during late winter and early spring. In mid-March, regimental orders for the Second Connecticut instructed men to bury filth and dig fresh vaults so as to "avoid the greatest danger of the troops growing sickly." Vaults were to be covered with fresh dirt every day at sunrise and again at 2 P.M. Soldiers were also reminded of the proscription against easing themselves anywhere besides the vaults. Those too ill to proceed to these designated sites were permitted, however, to relieve themselves in holes dug between their huts. The regimental quartermaster bore responsibility for inspecting the unit's camp and reporting deficient companies to the commanding officer.[98] Infractions continued, and at the end of the month the same regiment resorted to posting a permanent sentry in front of the camp to guard against men easing themselves in front of their huts.[99]

By April, springtime sanitary problems had reached a level requiring the commander in chief's intervention. Midway through that month, Washington's disciplinarian side showed through as he admonished his men for their "want and neglect" of latrines that had left an "intolerable smell" in some brigades. The dirty conditions necessitated that men clear the "filth and dirt" that had accumulated in front of, between, and behind the huts. Keeping the cantonment clean and healthy relied on taking the guidelines appropriate for a regimental camp's health and extending them to the whole of the Main Army.[100] The commander in chief also implemented new measures specific to the log-hut city. As warmer weather arrived, Washington had the clay removed from between the logs that made up the huts' walls in order to ventilate the interiors. Instructions for burning musket cartridges inside were meant to clear the foul air as well. These seem to have been reactive steps that failed to keep up with the rate at which soldiers made their surroundings unhealthy. By late spring, camp occupants had rendered Valley Forge, in the words of historian Jacqueline Thibaut, "overcrowded, damp, and garbage-laden."[101]

These conditions led to the plethora of ailments bred in the poorly constructed and arranged built environment at Valley Forge. Scholars estimate up to three thousand soldiers perished at Valley Forge, mostly from disease resulting from poor camp conditions.[102] John Laurens despaired in March that "the number of men unfit for duty by reason of their nakedness, the number sick in hospitals, and present under inoculation, certainly emaciate the effective column in our returns."[103] Uncleanliness also made huts breeding grounds for vermin, which then afflicted the dirty and ill-clothed soldiers. Anthony Wayne described pests "now devouring" his poorly clad troops in May. "Some hundreds" had succumbed to illness, with the wretched Pennsylvania line seemingly the worst affected.[104]

Conditions worsened through May and early June. Although the Continentals had successfully combated *variola* microbes, they now lay besieged by the accumulated human and animal waste rotting in the springtime Pennsylvania sun. The log-hut city might have afforded protection from wind and snow, but improperly administered, it became a breeding ground for dysentery, typhus, and other camp ailments. One Massachusetts soldier reported, "I have taken with the yellow fever which has like to have proved fatal."[105] Sgt. Jeremiah Greenman of Rhode Island recorded conditions "very sickly in camp" on May 30.[106] Capt. Paul Brigham related in his journal that Solomon Howe, physician's mate with the Eighth Connecticut, died on June 3 following a twenty-four-day bout with "putrid fever." Brigham himself spent the next night ill.[107] Dr. Joseph Clark of the New Jersey line recorded in his journal that a fever prevailed in camp in early June, "which in many instances proved fatal."[108]

Unhygienic conditions and camp disease ultimately accomplished what supply disruptions and Howe's Redcoats could not, driving the Continental Army from its log-hut city. On June 8, Washington wrote to Nathanael Greene, despairing of "the very sickly situation of the camp." The commander in chief believed that conditions would only grow worse and ordered his quartermaster general to reconnoiter new grounds on which to encamp. The army soon vacated its putrid huts and moved into tents.[109] Besieged by their own muck, the Continentals retreated to a new site, half a mile away. Even fifty years later, one veteran recalled the day he and his comrades "left our filthy huts and encamped in tents."[110] There they escaped, in the words of one major of the Pennsylvania line, "the disagreeable smell occasioned by our long stay."[111]

The combination of poor sanitation, inadequate shelter, and supply interruptions at Valley Forge rendered the Continental Army as disease-ridden in the spring of 1778 as it had been a year earlier during the height of the smallpox epidemic. The proportion of sick Continentals peaked in February at 35 percent.[112] The lack of adequate hospital facilities in the region aggravated the suffering of the sick and prolonged the time before they could return to active duty.[113] Even in June 1778, 27 percent of the army remained unfit for duty.[114] Based on these statistics, the Valley Forge encampment hardly qualified as the refreshing quarters that a regular army expected during the winter months. Whatever improvements in discipline and drill von Steuben's training regimen might have instilled in the ranks during early 1778, the army entered the active campaign season with more than a quarter of its men unavailable for combat. Over the course of the following months, Washington's men fought a bitter but indecisive engagement at Monmouth Court House, but otherwise achieved little.[115]

The Continental Army that emerged from the Valley Forge winter demonstrated a marked difference from the force that had gathered in northern New Jersey a year earlier. Nevertheless, the Valley Forge encampment stands as both a significant innovation in castrametation and a partial failure. The Continental Army pioneered a new method of wintering troops and maintained its hold on the countryside. Yet conditions in the log-hut city that winter stood at odds with the goal of providing soldiers with comfortable and healthy winter quarters. While the huts built at Valley Forge undoubtedly represented an improvement over the shanties used earlier in the war, their leaky roofs and flooded interiors made for unhealthy and unpleasant lodging. Ensuring a steady flow of supplies to concentrated winter camp likewise proved difficult. While the army did emerge from the camp well organized and better disciplined as a result of the beginnings of von Steuben's training program, given the hardships experienced at the log-hut city along the Schuylkill, Continental officers remained unsure whether the benefits of this new method of castrametation outweighed its detriments.

CHAPTER 5

"Much Improved in City Building"

1778–1779

After the drawn Battle of Monmouth on June 28, the British Army pulled back to Manhattan, while Washington marched his men northward. The Patriots began crossing the Hudson River in the middle of July. Through the summer, the Rebels camped near White Plains, north of New York City. There the Continentals enjoyed a healthy field camp at which they fully recovered their strength from the previous winter's exertions. An officer described the encamped troops as *"a most grand army."* Patriot strength peaked at 18,000 men in early October.[1]

The Continentals and Redcoats occupied roughly the same positions as a year earlier. Moving forward, the overall strategic situation in the region remained little changed until 1781. The British-held port city lay at the center of the operational zone, with a large garrison placing the surrounding area under the threat of attack. With France now allied to the United States, the revolutionaries hoped to eject the enemy from New York with the help of King Louis XVI's powerful navy. Without French support, however, the Continentals had little option but to stay on the defensive. The Hudson River provided an avenue of advance for Royal forces that threatened to cut communications between New England and the remainder of the colonies. In October 1777, Crown troops had thrust up the Hudson and dislodged the Patriots from their feeble fortifications in the Highlands.[2] Rebel strategy therefore centered on preventing another such attack by securing these vital mountains.[3]

The Revolutionaries had made only limited improvements to the military infrastructure in the New York region to support this positional strategy. Barracks stood at Fishkill and Peekskill in the Highlands. At West Point, the most important geographic location for defending the region, fortifications and housing lay incomplete.[4] Farther south and west, a network of magazines stretched through New Jersey to succor troops moving through the area. But that state still lacked barracks or towns sufficient to house a large army. In late 1778, the Continentals would again need to exchange their tents for winter lodging. They would be housing a larger army than ever before in a region still ill-prepared to receive it. Whether Washington's men would build another log-hut city, retire to billets in the interior, or seek out some other method remained uncertain.

In September 1778, the Continentals marched northward. The commander in chief placed his headquarters in Fredericksburg, New York, forty miles north of White Plains, and arranged his troops in an arc stretching from Danbury in Connecticut to West Point on the Hudson's left bank. These dispositions secured the Highlands while also leaving the army well placed to act in conjunction with the French fleet, should it arrive. The Patriots could also move eastward to counter a rumored British attack on Boston, although in actuality the army spent the following two months idle.[5]

Amid this relative calm, Washington addressed the question of winter quarters at a much earlier date than the previous year. The difficulties encountered in determining where and how to spend the winter in 1778 led the Continental commander to query his officers about the subject in mid-October. Doing so would hopefully yield an earlier decision and enable soldiers to get into quarters before snow blanketed the ground. He issued a circular to seven of his subordinates on October 14, requesting their opinions regarding how the army should arrange its forces for the coming winter. Washington asked first for recommendations for what dispositions the army should take. Respondents were to consider "the security of the army itself—its subsistence and accommodation-protection of the country—the support of our important posts." Washington asked whether the army should stay concentrated during the winter or divided into small cantonments, how soon it should enter quarters, and how to best secure its provisions and forage.[6] He supplemented his original circular with a council of war on October 16, once again asking his officers for suggestions regarding winter dispositions.[7] The commander in chief received responses from Major Generals Lord Stirling, Horatio Gates, Nathanael Greene, Johann de Kalb, Alexander McDougall, Israel Putnam, and Baron Friedrich von Steuben, as well as Brigadier Generals James Clinton, Henry Knox, Samuel Holden Parsons, William Maxwell, Peter Muhlenberg, William Smallwood, Anthony Wayne, and William Woodford.

Beyond their timing, the content of Washington's questions evinced a change in concerns from the previous year. While security of the army and protection of the country paralleled criteria covered before Valley Forge, the addition of subsistence and accommodation indicated the general realized that logistical feasibility and health deserved equal consideration. The emphasis on how winter quarters might be supplied represented the most important development from the pre–Valley Forge debate, when logistics had not been considered. Other lessons learned from Valley Forge were less clear. That the commander in chief included a dispersal into cantonments as an option for quarters indicates that His Excellency did not necessarily view the log-hut city as the army's best option. Several of his commanders felt similarly.

Disparate experiences with Continental winter quarters colored the generals' responses. Of the brigadiers, only Clinton and Parsons had not participated in the Valley Forge debate in December 1777. By contrast, more than half of the senior officers surveyed—de Kalb, Gates, McDougall, Putnam, and von Steuben—had not been present for the same discussion. Gates, McDougall, and Putnam had spent most or all of the 1777–78 winter in New York and had little exposure to the new housing methods pioneered on the Schuylkill. Consequently, Washington was to receive input from several generals unfamiliar with the log-hut city. Also, significantly absent from the 1778 consultations were any militia generals. Nor did Washington formally solicit advice from any state or national civilian politicians. New Jersey's governor William Livingston tendered a request for Continental troops, but submitted no formal plan. Unlike 1777, the decision for winter quarters in 1778 was to be exclusively the decision of Continental officers.

The Rebel commanders drew different conclusions from the previous winter and stood at odds on several issues. Estimations of the army's logistical capabilities varied from bullish to pessimistic, as did suppositions regarding the British Army's offensive potential. The respondents divided into three camps: those who supported a concentrated encampment in the Hudson Highlands, those who rejected a Highlands camp but otherwise accepted the idea of a concentrated encampment, and those who favored dispersing the army into cantonments in towns and villages.

The novelty of the log-hut city and its attendant health and supply issues led several of Washington's subordinates to proffer alternative methods of winter quarters. Major Generals Gates, Greene, and Stirling, as well as Brigadier General Maxwell, all suggested dispersed arrangements. Gates explicitly rejected the notion of returning to huts. He recognized that in December 1777, Washington's men "did build a town for their Winter Quarters" out of necessity but believed that current circumstances did not require a return to such an exigency. He felt uncertain that soldiers "would cheerfully do the same thing this year." Instead he proposed leaving small garrisons in forts in the Hudson Highlands and sending most of the army to winter in billets and barracks scattered throughout the Middle States. Brigadiers Paterson and Poor, who had both served under Gates in the Northern Department, endorsed the major general's plan.[8] Maxwell also suggested distended dispositions, with troops stationed from Baltimore up to Albany.[9] Stirling proposed cantoning brigades in various New Jersey towns between Hackensack and Trenton, with huts making up the difference.[10]

Greene likewise clung to more established models for wintering the army. In early October, prior to Washington's council of war, the Rhode Islander had surveyed the Continentals' options between quartering men in "small towns and the neighboring houses to those villages" or building huts as at Valley Forge. The quartermaster general argued in favor of billeting the army in towns, believing that the difficulties in gathering building materials would make it "utterly impossible" to "barrack the whole army."[11]

The officers opposed to the return to the log-hut city demonstrated an outlook derived from a limited understanding of European castrametation. In their preferences for billets and barracks, they revealed the influence of the orthodox maxims outlined by authors such as Turpin de Crissé, Bland, and Cuthbertson. These officers' predilections for such methods reflected their backgrounds. Gates had garnered experience as a brigade major in the British Army during the Seven Years' War. Stirling had served as a provisioning agent and aide-de-camp to Massachusetts governor William Shirley during that conflict. Greene had exhibited a partiality for European regularization throughout the war. The results of the experiment with new quartering techniques in 1777–78 had done nothing to diminish these generals' preference for traditional European approaches to shelter.

More recent experience in the wars of continental Europe informed a more nuanced understanding of castrametation among the army's foreign generals. In contrast to their American peers, both Johann de Kalb and Friedrich Wilhelm von Steuben favored hutting the army. Both men had served in Germany during the Seven Years' War. This theater had witnessed a proliferation of fortified camps that had sparked new interest in castrametation during the second half of the eighteenth century. Consequently, de Kalb and von Steuben would likely have known that prolonged encampments were developing into an increasingly frequent quartering option. While European armies did not use timber-built camps for winter quarters, the two German officers seemingly recognized that the Continentals could adapt such installations for winter shelter. De Kalb favored a compact arrangement, with troops hutted at their positions to ensure order and discipline.[12] Von Steuben objected to billeting for practical purposes, arguing that the region lacked any town "considerable enough to quarter a brigade." He also recognized that dispersing the army would undermine its order and discipline. The baron confidently expected the Continentals could endure the cold season provided they improved the quality of their huts from the previous year. Von Steuben called for "good barracks— covered with plank and not with earth."[13] Although he referred to his proposed shelters as "barracks," the timber structures built in the field rather than in towns or fortresses represented an improved version of the Valley Forge huts. Of the American officers, Henry Knox's views most closely paralleled the two foreign generals'. The well-read artillerist had evoked Frederick the Great in the previous year's quartering debate, indicating he may have better understood developments in European castrametation than some of his peers. Knox supported a return to log huts, provided they were of better quality than those built in the previous year.[14]

Strong support for the log-hut city also came from the brigadier generals who had served with the Main Army in Pennsylvania the preceding year. In contrast to their superiors, these officers did not stay tethered to orthodox European methods, nor did they indicate an awareness of more recent developments on the continent. Instead, the army's more junior generals showed faith in their soldiers' abilities to build their shelters for themselves. Most of the brigadiers had directly overseen their units' hut construction the previous year. In their responses to Washington's queries, they highlighted several of the problems encountered at Valley Forge and shared possible solutions. Muhlenberg, Smallwood, and Hand all voiced support for building another log-hut city, provided the army began construction as soon as possible. Anthony Wayne discerned that some units had experienced more success than others in constructing their huts at Valley Forge and that the whole army could copy these good examples.[15]

Beyond form, the generals also disagreed on the geography of winter quarters. The majority who suggested building at least one log-hut cantonment proffered various locations for it. Most favored a position in the Hudson Highlands. The importance of West Point, as well as the strategic similarities between the Philadelphia theater a year earlier and the army's current situation, shaped most of the generals' responses. In addition, the potential appearance of a French fleet in the area made a tighter arrangement of forces attractive, as this would ease the task of concentrating the army for a potential attack on New York.[16]

Neither the foreign generals nor most of the brigadiers addressed the potential logistical problems the army might face in their proposals. These officers shared this oversight with most contemporary military experts who mostly ignored matters of supply, particularly the logistics involved in provisioning winter quarters. Enlightenment-era warfare increasingly featured plentiful forage, well-organized bureaucracies, and well-integrated road and river networks that made for generally abundant provisions, reducing generals' need to trouble themselves with such matters. The Continental Army, however, possessed none of these advantages.

Logistical and defensive concerns stood in opposition to one another. To ease supply burdens, the army needed to reduce its concentrations and move some brigades closer to their sources of provisions. To do so, however, would leave individual wings of the army more vulnerable to attack, particularly if they wintered in places possessing less advantageous terrain. Essentially, the army could facilitate its supply only by sacrificing security. Balancing these two concerns would continue to flummox Continental leadership over the course of the following two winters.

Fortunately for the Rebel cause, several of Washington's subordinates did recognize the logistical problems inherent in supplying a large, stationary army through the winter. Alexander McDougall, who had commanded along the Hudson since April, claimed that supplying the whole army in a mountainous area devoid of forage would be impossible.[17] John Nixon, who had also served in the region, agreed.[18] Both officers suggested dividing the army between New Jersey, New York, and Connecticut to ease its supply burdens. The also argued that the mountainous terrain along the Hudson would permit a smaller force to defend West Point and its environs.

Several officers put forth detailed analyses of the army's logistical capabilities. Henry Knox suggested sending most of the Continentals to Connecticut, with only small detachments in New Jersey and along the Hudson. He recognized that foodstuffs would arrive from the south and west and highlighted the abundant forage and "the goodness of the roads below the mountains through the Jerseys" as a crucial line of communications.[19] Conversely, Lord Stirling inverted Knox's arrangement. He did not share Knox's optimism regarding forage and therefore weighted dispositions toward New Jersey, with smaller forces in New York and Connecticut. Based on "the state of cartage & forage," the Rebel Earl stated that "it is absolutely impractical to maintain the army in flour & grain in any situation on the east side of Hudson's River."[20]

The clearest articulation of provisioning winter quarters came from the quartermaster general. In a well argued response, Nathanael Greene assessed the army's options for Washington. He saw that, ideally, the Hudson Highlands made the most sense for a winter position from a strategic point of view. Wintering near West Point would, however, excessively strain the army's limited transportation assets. The Main Army had campaigned along the Hudson since July, drawing most of its provisions from Pennsylvania and southern New Jersey. Trenton, at the head of navigation along the Delaware, represented the principal supply hub in the theater. Carting these stores up to New York had exhausted much of the forage in New Jersey. Greene feared that if Washington placed his winter quarters along the Hudson, horse and ox teams would be unable to complete their journeys from the Delaware to camp. To conserve forage and avoid the logistical interruptions experienced at Valley Forge, Greene pressed Washington to winter in New Jersey.

Even within that state, distance from Trenton mattered. A northerly position in Bergen County would theoretically allow for easy cooperation with troops posted at West Point. Greene recognized, however, that this would also increase the strain on the army's logistical tail. These considerations led him to endorse Middlebrook instead. This locale, where the army had camped in June 1777, lay only twenty miles from Trenton. Teams victualing a Bergen position, forty miles farther away, would consume a substantially greater amount of forage. Ample roads over rolling piedmont terrain near Middlebrook would make for easy transportation.[21] He justified his views to General McDougall by claiming, "An active, vigilant general can guard against every kind of evil but that of want of provision and forage." The near disaster at Valley Forge likely colored Greene's perspective.[22]

By late October, General Washington had received input on potential winter quarters from a dozen subordinates. No clear consensus presented itself. On October 29, Washington himself offered his views on winter arrangements. In a letter to Greene, the Virginian considered placing Continental brigades near Danbury, Connecticut; in the Hudson Highlands; and at Middlebrook, New Jersey. These proposed sites reflected a blending of the various suggestions sent to Washington in October. Nevertheless, he did not endorse returning the army to huts. If the British diminished their New York garrison, he entertained the possibility of quartering the army deeper into the interior. He proposed quarters at Albany, Trenton, and Burlington, where "very good barracks" already existed and there was "adjacent country abounding in wheat and mills to manufacture it." Washington thereby displayed a preference for orthodox European methods favored by many of his senior commanders. Such an arrangement would also greatly reduce the army's reliance on supply trains, as the dispersed troops could subsist locally. Should the British stay in New York in strength, Washington indicated the Hudson Highlands would receive the bulk of his army. But the commander in chief had not yet reached a formal decision regarding the form of housing or winter dispositions by early November.[23] Alexander McDougall reported to New York governor George Clinton on November 5 that Washington stood "at a loss how to dispose of the army."[24]

Ultimately, logistics determined Washington's choice. In early November, the commander in chief received a report on the forage situation from Greene's subordinate, Col. Clement Biddle, the army's foragemaster. Biddle found that the Main Army's extended stay along the Hudson had depleted stocks of animal feed in New Jersey. The Continentals had more than five thousand animals transporting supplies and equipment. Further operations in New York would necessitate that forage be carted from more distant sources. This would require the hiring and feeding of extra animal teams to bring in forage for the primary teams. Biddle believed he would need a further 1,400 horses and oxen. Winter ice promised to suspend transport on the Delaware, meaning few provisions at Trenton would be restocked prior to the army's entering winter quarters. Concentrating the army for an offensive against New York or a winter encampment would, in Biddle's view, most likely exhaust forage supplies and render the army immobile and in danger of famine.[25]

Other members of the Quartermaster's Department corroborated Biddle's assessment. At Morristown, deputy quartermaster Col. James Burnside found himself unable to purchase forage for the teams passing through that town on their way to the Hudson Highlands. Burnside claimed that shortages derived from local farmers' unwillingness to sell to the army in exchange for inflated Continental currency. Describing the forage scarcity as "artificial," he believed supplies could be "had all winter" if the Quartermaster's Department could purchase the article in good quantities. In early November, however, New Jersey farmers appeared to be "determined to keep ahead of us." Whether the army had depleted the region's forage stocks or simply could no longer afford the item, the result was the same. Burnside complained that shortages had forced him to halt wagons at Morristown due to a lack of feed. This portended ill for a prolonged winter camp along the Hudson.[26]

Washington took time to carefully weigh the various options his subordinates had provided before acting. A month after first polling his officers, the commander in chief reached a decision regarding how the army should lodge. Despite the opposition of Gates's clique, Greene's suspicions, and his own misgivings, Washington decided hut encampments, rather than billets or barracks, made for the best winter shelter. In a letter to Israel Putnam, who was commanding the left wing of the Main Army, Washington articulated the benefits of huts. Compared to making quarters in private homes, a log-hut city promised "to be as little burdensome as possible to the inhabitants of the county" while also offering a compact deployment that would improve security, discipline, and administration. Reflecting a shift in Continental doctrine toward a wholesale acceptance of huts, Washington expressed his "desire that they should hut themselves as they did last winter at Valley Forge, wherever they can."[27] In a letter to Congress shortly before retiring to winter quarters, Washington wrote, "The troops must again have recourse to the expedient of hutting, as they did last year." Better supplied and in a less dangerous strategic juncture, however, he hoped his men would "be in a more comfortable situation than they were in the preceding winter."[28] The brigadiers' advocacy of the log-hut city had brought about a significant shift in Washington's thinking. Thus, in late 1778, the Continental Army had taken its first steps toward institutionalizing a new doctrine of castrametation.

With huts decided upon, Connecticut, the Hudson Highlands, and Middlebrook appeared likely to receive Continental brigades. The question remained as to where exactly the army should place its next log-hut cities. At Valley Forge, the Rebels had simply settled onto defensible high ground west of the Schuylkill with little consideration of how the ground would affect their ability to build, fuel, and maintain the camp. European castrametation texts highlighted the importance of access to fresh water, dry ground, and timber when placing temporary camps, and the Continentals extended these rules to apply to winter quarters as well. Wood, crucial for European camps as a fuel source, was to be doubly important to the Continental Army intent upon building timber houses. If the army intended to camp for up to six months, it would need well-drained ground upon which to build its huts. This ground also needed to be sufficiently unbroken to allow brigades to erect their shelters in a neat, orderly manner to facilitate assembly and discipline.

Satisfying these castrametation criteria further strengthened Middlebrook's case for receiving the bulk of the army. In late October, the Quartermaster's Department had surveyed sites suitable for encamping large portions of the Main Army. Sweeps in the Hudson Highlands revealed the difficulty of meeting these parameters while also staying in defensible terrain and close to supplies. Greene and Putnam surveyed the ground in the vicinity of King's Ferry and found "but one tract of woodland of sufficient extent to hut the army collectively." The rough country around Fishkill offered only enough room to encamp single brigades, and the broken ground appeared to offer few prospects for exercise or maneuver. Mostly divided into small farms, the Hudson Highlands lacked substantial woodlots beyond those small holdings of the individual farmers. According to Greene, if the soldiers encamped along the Hudson, "their situation in the Highlands will be little better than in a gaol."[29] Conversely, he described the region around Middlebrook as "plentiful country, naturally strong and difficult to access and surrounded with a great plenty of wood."[30] Thus, the hills north of the Raritan appeared ideal for wintering the army.

Although officers appeared nearly unanimous in their desire to enter winter quarters immediately, Washington announced a formal end to the campaign season only on November 27. The commander in chief's arrangements for the winter of 1778–79 ultimately incorporated elements of Stirling's, Knox's, and Greene's suggestions, though it bore the closest resemblance to the latter's plan.

To satisfy West Point's defensive requirements, three Massachusetts brigades encamped in the New York Highlands under Alexander McDougal. Brig. Gen. John Paterson's brigade held West Point itself on the Hudson's west bank, while Ebenezer Learned's and John Nixon's brigades wintered east of the river, near Fishkill and Peekskill, respectively.[31] Numbering 3,100 men, including militia detachments, the Massachusetts units did not pose the logistical problems Greene believed encamping the whole army at West Point would have entailed. McDougall's limited contingent likewise did not need as much open ground upon which to situate a camp, though the New York general encountered problems in securing shelter for even this small force, given the nature of the terrain.

On the left wing, two Connecticut brigades and one New Hampshire brigade under General Putnam quartered in a log-hut city near Redding, Connecticut, to solidify defenses in that state. In northeastern New Jersey, the North Carolina Brigade secured Bergen County as well as nearby Smith's Clove, an important pass in New York leading to the Hudson Highlands. Washington proposed an existing barrack in nearby Suffern for the Carolinians' quarters.[32] Reflecting a blend of Greene's and Stirling's proposals, seven brigades from Virginia, Maryland, and Pennsylvania occupied the main encampment at Middlebrook. The artillery went to nearby Pluckemin. The New Jersey Brigade provided forward outposts for the main camp, with regiments cantoned in and around Elizabethtown. A small force under Edward Hand garrisoned Minisink on the upper Delaware in New York. The limited availability of fodder for the army's vital supply trains necessitated the cavalry's dispersion, with regiments detached as far as Winchester, Virginia; Lancaster, Pennsylvania; and Durham, Connecticut. Only Lt. Col. Henry Lee's legion stayed near the Main Army, wintering in southern New Jersey.[33]

Washington's arrangements balanced logistical and strategic concerns. His concentrations guarded the key routes into the Hudson Highlands and afforded the troops safety from British attack. They were also mutually supporting. The troops at Middlebrook and Redding could respond to a threat at West Point within a few days. The distribution of forces also promised ease of supply and minimal burdens on local civilians. Explaining his arrangements to Congress, Washington claimed, "To have kept the troops in a collected state would have increased infinitely the expense and difficulty of subsisting them." Conversely, "To have divided them into smaller cantonments, would have made it far less practicable to maintain order and discipline among them." Further dispersal would have also constrained his ability to contest a British advance or to concentrate in order to launch his own attack should the opportunity arise.[34] After more than a month of deliberation, the commander in chief had struck a workable balance for winter dispositions. In rough outline, the dispositions

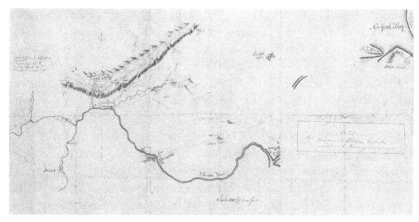

This map displays the location of the 1778–79 Continental cantonments at Middle-brook, with the Virginia and Maryland lines ensconced in the Watchung Mountains. Robert Erskine, "Road from Quibbletown to Amboy; Places by Bearings" (November 5, 1779). Erskine-Dewitt map. Continental Army. Surveying Department. New York Historical Society.

he selected would prove viable in winters through the end of the war. The late 1778 quartering debate, and its result, therefore ranks as one of Washington's significant strategic achievements.

In contrast to the Valley Forge winter, civilian leaders meddled little in the plans for the army's winter quarters around New York in late 1778. While congressional delegates voiced their concerns to Washington over the Southern Theater and expressed interest in an operation against Canada, they mostly deferred to Washington's authority on the matter of quarters. Washington denied congressional appeals for a detachment for Philadelphia, claiming he could not spare more men "without leaving this cantonment in so weak a state as to be liable to an insult during the winter."[35] The general likewise declined a request from New Jersey governor William Livingston for a deployment to Bergen and Monmouth Counties. The commander in chief claimed, "The safety of its inhabitants has been a particular consideration" in his distribution of forces. It was, however, "impossible to include every place." Livingston accepted Washington's judgment without protest.[36]

Overall, military considerations of rest, security, and ease of supply overwhelmingly guided the arrangement of Patriot forces for the winter. Washington clearly intended the 1778–79 winter to provide quarters of refreshment on the European model. Beyond keeping most brigades out of contact with the enemy, success in the endeavor depended on refining the army's approach to building and administering its camps. From December 1778 through June

1779, Continental generals and line officers worked to craft new innovations in castrametation.

While the generals deliberated, the Main Army stayed in its camps near Fredericksburg. As the leaves reddened and temperatures dropped, men built makeshift chimneys for their tents to keep warm. Spending day after day in these small, smoke-filled chambers surrounded by the dreary hillsides of the Hudson Highlands, soldiers grew anxious for final word on their destinations for winter. Many men along the Hudson harbored sour memories of the late-December trudge into Valley Forge and anxiously awaited news that they were to quit the field. Continental brigadier Jedidiah Huntington, one of the sharpest critics of the previous year's cantonment, postulated that Washington must have assumed the British were about to evacuate New York. Otherwise, why had the commander in chief waited so long to retire?[37] Lt. Col. John Laurens recalled Valley Forge when he informed his father, "All that I dread is the disadvantage of getting our troops late into winter quarters."[38] Some worried that they would stay at Fredericksburg, a locale well north of the previous year's winter quarters.[39] Others continued to harbor negative opinions of huts. In late November, Lt. Col. Henry Dearborn of the First New Hampshire Regiment noted that to his "great mortification found we were ordered to hut once more."[40]

For the soldiers headed to Middlebrook, the march from New York to the Raritan made for a difficult task. Regiments were to depart from Fredericksburg, head west to the Hudson, and trek along that river's eastern shore past Peekskill and on to King's Ferry. There they would take boats across the river and then proceed through Orange County to the New Jersey border. In New Jersey, the Continentals would avoid the barren mountains and disaffected inhabitants that Charles Lee's column encountered in 1776 in the Ramapos. Instead, they would proceed through the generally flat terrain near Paramus and Acquackanonk and down the left bank of the Passaic River to Newark. From the swampy banks the Passaic, they would then sojourn west through Springfield before finally arriving at Middlebrook. The trip would take nine days, with a route covering 106 miles. Soldiers would average between eleven and fifteen miles per day, though they would cover only four while crossing the Hudson. They would make up for the lost time with a nineteen mile trek on the final leg of the journey from Springfield to Middlebrook. The Maryland and Virginia lines proceeded as scheduled, but a British sortie up the Hudson on December 5 interrupted the Pennsylvania line's march as it halted to monitor enemy activity. Ultimately, nothing came of the British operation other than to delay the Pennsylvanians' progress toward Middlebrook.[41]

Consequently, the Virginians and Marylanders were the first to arrive. A profusion of timber, the most important article for building a log-hut city, stood nearby. Washington had dispatched Nathanael Greene to find specific locales near Middlebrook that possessed dry ground, access to fresh water, and ample wood.[42] By early December, the quartermaster general had nominated two prospective sites, which Washington then inspected himself on December 5. Two days later, he reached his final determination.[43] A contemporary newspaper advertisement described the countryside near the Virginians' encampment as "most-excellent timberland," while the vicinity of the artillery park at nearby Pluckemin featured eight thousand acres of timberland.[44] Given this plentiful wood supply, the defensive potential of the local hills, and the proximity to supply lines, Middlebrook made for an ideal site for a prolonged encampment.

If the Patriots' winter quarters were to provide a recuperative environment, officers and men needed to improve upon the quality of their shelters. Washington turned to the model he had prescribed at Valley Forge. Despite the haphazard arrangement those huts had taken, Washington had observed sufficient examples of successful shelters during that winter to convince him of log huts' overall viability. At the outset of the Middlebrook encampment, the commander in chief informed Major General Putnam of his goals for housing the army in the coming winter, writing, "There were several [huts] last winter at Valley Forge, which by the care of the officers were not only comfortable but commodious, and in which the men lived exceedingly well and preserved their health."[45] The task in late 1778 was to standardize this model throughout the army.

New guidelines for hut design and placement comprised the first step to improve conditions in the winter camp. Without a published text to serve as a guide, Washington implemented new construction regulations directly from headquarters. Through general orders, each regiment received instructions, developed by Greene, on how to build their huts in a manner that would minimize the worst failings of the Valley Forge shelters. Orders released on December 14 pointed out that "much of the sickness among the troops seems to have been occasioned by the improper method adopted in forming many of the huts last winter; some being sunk in the ground and others covered with earth." Washington's new commands prohibited earthen roofs and permitted only boards, slabs, or shingles for overhead coverings. Boards cut at regional sawmills and stockpiled during the autumn ensured an ample supply of good roofing materials. Washington's orders also banned the practice of sinking huts into the earth. The cabins at Middlebrook and afterward were to be sunk only deep enough to ensure a level floor. Plans for hut interiors also received an upgrade, with soldiers' bunks and storage raised off the ground to preserve arms and equipment from damage.[46]

Beyond improvements to design, soldiers' health and comfort also relied on the army's ability to build its huts quickly. At Valley Forge, the Continentals had only begun erecting their camp with snow already on the ground and weather turning cold. A lack of tools had further retarded hut construction, forcing most soldiers to remain in their tents into January. In 1778, access to sufficient numbers of tools would ensure both rapid and solid construction. The Continentals needed a large number of woodworking implements. A single regiment required more than 30 different types of tools and more than 150 total pieces of equipment.[47] In late 1778, the Main Army now operated amid a chain of magazines stretching northeastward from Trenton from which the men could draw tools.[48] The weeks leading up to the start of camp witnessed a burst of orders to local deputy quartermasters in search of tools. These officers sent entrenchment tools, crosscut saws, broad axes, adzes, and carpenters' hammers to Connecticut, the Hudson Highlands, and Middlebrook.[49] Gone were the days of a mess working with a single ax. Nevertheless, soldiers damaged or dulled their tools quickly in the process of building huts. Deputy Quartermaster Jacob Weiss declared of his saws on December 23 that "mine go fast," and he had "not above three or four hundred on hand."[50] Six days later, the army "had not one left."[51] Comparing the coming winter with Valley Forge, Capt. Samuel Shaw declared, "We shall all hands have to go to work, as the whole are to be hutted in the same manner as last year; and I hope we shall make quick way in the business, as Jack Frost is a very powerful stimulus to people in such a case."[52]

Despite better access to tools, hut construction proceeded at an uneven pace throughout the army. Early-arriving troops, such as Washington's guard, reported that they had left their tents for huts as early as December 16. The Pennsylvanians, who only reached Middlebrook in mid-December, remained, according to Wayne, "exposed to wind and weather in their old tents" until the new year.[53] The Pennsylvania enlisted men finished their homes by January's first week.[54] The Maryland brigades, which had spent 1777–78 billeted at Wilmington rather than the main hut complex at Valley Forge, lagged behind their more experienced comrades.[55] A Maryland captain did not move into his hut until the end of January.[56]

Sixty miles northeast of Middlebrook, the center of the Main Army, in the Hudson Highlands, faced greater challenges in building its winter quarters. The Patriots had labored on barracks at the various Highlands installations since 1776, but permanent shelter was still in short supply in late 1778. Washington instructed Alexander McDougall to make the completion of defenses at West Point his principal objective but also to disperse his forces to cover other posts stretching from King's Ferry northward toward Kingston, with light parties extended down to White Plains. The New York general thus bore responsibility for a command forty-five miles deep with a major river dividing his forces; winter weather would potentially interrupt crossings. He had to protect civilians in Westchester County, build defenses, and erect adequate shelter for his men. All of this in terrain that had been judged too difficult to hut and too hard to supply for the bulk of the army.[57] The broken terrain and the need to secure several vital locations prohibited more concentrated quartering.[58]

McDougall's forces unsurprisingly suffered the greatest delays in getting under winter coverings. John Nixon's brigade, which had started putting up its shelters at the beginning of December at Continental Village near Peekskill, made slow progress due to tool shortages.[59] One regiment lost its apportionment of axes and entrenching tools on its march from Fredericksburg.[60] To compensate, McDougall ordered the best axmen from regiments furthest along in hutting to aid sluggish units. Amid poor weather that had "retarded the finishing of the huts," the general also approved increased beef and flour rations for the uncovered men on December 28.[61] Even at the end of December, however, he expected his men were several days away from completing their huts.[62] Massachusetts private Zebulon Vaughan in Nixon's brigade complained in his diary on December 14, "Very hard for poor soldiers to work building our own houses." He did not move into his hut until January 5. In the interim, soldiers made do with their tents amid cold and windy conditions.[63]

Across the river at West Point, men faced similar difficulties. McDougall had overseen construction of defenses there in April. Under his direction, Brig. Gen. Samuel Holden Parsons and Col. Thaddeus Kosciuszko had planned a series of fortifications on the hills overlooking the Hudson. Fort Arnold represented the most significant work, supported by a series of smaller redoubts. Kosciuszko's plan also included several barracks, each two stories high and capable of holding six hundred men. The buildings were to be divided into rooms measuring nineteen feet by nineteen feet, holding eighteen beds stacked in nine bunks. The beds were only three feet wide and intended to hold two men each. By late autumn, one of these structures, known as the long barracks, stood to the west of Fort Arnold. Construction of other accommodations proceeded slowly, however, and many buildings would lie incomplete until well into the new year.[64]

In December, McDougall instructed the new garrison commander, John Paterson, to examine the barracks, huts, houses, and tents in the area to find suitable coverings for his men. He entrusted the brigadier to find proper hutting grounds for such soldiers as would require that type of shelter. For others, the major general recommended the best tents and marquees, despite the deficiencies of using these items in winter.[65] In January, McDougall received Paterson's tabulation of the available shelter options. These included eighteen small huts that could hold only four to six men each and sixteen larger structures that each held eighteen. An "old barrack" contained sixteen rooms, each capable of holding eighteen men. A "new barrack" was to feature twenty similarly sized rooms. Construction had apparently departed slightly from Kosciuszko's model. Paterson also estimated living space in the various fortifications, guardhouses, and civilian homes in the area. All told, the general listed lodgings for 54 officers and 1,516 men. These were, however, spread out across a multitude of structures that broke up unit cohesion.[66]

The small huts and old barracks were of poor quality. The few structures standing in early December failed to meet the Massachusetts troops' needs. One officer described the soldiers' situation as "poorly accommodated" in mid-December.[67] A lack of tools and building materials, difficult ground, and the prioritization of fortifications precluded the construction of a proper log-hut cantonment. Indeed, Paterson's officers found no good hutting grounds within three miles of the Point.[68] These various holdups validated Greene's belief that it would have been problematic to hut the whole army in that region given its rough terrain.

In contrast to the New York Highlands, Israel Putnam's wing in Connecticut made good progress in establishing its camp. Unlike the installations on the Hudson, the Connecticut log-hut city at Redding benefited from better terrain and more abundant timber.[69] Brigadier General Huntington took charge of selecting a site for a cantonment based on availability of wood and forage. On November 20, he reported finding both in abundance four miles east of Danbury.[70] Continental troops arrived in numbers at the start of December. Henry Dearborn and the New Hampshire Brigade commenced hut construction on December 4. By the fifteenth, the soldiers were finishing off their huts' roofs, with men actually entering their shelters between December 16 and 19. On December 24, Dearborn reported, "Our men are well clothed & well hutted."[71]

Putnam's Connecticut brigades suffered a delay, however, when he ordered them to the coast to guard against a feared British incursion. Pvt. Joseph Plumb Martin and his comrades thus spent a few cold, rainy nights in the Connecticut woods in late December. He recalled not finishing his hut by the start of the new year.[72] These soldiers turned in their tents to be dried and cleaned on January 4.[73] The delay in settling into quarters exacerbated the hardships these soldiers faced, adding exposure to the elements to lack of pay, bad uniforms, and inadequate provisions. Connecticut enlisted men gathered in front of their under-construction huts without orders and threatened to march off to Hartford to demand that their home state redress their grievances. General Putnam intervened and cajoled the recalcitrant soldiers to return to their huts, arresting the ringleaders of the protest for good measure.[74] Henceforth, the Redding camp remained quiet. An officer pronounced the entire force at Redding "all in finished huts and settled down" on January 10.[75] This would not be the last time, however, that Continental winter quarters hosted mutinous activities.

While some units might have proceeded slowly in building their shelters, throughout the Main Army, the quality of these structures had improved from the previous year. Continental officers kept their men disciplined during the crucial building phase of December 1778 and January 1779. With another campaign under their belts, company and regimental officers displayed better leadership than they had at Valley Forge. Brigade and regimental orders demonstrated greater supervision and attention to detail. Units succeeded in realizing the recently mandated hut designs. The cabins' solid roofs and improved foundations ensured that they would provide adequate protection from the elements.[76]

The Middlebrook huts' quality and uniformity caught the Continentals' attention. James Thacher described the construction of his hut at Middlebrook. It was built of logs notched together, and it had mud and clay plaster filling in the gaps between logs. These structures departed from the Valley Forge designs and adhered to Washington's newly implemented guidelines. Thacher's hut possessed a roof "formed of similar pieces of timber, and covered with hewn slabs," rather than the sod coverings of the previous year. A stone hearth topped by a log chimney covered in clay plaster now provided warmth. Thacher and his men also cut into the hut windows and doors attached to wooden hinges, another improvement over Valley Forge.[77] The Sixth Pennsylvania Regiment cleaned streets between huts and ensured the "ends of houses" were "trimmed in a neat manner." Lt. Col. Josiah Harmar of that unit described an orderly plan of encampment with enlisted men's huts placed at regular 4-yard intervals. A street 8 yards wide separated the hut lines, with officers quartered separately, 127 feet in the rear of the privates.[78]

Attentive officers ensured that the standardized dimensions for the structures were disseminated throughout the army during the winter of 1778–79. Washington's subordinates in both the Hudson Highlands and Connecticut implemented his new regulations for building camps. In New York, McDougall outlined plans for huts to sit uniformly in line along hillsides, facing southwest to benefit from maximum exposure to the sun.[79] He also arranged for upgraded hut interiors by issuing orders for making "guard beds," which he described as warmer than bunks and less wasteful of timber.[80] On the army's left wing, in Connecticut, Brig. Gen. Samuel Holden Parsons described dimensions and construction methods that were similar to those at Middlebrook. Brigade orders provided instructions for hut building at Redding that closely paralleled Washington's prescribed model. The fourteen-by-sixteen-foot hut standing six feet high had become standardized across the Main Army.[81] Like Thacher,

Parsons highlighted the additions of "proper roofs" made of wooden shingles. The well-ordered hut rows in Connecticut reminded the brigadier of the army's "present mode of camping."[82] Sgt. John Hawkins, also wintering at Redding, related that comrades erected their huts in orderly rows, with a "regular lane or alley" between each hut. He observed huts with uniformly arranged doors, chimneys, and windows.[83] Archeological studies indicate the Connecticut encampments, in accordance with Washington's orders, ended the practice of sinking huts below the frost line.[84]

The memory of the poor health experienced in the Valley Forge huts drove further refinements to castrametation. Shortly after construction began on the Middlebrook huts, Washington ordered additional enhancements to the camp's layout. Borrowing from techniques of European castrametation outlined by Bland and Cuthbertson for tent camps or barracks, general orders on December 24 directed soldiers to dig drainage ditches in front of every hut that would "secure troops from any inundation of water and much contribute to the health and convenience of the whole camp."[85] As soldiers finished their huts, officers commanded their men to dig their vaults and necessaries a minimum of 120 yards downhill from their living quarters. This measure ensured melting snow or heavy rains would not spread human waste into living quarters.[86]

In the Hudson Highlands, Alexander McDougall showed himself to be as conscientious in hutting as his commander in chief. He emphasized camp cleanliness to his men in his December 4 general orders, declaring, "Unless great care is taken of the present encampment and the intended cantonment to keep them clean, epidemical disorders will prevail in the huts in the spring." The evacuation of Valley Forge the previous June loomed large in the army's institutional memory. McDougall reminded his men that a disease-ridden cantonment would "oblige us to encamp in tents earlier than will be comfortable for the troops." To avoid such an eventuality, the major general implored his brigade commanders and their quartermasters to monitor their men's huts closely. He pointed out to his officers that maintaining a clean camp was "absolutely necessary for their [the soldiers'] health, and your honor." To provide for a sanitary camp, he issued orders to "dig deep necessary vaults" as soon as troops began to build their camps and before the ground froze further, making it impossible to excavate these vital tools of camp hygiene.[87] Later that month, soldiers in the Highlands received extracts from Washington's general orders outlining methods for keeping camps clean and dry.[88]

With the army settling into its new quarters, General Washington departed camp in mid-December to confer with national leaders in Philadelphia. Nathanael Greene accompanied him. The commander in chief entrusted Lord Stirling to command at Middlebrook. The crisis atmosphere of the first weeks at Valley Forge had given way to repose and recuperation in late 1778. By leaving winter quarters in the hands of a subordinate and spending a month in a major city, Washington emulated the conduct of European commanders during winter. Major General Stirling proved up to the task of overseeing the final stages of camp construction. He reported to Washington in late December that "although it has been cold in extreme the army is in great health and good spirits." Hutting proceeded as well as could be expected given the weather.[89]

The army demonstrated its growing construction skill by endeavoring to build more substantial structures than huts. At Pluckemin, five miles north of the main Middlebrook encampment, soldiers of Knox's Continental artillery worked to complete an assemblage of buildings intended to house the army's cannons, the artillery staff, and the Military Stores Department. Ultimately, this site provided quarters for twenty-two artillery companies, two artificers' companies, and a company of armorers, an estimated one thousand men. Soldiers labored from December through February to build the Pluckemin site. The artillery complex included enlisted men's barracks, separate officers' quarters, a guardhouse, a powder laboratory, an armorer's shop, a storage facility, and an "academy building" intended for instructing officers. Unlike the Continental Army's earlier attempts at barracks building, the Pluckemin structures went up with no interruptions and proved to be sturdy. The artillerists finished the academy by February 18, when the building hosted a large social gathering to celebrate the anniversary of the French alliance. The existence of such an imposing structure demonstrated a marked growth in organization and building skills compared to the assemblage of leaky huts that had quartered most of the army at Valley Forge.[90]

The rapid construction of the Pluckemin complex contrasted with the ongoing struggle to build good barracks in the Highlands. Ens. Oliver Rice of the Ninth Massachusetts Regiment informed his brother in January 1779 of good conditions at the Fishkill barracks. "Duty is very constant," he wrote, but "our provisions good, and men very healthy."[91] The barracks were apparently poorly built, however, and conditions worsened by spring. McDougall described the Ninth Massachusetts's buildings as "much out of repair" in late March. The general excused these soldiers from fatigue duty to work on mending chimneys and replacing their bunks.[92] By contrast, the simpler lodgings proved attractive alternatives. McDougall described those built by Nixon's brigade at Continental Village as "excellent huts."[93]

The relative ease with which the army put up its huts at Middlebrook contrasted sharply with its experience at Valley Forge. So, too, did its supply situation. Compared to Valley Forge, the Main Army at Middlebrook passed the winter with fewer shortages. Administrative improvements could claim some credit, with Nathanael Greene and Jeremiah Wadsworth firmly in place directing the Quartermaster's Department and the commissary, respectively.[94] The camp at Middlebrook encountered only a handful of logistical disruptions. Blame for these lay with the poor state of the nation's roads that were easily blocked by rapid changes in weather conditions. When frost hardened road surfaces, wagons made it to camp unimpeded, but when sudden thaws turned roads to mud, soldiers could expect delays to supply trains.[95] Mostly mild weather through much of early 1779 ensured that road conditions rarely reached the point of impassibility. One Raritan Valley resident recorded but two frosty nights during the first two weeks of February.[96] Aside from a period in early February when flour stocks dwindled to a four-days' supply, shortages never approached critical levels.[97] No "starve, dissolve, or disperse" missives came from Washington's headquarters or those of his subordinates.

Beyond the weather, credit for the relative bounty Continentals enjoyed lay with the careful thought Greene and his department had given to the selection of winter campsites that could be adequately provisioned. The course of the winter vindicated Greene's arguments for the benefits of posting the army closer to its supply hub at Trenton. In a country possessing deficient internal transportation networks, the Fighting Quaker had realized that a shift of even a few dozen miles closer to sources of food had a sizable impact. Fewer miles traveled meant less grain and grass consumed by supply teams, thereby conserving an article that remained scarce well into 1779. The rolling terrain between Trenton and Middlebrook also presented fewer obstructions than mountain roads leading into the Highlands.

The Main Army's center and right wings did not enjoy quite as bountiful supplies. Relying largely on New England, the Continentals in New York and Connecticut benefited from that region's abundance of cattle but suffered from its relative paucity of grain. The presence of two brigades under Maj. Gen. John Sullivan in Rhode Island further limited provisions. Heavy snows in December cut off the Redding troops from their magazine at Danbury.[98] Transportation difficulties further curbed what commissaries could effectively distribute.[99] Putnam's wing consequently experienced disruptions to flour in late December, leading to a brief eruption of plundering in nearby towns.[100] Nevertheless, the troops at Redding passed the rest of the winter without serious issue. The soldiers in the Hudson Highlands benefited from wintering along the great river. It afforded not only an avenue of transportation when unfrozen but also food. When the ice broke up in the middle of February, General McDougall requested every regiment under his command to furnish a list of men "who understand fishing with a net" so they could take advantage of "the season now approaching when fish may be caught in great abundance." Men enjoyed fish in their rations in mid-April.[101]

The Continentals spent the 1778–79 winter well rested in addition to well fed. The bulk of the Main Army conserved its strength while removed from contact with the enemy. In his memoirs, British commander in chief Gen. Sir Henry Clinton judged Washington's camp at Middlebrook "too strong" to contemplate attacking.[102] Crown forces consequently spent the winter holding positions in and around the city of New York. The dense settlement of the area under British control left numerous houses and public buildings available to shelter much of Clinton's army in the typical European fashion for winter quarters. The prolonged occupation of the region also gave the Redcoats and Hessians ample time to construct sturdy barracks to supplement their billets. Outlying detachments relied on rustic huts, but nothing resembling the log-hut city took shape within British lines.[103]

Geography afforded Washington's men respite. The Hudson River and Newark Bay formed a limited natural barrier between Patriot- and Crown-held territories. The British did send parties into New Jersey, and local inhabitants continued to bring supplies into New York despite the prohibitions of the state government. Neither side showed as much interest in waging *petite guerre* in the state in early 1779 as they had in Pennsylvania the year before. Given the sedentary dispositions of both armies, only the forward-deployed North Carolina and New Jersey brigades experienced any fighting in early 1779. William Maxwell's New Jerseyans in Essex County bore much responsibility for outpost duty throughout the winter. Even here, a British raid on Elizabethtown on February 25 stood as the only significant skirmish to occur in New Jersey during the winter.[104]

Nevertheless, the New Jersey regiments suffered from exhaustion and interruptions to training due to their detached posting. Lacking decent uniforms, the men took refuge in their warm billets while officers postponed marches and drill.[105] In March, Col. Israel Shreve, commanding the Second New Jersey Regiment billeting in Newark, complained that his goal to emerge from the winter with his men well organized and better disciplined was "now destroyed" because he had been ordered to send several companies to cover outlying villages.[106] Maxwell, Shreve's superior, likewise felt that keeping the brigade on forward deployment deprived it of the opportunities for discipline and refreshment that winter should have afforded, complaining, "Duty has really been hard here."[107] The sufferings of the New Jersey Brigade indicate how the rest of the army might have been negatively affected had it been broken up into smaller cantonments in New Jersey's towns and villages. Instead, the regiments that were concentrated at Middlebrook avoided any such hardships.

The center and left wings of the Main Army also contributed troops to forward outposts. In Connecticut, General Putnam detached small elements from his three brigades to guard that state's long, vulnerable shoreline. Militia, rather than regulars, provided Connecticut's first line of defense, however, and coastal raids in the early spring destroyed stocks of provisions and took prisoners. Connecticut governor Jonathan Trumbull beseeched Washington for up to two Continental regiments to guard the coastline. Washington refused the request, just as he had Livingston's in December 1779.[108] Throughout the winter, small forward outposts under Brig. Gen. Samuel Holden Parsons monitored British activity and relayed intelligence back to higher headquarters. Parsons would further refine his skills in leading detached troops during subsequent winters.[109]

In New York, McDougall deployed company-size Continental contingents to bolster the local militia in Westchester County. These posts afforded units the opportunity to spend a few weeks in the more abundant countryside of Westchester rather than in the sparse Highlands. Forward deployments also freed up scarce lodgings.[110] The lack of a natural barrier led to persistent skirmishing over forage that followed a pattern similar to the previous year's in Pennsylvania. McDougall emphasized to his outpost commanders the necessity of gaining intelligence and developing a familiarity with local terrain. He also showed attentiveness toward tactics in outpost operations. He ordered Lt. Col. Aaron Burr, the outpost commander that January, to place his men no more than half a mile apart at night to prevent ambush. To maintain secrecy on patrol, he recommended troops wrap their shoes in rags to muffle their feet on frozen ground.[111] British troops in this region kept on the defensive through the winter. Overall, Washington and his senior subordinates prioritized resting and maintaining the cohesion of their forces over guarding against British depredations on civilian communities.[112]

The Main Army maintained its chain of cantonments around New York through spring with few alterations to the arrangement of troops. In April, Washington dispatched Poor's, Hand's, and Maxwell's brigades to join Major General Sullivan's contingent gathering near Easton, Pennsylvania, to march against the Iroquois in New York.[113] Consolidation in the Virginia line left Washington with six brigades at Middlebrook at the start of the new campaign season. Even with the departure of Sullivan's wing, the diversion of other forces from Rhode Island to the New York theater concentrated fourteen well-rested brigades to contest Clinton's army in the Hudson Valley.

The transition from winter to spring again raised concerns over camp illness. To ensure soldiers' health, officers had to maintain good sanitation. Enhancements to hygiene at Middlebrook derived from both better camp designs and improved administration by Continental officers. Units better addressed the problem of camp residents fouling the ground near the huts rather than using proper necessaries. The Pennsylvania line threatened soldiers with the loss of one dollar of pay every time they were caught easing themselves in improper locations. This relatively trivial fine indicates that the problem might have proven less pressing at Middlebrook than at Valley Forge. Camp followers faced harsher punishments. Any woman or child guilty of the same infraction was to be expelled from the camp.[114] Regimental commanders in New York likewise detailed officers to monitor the cleanliness of huts and barracks rooms. McDougall also directed his men to make soap, "as without it they can't be kept clean."[115]

The arrival of warm weather in April 1779 led to further invectives against uncleanliness. The concurrent arrival of recruits brought inexperienced soldiers to camp, exacerbating hygiene issues. With the "hot season" approaching, Washington sought to prevent the putrid conditions that had besieged Valley Forge. He admonished soldiers for "the smell in front of the parade ground," which was "so very offensive, and if not soon prevented, must be attended with very bad consequences." Soldiers were to clear animal bones from the ground around their huts and bury them in vaults "sunk at a proper distance" from camp. New duties also included covering vaults at least three times each week.[116] Other routine activities found men sweeping clean the streets between their huts.[117] In late April, soldiers carried "filth and dirt" gathered in front of their huts down to a nearby creek to be collected "in one heap."[118] Washington also reminded his men to properly cook their food. Indicative of the growing expectations the commander in chief had for his officer corps, he emphasized that brigade commanders bore ultimate responsibility for the health and cleanliness of their men.[119] Throughout the Main Army, officers demonstrated a better understanding of the attentiveness and discipline required to maintain hygiene in camp. Veteran soldiers also seem to have better adhered to their officers' instructions. No one present at Middlebrook mentioned foul smells or garbage littering company streets in late May. Neither Middlebrook, the Hudson Highlands, nor Redding witnessed rotten conditions requiring evacuation come spring.

Beyond camp ailments, smallpox also appeared to be in retreat in the spring of 1779. The army experienced less turnover in the ranks than in previous years. With the war seemingly stagnating, the profusion of recruits seen in 1777 and 1778 failed to materialize. While this portended future manpower shortages, it also made light work for Continental doctors. Immediate inoculation of new arrivals had become standard practice. Brigade commanders and hospital staff knew their duty without needing special instructions. The commander in chief rarely mentioned smallpox in his correspondence from Middlebrook. Overall, the army's personnel by 1779 had become what Civil War historian Kathryn

Shivley Meier has termed "seasoned soldiers." The men had developed immunities to diseases and inured themselves to the rigors of life in the field.[120]

In addition to health, spring recruitment tested the orderly arrangement of the Patriot camps. In the Maryland brigades, new arrivals built huts in front of and beside the existing encampment with little regard for uniformity. Brig. Gen. William Smallwood, commanding the Maryland line, condemned the "disorder those huts generally produce." He recognized that the indiscipline and inexperience of the recruits showed in the disordered built environment they erected. In what would become a standard disciplinary measure within the Main Army, Smallwood ordered any new hut that did not conform to the camp's plan to be pulled down and rebuilt.[121]

By late spring, forage rather than disease or enemy action preoccupied the army's senior commanders.[122] Although weather had been generally mild through the winter, April had witnessed frosts followed by a drought that reduced the availability of local food and fodder.[123] By late spring, New Jersey's pastures had recovered slightly, though there remained barely enough grain and hay in the state to subsist the horses with the army. Conserving forage during the winter, however, had ensured that sufficient stocks remained available in June when the army transitioned to active operations. Emergency procurements subsequently kept wagons in motion when the army marched northward to West Point, where it stayed for most of the summer.[124] Not until grass grew and grain ripened in the late July did forage return in relative abundance.[125]

The anxiety that Patriot officers expressed over forage deficiencies throughout 1778 and 1779 highlights the indispensability of that article to maintaining supply trains. Given the difficulties the army encountered even in the summer of 1779, it is likely that concentrating a larger portion of the Main Army in the Hudson Highlands for winter quarters would have produced a logistical calamity similar to the 1777–78 winter. At Valley Forge, the army had, to its detriment, largely ignored logistics in locating its quarters. At Middlebrook, the Rebels reaped the benefits of a well-fed camp thanks to Greene's careful assessments of the country's ability to supply the soldiers. Greene had effectively pioneered a new understanding of the logistics of supplying winter encampments that no European writers had discovered in their works.

Overall, the Continentals emerged from winter quarters in better shape than they had the previous year. As a result of soldiers' and officers' efforts, the army exhibited better health and discipline. Officers who had resided at both winter camps remarked on the improved quality of their quarters and the hale condition of their soldiers. In a March letter to Lafayette, Washington claimed his men were "better clad and more healthy than they have ever been since the formation of the army."[126] Dr. Samuel Adams, stationed with the artillery at Pluckemin, declared, "Our army is remarkably healthy" in May 1779.[127]

Elsewhere in the army's arc of camps around New York, similar conditions prevailed. At Redding, Brig. Gen. Jedediah Huntington happily reported to his father in mid-March that "a remarkable degree of health prevails in this division," which had not lost a man in the four months since entering winter quarters.[128] A Connecticut soldier at Redding recalled having "had a comfortable winter."[129] Chaplain David Avery, stationed in the Hudson Highlands, recorded the soldiers wintering at Peekskill to be "in good health."[130] Another chaplain, Enos Hitchcock, found the men at West Point in "very fine health and spirits" in April.[131] Lt. Henry Sewall believed the troops at the fortress stood in good form in late May. If the British attacked, he confidently asserted, "they will meet with a *warm reception*."[132] Compared to the previous year at Valley Forge, when one in three Patriot soldiers had come down with illness, the Continental Army emerged from winter quarters in the spring of 1779 with only 9.4 percent of its manpower on the sick lists.[133]

Many officers also showed greater sureness in the army's ability to build and maintain winter shelter effectively. Observers took note of the encampments themselves, which exuded a new orderliness. James Thacher described Middlebrook as "a regular uniform compact village."[134] Anthony Wayne commented that his Pennsylvanians' camp's "regularity is equal to any on the continent. Its internal police is at least as regular as that of Philadelphia." Contrasting Middlebrook with Valley Forge, Wayne assured Washington, "We are much improved in city building."[135] Washington responded that the Pennsylvanians' "barracks appear to be well constructed for the accommodation of the troops, and judiciously disposed."[136] Given the army's success at constructing and maintaining its winter quarters, Wayne stood confident that the Continentals could now pass the winter "as healthy and as regular an army as ever made a winter's campaign."[137]

Over the course of the 1778–79 winter, the Continental Army developed a new doctrine of castrametation. The clearest manifestation of this doctrine came in the built form of the log-hut city, which departed so drastically from contemporary methods of winter quarters. By implementing new standards of construction and gleaning European maxims for camp sanitation and applying them to winter quarters, the army overcame the worst failings of the Valley Forge hut city. The Continental Army also developed a clearer understanding of the logistics of supplying winter quarters, particularly in its attention to how access to roads, proximity to magazines, and availability of forage limited where the army could and could not easily quarter. The Patriots had also honed a better appreciation for what landscapes could best support a prolonged, stationary camp. Experienced officers, better-disciplined enlisted men, and the attentiveness of senior commanders ensured that the army put into practice the combination of old maxims and new ideas that comprised Continental thinking on castrametation. In the late spring of 1779, the Patriot cause reaped the rewards of these efforts as the Continentals entered the new campaign healthy and confident.

The buildings the Continental Army erected during the 1778–79 winter would continue to find employment as winter shelter, hospitals, and storehouses in subsequent years. Changes in Continental strategy made the presence of such instillations imperative. In January 1779, Nathanael Greene explained to Washington what he viewed to be the "principle objects" of the next campaign. He stressed the importance of taking "a position favorable for subsisting the army with ease and at the least expense," along with an offensive against the Iroquois and an attack on New York. In his view, maintaining the army in New Jersey best satisfied the first criterion.[138] Due to the army's discerning selection of sites upon which to build its quarters, the Continentals now had military infrastructure standing in areas that events had proven could be easily supplied and secured. Faced with declining operational mobility in the New York region, keeping the army at cantonments for half the year presented an increasingly attractive option. Nevertheless, the war continued to bring the unexpected, and the Continental Army would once again need to reevaluate its positions come the following winter.

CHAPTER 6

"The Doctrine
of Huttification"

1779–1780

Sprung from successful winter quarters, the Continentals achieved several victories during the summer of 1779. Maj. Gen. John Sullivan directed a campaign in western New York against the Iroquois heartland. His four brigades encountered few problems with health, discipline, or supply, although they failed to end raids on the frontier. Along the Hudson, Washington husbanded his remaining forces to monitor the British. Small-scale surprise attacks at Stony Point in July and Paulus Hook in August defeated isolated Redcoat garrisons and helped maintain Patriot control of the river north of Manhattan. In the autumn, Sullivan's forces returned to New York and New Jersey, and Washington prepared to enact his long-held goal of attacking the city in conjunction with the French fleet.[1]

These successes aside, late 1779 brought new challenges to Washington's Continentals. A buildup in the British garrison in New York left the Rebels uncertain of enemy intentions. The revolutionaries could not expect their opponents to stay quiescent for another winter. In addition, expiring enlistments, desertion, and the dispatch of brigades to reinforce the beleaguered Southern Theater reduced Patriot manpower. At the same time, declining finances and congressional mismanagement threatened to undermine the always-rickety supply apparatus. Finally, although the Continentals could not foresee it, the coming winter would be one of the worst in memory. Thus, 1779–80 would present the army with a new test to its quartering system.

In the autumn of 1779, Washington held position along the Hudson near West Point, awaiting the potential arrival of French reinforcements under Charles Hector, Comte D'Estaing. If the French fleet arrived before winter, the commander in chief hoped to launch an attack on New York. The local infrastructure would support this offensive. Storehouses and barracks stood at Peekskill and Fishkill, and in September Washington ordered a new barracks construction program at the West Point fortifications to house up to three thousand men.[2] In New Jersey, artificers and hospital staff occupied the huts at Middlebrook and barracks at Pluckemin after the army's departure in June. Washington also directed new flat-bottom boats, instrumental for an assault on Manhattan, to be repaired and stored at Middlebrook. Morristown held military storehouses containing camp equipage. The Continentals also maintained their magazines along the route from Trenton to West Point, New York.[3]

If the attack did not take place, Washington preferred New Jersey for winter quarters. Through early autumn, the commander in chief continued to view ease of supply as the most important criterion in determining the location to which his troops retired. Secondarily, he sought locations affording ample resources for hut construction, dry ground, and terrain that his men could adequately fortify. The slopes of the Watchungs north of the Raritan River had satisfied all these conditions with the Middlebrook site. In the fall of 1779, it appeared this area would do so once more. In September and October, the Continental commander favored Quibbletown, ten miles east of the 1778–79 huts. There the army could build a fortified camp in the Watchungs and enjoy easy communications with Trenton and the other storehouses in the region. The Hudson Highlands and Connecticut would again receive troops as well.[4]

The previous two winter encampments had highlighted the importance of retiring to winter quarters as early as possible. Major General Greene demonstrated greater attentiveness to preparations as his second full winter as quartermaster general approached. In late September, Greene began to gather supplies for the planned winter quarters at Quibbletown, as well as for troops who would presumably winter in Connecticut.[5] Through the early autumn, senior Continental commanders appeared to have firmly established their preliminary arrangements for winter quarters. This portended a smooth retirement from active operations.

Events in late October and early November upset these arrangements, however, forcing Washington to reevaluate his plans for winter dispositions. The disruption came in the form of a late-October raid by a party of four hundred infantry and one hundred cavalry of Lt. Col. John Graves Simcoe's Queen's Rangers, a Loyalist unit. They landed at Perth Amboy on October 27 and marched past Quibbletown and on to Somerset Court House, in the vicinity of Middlebrook. Continental officers struggled to discern the objective of the attack, with Virginia troops camped along the New York border rushing southward to guard Morristown rather than Middlebrook.[6] Simcoe's force reached the vicinity of the old log-hut city, where they set fire to artificers' huts, burned seventy tons of hay and fourteen bushels of grain, and destroyed eighteen boats as well as other equipment. During the Rangers' withdrawal, they encountered spirited resistance from the New Jersey militia, resulting in Simcoe's capture.[7]

While the overall damage had been light, Simcoe's raid nevertheless revealed the vulnerability of Patriot posts in the Raritan Valley. The approaches to Middlebrook benefited from no natural barriers. Only fifteen miles of flat terrain separated Middlebrook from Perth Amboy, where the British had shown they could land with impunity. The October raid raised the question of whether the army would have enough warning to mount a proper defense should it decide to camp along the Watchungs. Local Patriot leaders recognized this area's vulnerability immediately after the raid and bombarded Washington and Greene with their concerns for the protection of supplies already gathered in the area.[8]

Simcoe's raid compelled Washington to reconsider his plans for winter dispositions. Unlike previous years, the form of quarters was not in doubt. Soldiers would lodge in a log-hut city. But where should they build it? In similar situations previously, Washington had held a council of war to solicit his subordinates' opinions on such matters. In 1779 he seems to have eschewed such an approach. Only one of his generals, Maj. Gen. Arthur St. Clair, offered input on the matter. Writing to Washington on November 2, 1779, St. Clair worried that a winter attack on the army's quarters could lead to catastrophe. If posted "in the vicinity of the enemy," this diminished force would be "liable to have their quarters beat up." If induced to retreat to a new position in the middle of winter, the army would be left "exposed to the loss of their baggage and artillery" as well as their horses. Thus, a remote encampment appeared to be the army's best option.

Yet a more inaccessible location presented its own set of problems. St. Clair observed that placing the army at a greater distance from New York City would expose New Jersey to further British raids. Sending most of the army to West Point would completely expose its lines of communication through New Jersey and force Patriot supply trains to travel through "less abundant country." Distance from the army's primary sources of supply to the west and south again nullified the possibility of a more secure encampment in the Hudson Highlands. Pointing out the Rebels' dilemma, St. Clair lamented that "difficulties present themselves on all sides." As a compromise, he proposed winter quarters within a few hours' march of the Watchung Mountains, "a barrier of considerable importance." These hills would provide security for the cantoned army while still affording it a position close to its principal supply sources.[9]

Washington reconsidered his planned site for the army's winter quarters in light of the circumstances St. Clair had outlined. European writers, including Turpin de Crissé and Frederick the Great, had praised the benefits of using terrain to secure an encampment. Washington's new plan for winter quarters bore the mark of these concepts and St. Clair's advice. Rather than use the Watchungs' slopes as a foundation for a fortified camp, he chose instead to treat them as an impediment to any potential enemy advance. An encampment west of the range would place two parallel ridges between the British in New York and the log-hut city. This topography would limit the avenues of approach available to any British attack. Observation posts along the ridgeline would give ample warning. West of the Watchungs lay the broken ground of the New Jersey Highlands. This terrain promised to further inhibit an aggressor and provide a stronger position in which to erect a camp. Morristown, the site of Washington's headquarters in early 1777, lay at the heart of this region. Consequently, in early November, the commander in chief preferred that village rather than Quibbletown.

Wintering west of the Watchungs would exchange ease of provision for ease of defense. To its debit, a Morristown camp would extend supply lines to Trenton another fifteen miles from what they had been at Middlebrook. Washington's proposal thereby gambled that the Quartermaster's Department could maintain roads and stock forage in quantities to keep wagon trains moving to camp throughout the winter. Major General Greene did not object to Morristown in early November and made arrangements for the construction of another log-hut city.[10]

Greene soon discovered, however, that finding suitable sites for winter quarters presented a significant challenge. Throughout November, Greene and his subordinates scouted potential spots for winter quarters near Morristown. The quartermaster ordered his men to conduct what was essentially a topographic survey of northern New Jersey. They were to note the "water, wood, and make of ground" for each locale, the state of the roads, and the presence of houses in which officers might quarter. Greene made abundant timber the most important criterion, as it had been the previous year.[11]

In a twist of environmental irony, the same geographic features that made northwestern New Jersey so appealing as a remote and easily defended location also made it unsatisfactory for building and supplying a large camp. Natural features including ridgelines, lakes, and swamps broke up the terrain. Much of the ground was too damp, ridges were too steep, and woodlands too small and dispersed to be useful to the army.[12] At Canoe Brook, east of Morristown, Greene discovered "a great quantity of wood"; however, he found that the "ground is so wet and swampy that it is totally unfit for an encampment."

Human land-use patterns also proved unhelpful. Of the territory in eastern Morris County, Greene lamented "all this country is divided into small farms each of which has only a small wood lot."[13] Greene had discerned an important difference in the development of the region around Morristown compared to the vicinity of Middlebrook, which had hosted the army the previous year. Most of Morris County's population hailed from New England. Morris residents shared New Englanders' tendencies toward small landholdings that left the county with few large woodlots. The rough and rocky glacial hills of the New Jersey Highlands further contributed to this variegated configuration of landholding. Individual farms included the small woodlots Greene observed, but their expansive distribution promised to inconvenience the army in its search for lumber. Conversely, Middlebrook had lain closer to the Raritan Valley, which had long served as a source of cordwood for New York.[14]

Reports from Greene's staff featured detailed studies of the region's landscapes, but no standout choice for a campsite. Morristown's deputy quartermaster Col. James Abeel, joined by Maj. Gen. Lord Stirling, a resident of nearby Basking Ridge, found a locale between the parallel ridges of the Watchungs near Stirling's home. Greene rejected this proposal, however, due to an inadequate local wood supply. Clement Biddle advocated for the vicinity of Scotch Plains near Quibbletown because of an abundance of hay, but his superior dismissed this since it lay exposed to a British attack.[15] Another survey by Abeel farther north found a favorable site near Morristown. Abeel described the region as "well covered with timber & pretty well watered the ground is dry & if the tract is large enough I believe will be the best I have as yet seen."[16] Greene remained unconvinced. Not content to leave the search to his subordinates, he toured the Parsippany region north of Morristown. The Rhode Islander dedicated two days to this survey, but his efforts and those of his staff yielded no conclusive solutions by the middle of the month.[17]

Beyond finding hutting grounds, reconciling the conflicting criteria of defensibility and ease of supply also perplexed the Continentals. Greene summed up the conundrum to Washington in a November 14 letter, stating, "It is not always in the power of a general to take a position most favorable to his wishes on account of provision & forage, or to place himself in the most advantageous point of view, for covering the country and securing his capital posts." As Greene had in 1778, he reiterated that, all other troubles aside, "there is no contending with hunger."[18] Nevertheless, the commander in chief vacillated between logistical and defensive considerations. Washington bemoaned to Maj. Gen. Alexander McDougall that he found "it rather difficult to fix upon a line of winter cantonments that will answer the double purposes of security and subsistence" and pointed out that "these two points militate strongly against each other."[19] The lack of decent ground for hutting added a third dimension to the debate between supply and security. After receiving orders to plan hut arrangements for the winter camp on November 17, Greene responded to Washington, "It is very difficult to find a piece of ground with all the requisites for hutting the army to advantage." He despaired "of getting a position perfectly to my liking, or that will be entirely satisfactory to your excellency."[20]

The Main Army was in a situation similar to that before Valley Forge. The enemy occupied a principal city, with Rebel troops hovering in the countryside beyond. Congress pressured Washington to mount an offensive to retake the town despite the lateness of the season. The need to cooperate with the French fleet to undertake such an operation added a further complication. The original plan for a strong, concentrated forward camp near Quibbletown hinted at an offensive posture. Washington seems to have held out hope for the French arrival through the middle of November. Nevertheless, he hedged his bets by sending Greene and staff on a search for a more secure cantonment site should the fleet disappoint. Concurrently, the enemy buildup in New York and the bold Simcoe raid pointed toward a potential British offensive. Consequently, uncertainty reigned over the commander in chief's decision-making through November.[21]

Throughout the second half of the month, Greene's staff continued to scour northern New Jersey for acceptable campsites. So befuddling was the geography of castrametation that Greene ignored Washington's defensive concerns and scouted terrain east of the Watchungs. In late November, Greene's subordinates presented a potential position at Acquackanonk. This site lay twenty miles east of Morristown, at the foot of the mountains along the Passaic River. Greene's scouts believed this place could accommodate the entire army, and it appeared ideally suited to the army's castrametation criteria. The locale would increase transportation from Trenton, but it enjoyed good local forage and an abundance of houses for senior officers' quarters and was closer to West Point.

Greene's strong support for Acquackanonk indicated his preference for a position that would facilitate hutting. In a November 23 letter to Washington, he contrasted the Acquackanonk site with an area that he was reconnoitering near Basking Ridge. The latter stood closer to Morristown and west of the Watchungs; however, Greene explained that it offered no opportunity to hut troops together except for an area featuring ground that was "spongy and cold." Conversely, Greene declared that Acquackanonk "pleases me much the best." He offered to halt the army's march in Parsippany to divert it to the Passaic should Washington opt for that locale.[22]

Concurrently, Brig. Gen. Anthony Wayne added a third contender. The Pennsylvanian, who had shown a keen understanding of the resources needed for hut building at Middlebrook, viewed a site far to the south in the Sourland Mountains in Somerset County. Greene informed Washington that Wayne had found that this position equaled Acquackanonk as a place that was as "preferable to any we can fix upon." Greene contrasted the two places, one "very favorable for West Point," the other only fifteen miles from Trenton, highlighting the strategic and logistical sides of the dilemma facing the Continentals. Quartering at Acquackanonk would extend supply lines from the south and uncover the middle of New Jersey, which had already been revealed as vulnerable by Simcoe's October raid. On the other hand, wintering in the Sourlands would leave the army well provisioned but far from West Point. Additionally, the southerly site lacked the rugged defensibility of Morristown and would expose much of the northern part of the state to attack.[23]

With November entering its final week, the need to stow tents and begin hut construction before winter's onset made a final quartering decision imperative. The exasperated quartermaster general complained, "I am almost worn out with fatigue," and said he had "been perplexed not a little to find out where to fix the army. I have rode hot and cold, wet and dry, night and day, in traversing the Country, in search of the most proper place for quartering the troops."[24] While Morristown's vicinity offered the best balance of security and logistical feasibility, so far the surrounding landscapes had not revealed any sites acceptable for building a log-hut city.

Ultimately, Greene's staff solved the quartering predicament by finding a suitable campsite near Morristown. Drawing on a report from Colonel Abeel, Greene told Washington on November 27 that between Morristown and Mendham a "very good position may be had at Jockey Hollow." The locale possessed a few disadvantages, specifically hilly terrain that would break the cantonment into individual brigade camps. To Jockey Hollow's credit, dry ground, abundant wood, and fresh water supplies would satisfy the army's needs. Rough terrain and distance from New York promised to impede any attack on the cantonment. The Rhode Islander recognized, however, that with a location in the mountains, "the transportation will be more heavy and difficult to keep up." Jockey Hollow fulfilled Washington's desire for security while remaining close enough to both West Point and central New Jersey to cover those positions.[25]

Washington wrote to Greene on November 30 to declare his final choice for Jockey Hollow. Concerns for the army's safety undergirded his decision. The need to detach forces to the South and the pending expiration of enlistments induced the Continental commander to "seek a more remote position than we would otherwise have done." Washington perceived the strategic picture from his vantage point as commander in chief, which transcended a specific focus on logistics. He thus ordered Greene to begin laying out ground for the encampment.[26]

In the Continental commander's final determination, the First and Second Pennsylvania, First and Second Connecticut, and First and Second Maryland

Brigades, as well as the New York Brigade and mixed brigades under Brigadier Generals Edward Hand and John Stark, camped at Jockey Hollow. Midway through November, Washington had planned to camp his brigades in one or two lines, making for a powerful defensive arrangement similar to that of Valley Forge.[27] As Greene had predicted, the terrain forced these units to camp separately, with broken ground separating the brigades. William Maxwell's New Jersey Brigade built its huts one mile south of the main encampment at Ayre's Forge. The Virginia line briefly began work on huts near this site before being dispatched to reinforce the South. As distance from New York minimized the risk of a surprise British attack, however, the Continental generals opted to leave the camp unfortified. As originally planned, the four Massachusetts brigades wintered in the Hudson Highlands. The New Hampshire Brigade and cavalry returned to Connecticut.[28]

Continentals of all ranks had waited impatiently for Washington's decision. Capt. Moses White wrote in early November from Peekskill: "Winter quarters are what we are all looking for. The general I believe waits for nothing." White obviously did not know of the extended search and attendant difficulties then underway.[29] Massachusetts troops presumed they would remain along the Hudson and therefore held fewer concerns, as they did not face a long march into New Jersey.[30] Those headed for more distant locales expressed their displeasure. On November 29, Dr. Samuel Tenney of the New Hampshire Brigade complained, "Our unhappiness now is that we have to build winter quarters at a time when we should be in them." Tenney contrasted the relative inactivity of the Main Army over the summer, spent in "idleness & luxury," with the coming winter months promising "penury & fatigue."[31]

Even after Washington's decision, it took several days for information regarding the choice of quarters to reach officers throughout the Main Army. Virginia troops billeted in Morristown at the end of November as they anxiously waited to learn the location of their hut sites.[32] On December 3, the commander of Washington's guard, Maj. Caleb Gibbs, remained uncertain as to where to direct the commander in chief's baggage.[33] Nathanael Greene likened the Continentals to the "wandering Jews in search of a Jerusalem, not having fixt upon a position for hutting the Army."[34] Capt. Samuel Richards of Connecticut complained, "Our army—as usual—lay out uncovered until the enemy retired."[35] Washington might have countered Richards's criticism that a few weeks spent marching and camping in the snow ensured that the army would not suffer a surprise attack as it entered winter quarters.

The Continentals again began work on their quarters later into the season that they might have liked due to the delays the November search had imposed. The weather turned cold and snowy earlier than in years past, further adding to soldiers' miseries. Connecticut troops found up to two feet of snow lying on the ground when they arrived at their hutting grounds in early December.[36] John Stark's brigade of New England troops did not even depart their positions near Danbury, Connecticut, until December 5. Tent shortages meant that some men had to spend nights, in paymaster Nathaniel Beers's words, in "quarters in the woods without any other coverings than bushes and in a severe storm of snow." Stark's men did not arrive at Morristown and begin constructing huts until December 14.[37]

Upon arrival, soldiers labored with more experience and greater confidence in hut building than at Valley Forge or Middlebrook. The Rebels now accepted the construction of log cities as standard practice for winter quarters. Col. Alexander Scammell described the rise of the encampment at Jockey Hollow as part of the "doctrine of huttification."[38] Perhaps comparing the huts to the temporary late-season quarters in European warfare, Maj. Gen. Johann de Kalb referred to the Jockey Hollow shelters as "shanties." Nevertheless, he considered the practice commonplace, writing of "winter-quarters in the woods, *as usual.*"[39]

For the first time, some of the castrametation knowledge gained during the war was now codified in print. Baron Wilhelm von Steuben's *Regulations for the Order and Discipline of the Troops of the United States*, first published in the spring of 1779, represents the Continentals' first military manual. While primarily remembered as drill book, it also includes sections detailing the arrangement of shelters and placement of latrines in camp. Officers no longer had to refer to older treatises or rely on daily directives issued from headquarters. Von Steuben outlined the duties intrinsic to planning the army's camps in a manner similar to European manuals. The quartermaster was to establish a "line of encampment" and mark out the grounds upon which brigades were to camp. Brigade quartermasters were then to select grounds for subordinate regiments. Regimental quartermasters followed by determining sites for individual companies, kitchens, and other ancillary buildings. Von Steuben's regulations mention only tents, but the duties outlined for marking out camps carry over to winter quarters as well.[40]

Matters not included in the army's new manual, such as guidelines for the overall layout of the log-hut city and protocols for hut designs, remained under Washington's and Greene's purview. Just as these generals had discerned and disseminated the best practices for hut construction after Valley Forge, at Morristown they adopted a plan for arranging huts, drawing from successes at the previous winter encampment. For 1779–80, Washington ordered Greene to develop a hutting arrangement based on the most successful layout used at Middlebrook. Again, those of the Pennsylvania line provided a model for the rest of the army.[41]

New disciplinary measures facilitated sturdy and uniform construction. Washington implemented stringent punishments for units that failed to properly erect their shelters. He borrowed from methods first put in place by Maryland brigadier general William Smallwood at Middlebrook. The commander in chief decreed to Nathanael Greene that "the dimensions of the soldiers' barracks [were] to be given out and not departed from in the least particular, under pain of having those pulled down which differ from the model."[42] Washington informed the army in a general order two days later that "any hut not exactly conforming to the plan" was to come down.[43] Soldiers evidently adhered to these orders. Troops in the New Jersey Brigade tore down a deficient hut in advance of an inspection tour.[44] In March, Pennsylvania soldiers took down a poorly built guardhouse and rebuilt it.[45] Beyond punishment, the army also offered rewards to soldiers for sound hut construction. In contrast to the Valley Forge winter, in 1780 Continental commanders did away with monetary awards, due to either the depreciation of currency or its lack of motivation for enlisted men. Instead, soldiers completing their huts the fastest and within specifications received two gallons of whiskey as a reward. Those who built their hut closest to the prescribed model received four gallons.[46]

Despite the Continentals' improving experience and training, building huts in late December distressed soldiers more than in previous years. The long march to quarters had damaged uniforms, and two weeks of hut building left the rank and file's clothes in tatters.[47] Snow and cold further hindered hut building at Morristown despite threats, incentives, and the devotion of manpower to construction. Maj. Gen. Johann de Kalb complained, "The severe frost greatly retards our work and does not even permit us to complete our chimneys."[48] "It is so cold we can't get ours built," complained one Pennsylvania lieutenant.[49] For some, working on huts amid cold and snow also led to injuries. John Faust, a private with the Ninth Pennsylvania, "was disabled by building huts at Jockey Hollow" and spent the rest of the war in the invalid regiment.[50] The late decision on a campsite also delayed the arrival of tools. Joseph Plumb Martin recalled that his comrades pilfered implements from neighboring civilian inhabitants to "expedite the erection and completion of their dwelling places."[51]

Despite these difficulties, experienced troops persevered to get their shelters standing. Common soldiers demonstrated improved construction skills. Pennsylvania soldiers, veterans of two previous log-hut cities, started work on their cabins on December 5 and began to occupy them a week later.[52] Officers in the smaller New York Brigade moved into their huts on December 22, two weeks after construction began.[53] The commander in chief's guard once again finished its huts in under a week.[54] The Maryland line improved on its tardy performance of the previous year, with enlisted men well covered by December 24 and officers expecting to finish their huts by New Year's Day.[55] Stark's brigade, despite arriving in the middle of the month, finished its enlisted men's huts by December's final week.[56]

Martial pride endured and sustained units through the process of construction and habitation. Von Steuben's 1779 reforms outlined the supervisory duties for regimental officers and noncommissioned officers, and at Morristown their attentiveness toward hut construction reflected the army's increasing administrative skill.[57] Officers made sure to lay out hut sites close to available timber.[58] Regiments invested great attention to detail in building their shelters. Ens. Jeremiah Greenman's Rhode Island comrades worked through the end of February 1780, "fixing our hut to make it as complete as we can considering our situation."[59] Regimental officers bore the hardship of exposure while their men worked on their shelters. Lt. Col. Ebenezer Huntington, serving in Stark's brigade, did not move into a cabin until January 22, 1780. Even then, this structure was a captain's; Huntington did not expect to complete his own hut until the end of February.[60]

In the face of harsh weather, the Main Army at Morristown endured the winter of 1779–80 securely ensconced in its best-ordered log-hut city to date. An anonymous sketch of Stark's brigade's encampment at Jockey Hollow indicates that soldiers generally followed the new guidelines for camp construction. The drawing reflects the emphasis on uniformity in design and orderly layout. It depicts two neat rows of huts at the lowest level, presumably those of

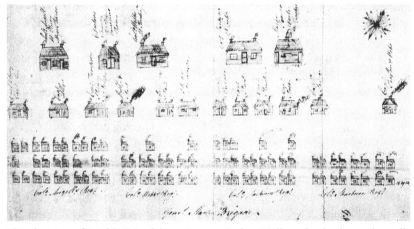

This drawing of Stark's Brigade's position at Jockey Hollow clearly shows the well-ordered encampment that Continentals built in 1780. Anonymous, "General Stark's Brigade." Historic Photograph Collection, Group A, number 0338. Morristown National Historical Park, Morristown, New Jersey.

the enlisted men. Ensigns' and lieutenants' huts stand at greater intervals on a third row, with captains' huts occupying a fourth row.[61]

Archaeological work at Jockey Hollow has largely confirmed the accuracy of the sketch, indicating that the army closely adhered to guidelines for building huts and laying out the encampment. Archaeologists studying the First Connecticut Brigade's encampment have found the remains of huts arrayed in two parallel lines of thirty-four structures each. This number corresponds with the brigade's listed strength of roughly nine hundred men in early 1780. Material remains also indicate most huts conformed to the fourteen-by-sixteen-foot dimensions regulations prescribed. Officers apparently had more latitude in the construction of their own dwellings. Both soldiers and officers placed doors and chimneys in various locations. Soldiers adhered to Washington's stipulation that they sink the shelters into the ground only far enough to provide for level floors. While no other brigade sites have received archaeologists' attention, the material evidence studied at Jockey Hollow stands in sharp contrast to the haphazard layout observed at Valley Forge.[62]

Commanders also recognized that well-built structures might have future value and should be kept intact. When the Virginia line departed for the South in early December, Washington prohibited any other units from appropriating the building materials gathered at the Virginians' hut sites without his

This replica hut at Jockey Hollow highlights the refinements to shelter building compared to the Valley Forge winter. "Reproduction Soldiers' Hut." Morristown National Historical Park, Morristown, New Jersey. Author's collection.

permission.[63] When the New Jersey Brigade moved into vacated huts at Jockey Hollow in April, General Maxwell forbade "the destroying any of the huts in our present encampment." He stipulated a punishment of twenty lashes for any soldier found "destroying or carrying away any part of the huts."[64]

Elsewhere in the Main Army's deployment around New York, Continentals similarly grappled with bad weather and varied terrain in building their winter shelter. Enoch Poor's New Hampshire Brigade wintered near its hut sites from the previous year, though the troops did build an entirely new complex at Ridgebury rather than reuse the cantonment at nearby Redding. Poor might have opted for a more defensible locale since his was the only formation in the area. Regardless, the New Hampshire men recorded good progress in building their new homes, with huts rising in two weeks. The brigade enjoyed an uneventful winter at Ridgebury, residing there from December through April, when it relocated to West Point.[65]

The situation along the Hudson had changed from the previous year. Patriot commanders sought a more compact arrangement for 1779–80, facilitated, they hoped, by newly built barracks. Work in the Highlands continued throughout the summer and fall of 1779. Redoubts and bombproofs competed with barracks for limited resources, however, and by November the complex still lacked the required shelter. Maj. Gen. Alexander McDougall, the presumptive commander in the Highlands for the winter, painted a dismal picture in a November 6 letter to Washington. Transportation shortages brought on by a lack of forage retarded construction. Masons were hard at work raising chimneys, but McDougall feared, "Such is the advanced season, that if a considerable garrison is to be left here, they have not a moment's time to spare to cover themselves." The fortress garrison had to transport its building materials, "even the water to make mortar," from afar. Troops lacked enough boards to make barracks, and McDougall viewed the only suitable hutting grounds as too far from the defensive works to cover them. He feared that if the Massachusetts line wintered in the Highlands, it would have to shelter in tents. This prospect would understandably discourage reenlistments.[66]

The commander in chief sympathized with some of McDougall's concerns. Preparations for the attack on New York had diverted most of the artificers to work on boats rather than barracks. With the offensive unlikely by November, Washington promised to return these skilled laborers to the Highlands as soon as possible. He also directed boards to West Point to accelerate construction. To economize, Washington ordered McDougall to concentrate his efforts on erecting the principal barracks at Fort Arnold and finishing those already underway. Garrisons for smaller works would have to seek refuge within their redoubts and bombproofs. McDougall's frequent complaints also led the commander in chief to seek a more confident leader for the Highlands posts. Once Washington had settled winter dispositions, he informed McDougall that the latter would be relieved.[67] Suffering from kidney stones, McDougall acquiesced with little protest.[68]

With McDougall relieved in late November, Washington appointed Maj. Gen. William Heath to command in the Highlands. Before McDougall departed, he and his staff had discovered good hutting grounds across the Hudson from West Point, near the home of Elijah Budd, which was suitable for a brigade. McDougall also found that the abandoned huts built at Continental Village remained in good condition and could be reoccupied with little effort.[69] Washington briefed Heath on these developments. The new commander duly sent John Nixon's brigade to reoccupy its old huts and John Glover's to the suggested campsite. The remaining brigades would winter at West Point itself.[70] Washington ordered all the masons present in the Massachusetts line's ranks to proceed to the Highlands to aid in building barracks at West Point.[71] Heath arrived there on December 4 and appointed Brig. Gen. John Paterson to again command the works and garrison of the fortress. Heath ordered an immediate report on the state of barracks "repairing or building" and pressed for the expeditious delivery of timber before the Hudson froze in order to speed along the completion of barracks and huts.[72]

Huts again proved a viable alternative. Quartermasters at Fishkill had stockpiled hutting tools during the previous summer, ensuring that the axes, saws, and other vital items were available when the soldiers arrived in December.[73] Glover's and Nixon's brigades east of the Hudson seem to have had the easiest time, with Nixon's men in particular needing only to mend standing structures.[74] Benjamin Gilbert, serving in the Fifth Massachusetts, part of Nixon's brigade, recorded striking tents and occupying a hut on the same day, December 10.[75]

The men wintering west of the Hudson encountered greater difficulties. Despite the existence of a "great barrack," most men faced the prospect of poor accommodations. Heath infused new energy into the garrison and on December 1 ordered fatigue parties, carpenters, and masons to labor on the barracks, as "every exertion is necessary to cover the troops." These orders were to stand "till the barracks are fit to receive the troops."[76] Construction placed heavy demands on stocks of tools and wore them out quickly.[77] Men finished huts adjacent to outlying redoubts by December 22, but work continued on the main barracks. Dr. Samuel Adams, surgeon with the Third Artillery Regiment, was one of the fortunate men who moved into a barrack on December 12.[78]

Others were not so lucky. One Massachusetts soldier, Isaac Glynn, lamented, "To our sorrow, all the barracks were full when we arrived, and we had to stay in tents."[79] Heath awarded men still in tents an extra gill of rum on January 7 "on account of the extreme cold weather."[80] The general confirmed on January 25 that some troops were still covered only by linen. The local environment contributed to this delay. Unlike the embowered force at Morristown, the West Point vicinity lacked nearby quantities of timber. Heath lamented that the garrison was "obliged to be on almost constant fatigue, dragging materials for their barracks, and all their fuel on hand sleds more than a mile." Washington's men in New Jersey, in contrast, could easily cut their wood from the forest that surrounded their hut complex.[81]

The winter of 1779–80 proved to be a particularly harsh time to be without good coverings. With temperatures dropping, snow falling, and many without shelter, men viewed the coming months with trepidation. Henry Sewall recorded an ominous entry in his diary near West Point on December 13: "If we fear the dangers in the *field*, we are not secure from the arrest of death in *winter quarters*."[82] Even soldiers living in barracks faced hardship due to the climate. A lack of wood left hearths cold. Soldiers responded by keeping to their beds much of the day or moving in with neighbors who still had fuel. Samuel Adams entered the new year without flames to warm him. On January 5, he finally obtained some wood. "Oh! The pleasures of a good fire," he exclaimed in his diary.[83] Amid the horrible weather, he related a story to his wife in which several men had their tents blown away by the wind and found themselves covered in snow when they awoke. Others had their tents covered in snow for up to forty-eight hours before their neighbors dug them out. In such circumstances, Adams saw the benefits of life in a barrack. He declared himself to be in good health.[84] Not everyone had the same good fortune. Isaac Glynn complained of the cold wind that came down the river and swept the barren plain on the Point. "We suffered very much" he declared, and "none but those who were there can tell what we endured."[85] John Paterson described a number of his soldiers "frozen lying in a field getting their wood."[86] Perhaps relating the same incident, Heath's aide-de-camp noted light infantrymen "found frozen to death in the snow" on January 10.[87]

To add to the misery along the Hudson, three fires broke out at West Point during January and early February. Repairing the damaged works diverted manpower from work on the barracks.[88] The most serious blaze occurred on January 23, consuming tents, paperwork, and the personal baggage of several officers. Most harmful to the poorly covered garrison was the loss of 500 of 750 axes, 6 of 17 saws, all 36 planes, and more than 150 other pieces of camp equipment.[89] Investigation revealed that the forts and barracks represented considerable fire hazards. Heath pointed out to Washington that the barracks had been "built in winter and in a hurry." Badly made chimneys with wooden mantels made for easy kindling, as did stoves. Poor construction allowed for drafts in windy conditions, which spread sparks throughout interiors. One officer informed Heath that "the garrison in hard blowing weather are almost afraid to close their eyes, lest fire should break out." Heath had not been ignorant of these conditions. His general orders of January 10 directed men to keep their chimneys clean regardless of whether they resided in huts, barracks, guard-houses, or bombproofs. Men were to pay great attention to stoves. If soldiers did discover a fire, they were to report it immediately, and all available men were to work to extinguish it. Heath felt that more substantial measures were needed, and he pressed Washington for a proper "water engine" to combat fire. Fortunately for the Rebels, no further conflagrations occurred.[90]

The griefs of snow, cold, and fire all paled in comparison to the provisioning crisis that began in December and climaxed in the first weeks of January. The Middlebrook winter had seen nothing like it. Valley Forge had witnessed some suffering, but not to the extent that soldiers at Morristown and the Highlands experienced in the new year. Much of the responsibility for shortages lay with issues external to the Continentals' scheme for winter quarters. Scholarly consensus holds that the collapse of the Continental logistical system in late 1779 originated from fiscal, administrative, and environmental sources. Of these, fiscal problems receive the majority of the blame. By 1779, the Continental dollar that Congress had printed to finance its war effort had inflated to near worthlessness. Inflation had begun to diminish the army's purchasing power earlier in the war, but the crisis became acute by late 1779. Deficient currency made it difficult to buy food and forage, as well as hire wagon teams.[91]

The Continentals at Morristown had the misfortune of going into quarters at a moment when climate conspired with finance to further curtail the army's ability to secure victuals. Through November, drought conditions prevailed in northern New Jersey and southern New York, leaving rivers and streams too dry to drive mills' water wheels to grind grain. Consequently, the Continental Army suffered a 25 percent decrease in its flour ration in November, nearly a month before the first significant snowfalls. Wetter weather to the south helped magazines in and around Trenton to maintain full stocks of flour, but the Continentals alleviated their grain crisis only by emptying these storehouses in early December. Forage levels did not fall as low as they had in early 1779, but they threatened to give out should the army continue to cart supplies over long distances.[92]

Washington informed Congress of the army's distress in mid-December, declaring, "I find our prospects are infinitely worse than they have been at any period of the War, and that unless some expedient can be instantly adopted a dissolution of the army for want of subsistence is unavoidable." The flour shortage had left part of the army without bread for several days. Washington explained that whereas the Continentals had previously suffered interruptions in supply due to administrative mishaps, the current crisis originated from "the absolute emptiness of our magazines everywhere and the total want of money or credit to replenish them."[93] Unlike the exaggerations the commander in chief might have used in dealing with Congress at Valley Forge, his writings in late 1779 were sincere. With roads blanketed in snow, however, the Continentals would have found great difficulty in dispersing to new quarters.

Congress responded with uncharacteristic alacrity to the commander in chief's pleas. It assisted the army by appealing to Connecticut, Pennsylvania, Maryland, Delaware, and Virginia to immediately send forward their quotas of flour and wheat originally intended for the spring campaign. Delaware's and New Jersey's quotas of ten thousand and eight thousand barrels, respectively, were to be sent immediately. The other states were to follow shortly afterward. New Jersey's government enacted a law on December 25 to streamline procurement within its borders by appointing a single superintendent of purchases to oversee the acquisition of food and forage. New Jersey also established a system of county contractors to make the purchases and extended a ban on the private hoarding of provisions until April 1. Maryland enacted similar measures and sent to Morristown provisions that had been previously gathered to supply the French expeditionary force.[94] These measures proved a last gasp of Congress's direction of supply efforts. In March, the national government enacted a state-specific system of provisioning. Henceforth, individual states would bear responsibility for collecting provisions and delivering them to magazines.[95]

The decision to build a log-hut city at Jockey Hollow also bore responsibility for the supply shortages. Nathanael Greene had recognized in November that transportation to the site would present a greater problem than less remote locales. Roads to Morristown traversed the rough ground of the New Jersey Highlands rather than the rolling hills of the Raritan piedmont that led to Middlebrook. Jockey Hollow's additional distance from Trenton exacerbated the situation. Under typical climactic conditions, the Patriots might have overcome these issues. Instead, the Continentals faced the worst winter in living memory. For an army in the process of building a city for ten thousand men in hilly terrain, snowfall over mountain roads brought potentially fatal interruptions to the flow of supplies. Greene's words on not contending with hunger would ring true.

Heavy snows arrived in early January, provoking the greatest scarcity of provisions of the entire winter. A storm beginning on January 2 left what one observer called "a prodigious quantity of snow" on the ground by January 6. High winds blew the snow into drifts that "filled up the roads to the top of the fences," making it "impossible to travel."[96] At Continental Village, Sgt.

Benjamin Gilbert recorded snow "midleg deep in the hut" on January 2.[97] The next day, James Thacher recorded in his journal, "The snow is now from four to six feet deep, which so obstructs the roads as to prevent our receiving a supply of provisions."[98] Washington informed Congress that "the late violent snow storm has so blocked up the roads that it will be some days before the scanty supplies in this quarter can be brought to camp."[99]

Unlike the Valley Forge winter, starvation, rather than mere hunger, genuinely threatened the army in January 1780. Indicative of the impending threat of dissolution, some rank and file at Jockey Hollow plundered local inhabitants to make up for what their commissaries failed to provide.[100] Nathan Beers declared on January 2, "No provision for two days past."[101] A New York officer described the gruesome extremities to which hunger drove his comrades, writing "During our hungry time, I eat several meals of dog, and it relished very well."[102] Joseph Plumb Martin recalled eating only "a little black birch bark which I gnawed off a stick of wood, if that can be called victuals."[103] Capt. Moses White wrote his brother from Jockey Hollow on January 2, despairing, "Between god almighty and the commissaries, we are all starving to death."[104]

The hunger resulting from the January snowfalls left the army in danger of collapse. Commissary Royal Flint informed Washington on January 3 that with New England cattle drives cut off, New Jersey represented the army's only option for supplies. The alternative was starvation. Flint saw a solution in the form of immediate impressment, what he described as an "immediate recourse to military authority for relief."[105] To provide this relief, Washington did indeed beseech the support of the population of New Jersey itself. In a letter to the county magistrates on January 8, Washington blamed "the uncommon vigor of the winter," which had obstructed road travel and led the Continentals to empty local stores and plunder nearby farms when bread and meat ran out. He outlined a plan by which each New Jersey county would provide a quantity of cattle and grain in proportion to its population. County magistrates were to oversee the collection of supplies, with Continental officers monitoring the counties' efforts. Farmers received certificates that they could redeem later for fair payment for the goods provided. If they did not come through, however, Washington hinted the army would take what it needed.[106] Swayed by either conscience or fear of military confiscation, the civilian population turned out to support the Continentals gathered in defense of the state. The commander in chief reported to Maj. Gen. William Heath in mid-January that the counties had "with great readiness complied with the requisition, and I flatter myself, that with economy we shall be enabled to live till we can be furnished in the usual manner."[107] Col. Joseph Lewis, commissary at Morristown, reported that supplies had "come in very well" to camp from January 12 to 15.[108]

The soldiers near West Point also suffered interruptions in supply shipments due to the heavy snowfall, which had reduced the garrison to a two-day supply of meat in early January. Officers of the Third and Fourth Massachusetts Brigades described shortages as "more severe than at any other time" in a letter to Major General Heath. Operating independently of Washington's orders, Heath's subordinates similarly impressed local foodstuffs and wagon teams to bring supplies to areas in need.[109]

To move supplies to camp, the Continentals adapted their transportation methods to suit winter conditions. Washington employed the militia as volunteer teamsters and to help break open roads.[110] Continentals not busy with other tasks in camp also cleared roads.[111] In the Highlands, when snow drifts blocked the teams from reaching camp, soldiers hauled a shipment of pork on their backs to its destination. Col. William Shephard, directing foraging operations under Heath's command, issued his detachments with "rackets," meaning snowshoes, which were needed to overcome the immense snow drifts. Heath ordered fatigue parties out of West Point to break the roads, emphasizing in his orders that opening communication in the Highlands ensured not only the supply of the garrisons there but also the continued flow of provisions to Morristown.[112]

Officers also turned the snow-covered ground to their advantage.[113] Sleds supplanted wagons since they could more easily transit snowy terrain than wagons. Writing from Morristown on January 18, Capt. John Patten of the Delaware Regiment reported that "provisions are now coming in fast" and would continue to do so unless the weather once again sealed off the roads.[114] Washington observed to Maj. Gen. William Heath, "Our dependence is upon the continuance of the frost," which allowed the army to maintain its supply trains via sled.[115]

Impressment successfully kept the Main Army together through the January crisis. Improving weather made it possible to clear the roads and bring supplies into camp, and through February the rank and file enjoyed a relative abundance of provisions. Given the ongoing financial crisis and ramshackle transportation network, however, provisioning the camps remained problematic. Greene reported in early February, "We have now a tolerable supply; but we have no magazines or money to form any; and therefore our stock cannot last long."[116] The fragile lines of communication running along inadequate mountain roads lay at the mercy of the weather. Shortages abated for only six weeks between mid-January and the beginning of March. Melting snows then removed the option of sled transport and turned the state's roads to mud. The unsettled weather of early spring hindered crossings of the Delaware, disrupting the flow of provisions from Pennsylvania.[117] A lack of funds made it difficult to hire wagon teams, reducing the army's ability to transport supplies from distant mills in March.[118] The brigades near West Point likewise suffered a scarcity of bread at the end of that month.[119]

Throughout spring, the Main Army continued its hand-to-mouth existence. While no periods of outright starvation recurred, officers and men nevertheless struggled to maintain a steady flow of food. Warm weather in April yielded passable roads and uncovered pastures, removing the main environmental impediments to transportation. Nevertheless, interruptions persisted, brought on by sudden rains, administrative foul-ups, and civilian resistance to impressment. Even in late May, the army found itself in want of meat.[120] On the twenty-sixth of that month Washington again complained that his men were "reduced to a situation of extremity."[121]

Only in June did the Continentals' logistical difficulties began to subside. Just as finance, climate, geography, and strategy had conspired to render the army hungry through the winter, these factors now combined to restore a steadier flow of foodstuffs. With the roads now dry, cattle and wagon trains moved with ease. The declining size of the army also lightened its burden on the region. The First and Second Maryland Brigades departed for the Southern Department in March, while the New York Brigade left for Albany a month later. Expiring enlistments and desertions reduced Washington's numbers to roughly five thousand by June, less than half of what he had brought to Morris County the previous December.

While the Continentals grappled with starvation at Morristown and West Point, detachments posted closer to New York City faced a more conventional enemy. British and Hessian forces had maintained their winter quarters in New York, their strength diminished by the detachment of eight thousand men for an expedition against Charleston, South Carolina. The troops left behind under Maj. Gen. Wilhelm von Knyphausen occupied a mix of public buildings, houses, fortifications, barracks, and huts as they had the previous year.[122] One German soldier recorded that his regiment wintered in an old brewery along the banks of the Hudson.[123] Thirty miles separated Crown and Rebel quarters. To dissuade enemy raids on the countryside and curtail illegal trade, Washington again posted troops opposite New York.

The Rebels refined their approach to outpost duty just as they did to building quarters. For 1779–80, Washington opted not to permanently detach a single brigade to the waterfront opposite Staten Island, referred to as the Sound. Given the ineffectiveness and exhaustion William Maxwell's troops had experienced in 1778–79, Washington chose instead to rotate troops in from Morristown every one to two months. This system allowed soldiers to return to the main encampment for rest and training, tested units in more active operations, and eased the logistical burden of supplying the entire force in one place. For the first month of winter, Washington appointed Samuel Holden Parsons commander of the outposts along the New Jersey waterfront. The brigadier had served in a similar capacity along the Connecticut coast the previous year and brought his experience in gathering intelligence to the shores of Newark Bay.[124]

Unlike the previous winter, early 1780 witnessed numerous small-scale engagements in New Jersey. The extreme cold that arrived in the Northeast that winter covered the region's littoral waterways with ice, facilitating the movement of Patriot and British forces. On January 14, Washington sent a Patriot contingent of 2,600 men equipped with sleighs to traverse the snow-covered New Jersey countryside to raid British and Loyalist positions on Staten Island. Washington sought to seize supplies at the enemy's expense and destroy their lodgings if possible, a further refinement of the forage- and quarters-focused partisan war he had waged during winters since 1777. The attack failed to achieve surprise, however, and undisciplined militia plundered civilian inhabitants. The raiding party, under Lord Stirling's command, managed to withdraw before British reinforcements arrived. Ultimately the foray gained and lost little.[125]

Over the following months, the enemy tested the Rebels' defensive capabilities. Throughout the remainder of January and February, British forces retaliated against the Patriot outposts in New Jersey. The dispersal of Continental troops deriving from the lack of shelter inhibited the outposts from mounting a strong defense. British and Loyalist raiders struck Essex County on the night of January 25–26, burning the Presbyterian meetinghouse and courthouse in Elizabethtown, as well as the Newark Academy, which had been used to quarter Continental detachments in that town.[126] The outpost commander in January, Col. Moses Hazen, did not have experience in such operations. Following the raid, Washington superseded the colonel and dispatched Maj. Gen. Arthur St. Clair to "investigate the causes of the late misfortune & disgrace."[127] St. Clair's assessment found Continental units widely spread and therefore vulnerable, but the absence of concentrated housing in the region meant that these dispositions were as compact as "the nature of the cantonment will allow." With further reinforcement unlikely, St. Clair reduced the garrisons of forward towns and called for mounted patrols to replace stationary guards to better secure the ground between posts. The Continentals appealed to the New Jersey government to provide the necessary animals.[128]

St. Clair's adjustments limited the damage subsequent British attacks inflicted. On February 11, Rebel positions resisted British raids targeting Elizabethtown, Rahway, and Woodbridge. With outposts "timely apprised" of the enemy's approach thanks to the newly implemented mounted patrols, the defenders withdrew with minimal casualties.[129] Outposts proved similarly effective in responding to a raid against Newark on February 19. Crown forces captured two civilians, but St. Clair suffered no military losses in the skirmish. While the British lost no men either, they did abandon twenty head of cattle that had been collected during their advance.[130]

These actions deterred further British expeditions. The New York garrison therefore fell quiet, while Patriot outposts turned to curtailing illicit trade along the Sound. Stymied in Essex, on March 23 and April 15, the British instead raided into Bergen County. Thereafter, the wet weather that characterized much of May left the ground in New Jersey unsuitable for even small operations. In addition, the spring thaw opened New York to steadier resupply. This lessened the British garrison's need to supplement provisions with foraging in New Jersey.[131]

Across the Hudson, Patriot forces also engaged the British in New York. With the Continentals firmly emplaced around West Point, militiamen played a larger role in manning forward posts in New York than they did in New Jersey. Fighting erupted in southwestern Connecticut in mid-January, near that state's border with New York. In these partisan actions, Connecticut's Whig militia came off worse. In New York, a Crown raiding party struck a forward-deployed Continental regiment in early February, killing or wounding almost forty and taking more than ninety prisoners. Despite these setbacks, Continental leaders resisted pressure to detach regulars from winter quarters to bolster the outpost lines. Washington denied a request from the Connecticut government for troops to guard against raids in March 1780. Throughout the winter, the bulk of the Main Army's troops stayed in their cantonments.[132]

Although the army suffered from cold, hunger, combat casualties, desertion, and expiring enlistments, it lost few men to disease. This success resulted from Continental officers' increased attentiveness and adaptability in matters of camp hygiene. The severe weather experienced through the 1779–80 winter necessitated further refinements to Continental Army castrametation to ensure good health. In a general order dated February 16, 1780, Washington established methods for dealing with snow accumulation and minimizing the threat of flooding during thaws. Troops were to take "particular care" to remove snow from huts built on hillsides. Trenches "dug round" each hut would ensure proper drainage. Otherwise, Washington expected "soldiers will sleep amidst continual damps, and their health will consequently be injured."[133] The frequent snowfalls witnessed at Morristown made such measures more vital than they had been during the mild Middlebrook winter, but Washington's measures proved effective. An observer at Morristown judged the cantonment "comfortably hutted and in good health" in mid-February despite deficiencies in clothing and provisions.[134]

In the Hudson Highlands, the four Massachusetts brigades also strove to keep their cantonments salubrious. There the presence of barracks and fortifications in addition to huts complicated the Continentals' task. During January, officers at West Point admonished their men for "easing themselves" on the snow and ground. In response, general orders directed regiments to dig proper vaults convenient to every unit. Men were forbidden from relieving themselves anywhere else.[135] This reproof seems to have had the desired effect as commanders in the Highlands issued no further orders regarding camp hygiene until May. Then, as at Morristown, the Massachusetts soldiers addressed camp cleanliness amid warming temperatures. Maj. Gen. Robert Howe, who had succeeded Heath in February, directed brigade commanders to establish procedures for carrying filth from huts and barracks to be buried and burned.[136]

Keeping barracks that each held dozens of men clean eluded the Continentals despite officers' frequent admonishments. Daniel Granger dwelled in barracks during the summer of 1780 as a fifteen-year-old and recalled they "had been left extremely dirty." His memoir related that the structures were "infected with millions of fleas & other insects." The young private opted to sleep outside on a flat rock "to have one night's comfort."[137] Joseph Plumb Martin likewise recalled that when living in the "old barracks" in late 1780, "there were rats enough, had there been men, to garrison twenty West Points."[138]

Maintaining hygienic conditions in the log-hut city proved easier. As winter transitioned to spring, the army at Morristown worked to maintain a salubrious camp amid melting snows and rising temperatures. With most huts now featuring doors and windows consisting of square holes covered with shutters, Washington ordered them to be opened "every fair day" beginning in March 1780. Soldiers' bedding and straw were to be "frequently aired."[139] Experienced line officers enforced sanitation regulations. In Col. Moses Hazen's regiment, subalterns led noncommissioned officers in inspection details monitoring cleanliness in camp. They ensured that filth was "removed from the huts and utensils" kept "perfectly clean."[140] Sherburne's additional regiment appointed an officer in March to oversee the removal of filth from the brigade guard hut.[141] That same month the artillery brigade detailed its acting quartermaster as a temporary superintendent to supervise cleaning the artillery park. Under the quartermaster's direction, the gunners carried "all the filth, dirt, and brush" accumulated between their huts fifty feet beyond their camp perimeter and set it ablaze.[142]

Smallpox presented only a minor concern. Inoculated veterans filled the ranks, minimizing the risk of a *variola* outbreak. For the small number of new soldiers, brigade and regimental officers showed themselves capable of administering quarantine and inoculation procedures without the commander in chief's intervention. In May 1780, Connecticut officers ordered men who had already had the disease to clean out the recently vacated Maryland line huts and prepare them for occupation. Soldiers who had yet to suffer the illness were held back from the new quarters.[143]

Such measures proved effective. The Morristown encampment, despite its size and concentration, did not host any of the problems of illness that had plagued the Continentals at Valley Forge two years earlier. The percentage of sick rank and file hovered in the range of 9–11 percent for the duration of the winter, essentially where it had rested since the sanitary reforms implemented at Middlebrook had taken hold.[144] Conditions in the Highlands were similarly good. One Massachusetts lieutenant pronounced, "All yet remain in good health" in May.[145]

This was a positive takeaway considering the previous six months of cold, hunger, and skirmishes. The Main Army at Morristown dwindled to some four thousand men by June. Three brigades departed for other theaters, while expiring enlistments and desertion left the remaining units understrength. At Jockey Hollow, food shortages contributed to the brief mutiny of the Connecticut line in late May. These soldiers returned from outpost duty to find scant provisions at the cantonment. Coming the heels of weeks on frontline patrolling, two Connecticut regiments assembled without orders and attempted to march out of camp. As at Redding the previous year, the appeals of trusted officers convinced the soldiers to return to their huts before the protest exploded into a full mutiny. Nevertheless, the event revealed that Patriot morale and discipline were eroding by this point in the war.[146] Finally, word of the Patriot disaster at Charleston, South Carolina, reached New Jersey at the beginning of June. There nearly five thousand Continentals and militia had surrendered to Gen. Sir Henry Clinton on May 12. After the fall of the South's largest city, Royal troops were expected to return to New York.[147]

The Continentals and their cantonments faced a significant test that month. Bolstered by reports of mutiny and desertion in the Continental camp and widespread disaffection among the civilian population, Hessian lieutenant general Wilhelm von Knyphausen resolved to launch an offensive into New Jersey on the night of June 6. He targeted Morristown via a march from Staten Island through the gap in the Watchungs near Chatham. The Rebels' reliance on the log-hut city at Jockey Hollow as a fixed base offered the British a discernable objective for a limited attack. The loss of the supplies and infrastructure concentrated at Morristown presented a potentially crippling blow to the Main Army in New Jersey.[148] Sir Henry Clinton, in his memoirs, highlighted the attractive prospect of seizing the Continentals' "grand depot of military stores at Morristown and capture or disperse the force that covered them."[149]

Although the Patriots faced six thousand Hessians, Redcoats, and Loyalists, they successfully employed the flexible defense they had developed in combating enemy raids over the winter. Maxwell's New Jersey Brigade, manning the outpost line since mid-May, accurately reported the size and direction of the enemy invasion to Washington on June 7 while avoiding a general engagement against a superior force. The commander in chief, properly warned, sent away whatever supplies and stores could be moved from Morristown and prepared to reinforce Maxwell with the soldiers at Jockey Hollow. By late afternoon, the six brigades had arrived to defend the gap near Chatham. Royal troops faced the prospect of attacking a prepared enemy that was holding the high ground, with a hostile militia threatening their flanks and rear. When word arrived that Clinton's force from the Carolinas would soon return with reinforcements for a stronger attack, Knyphasuen retired to Elizabethtown after burning the village of Connecticut Farms.[150]

Two weeks later, Clinton launched another sortie into New Jersey to hold the Rebels' attention while he planned to send a second group up the Hudson against West Point. Washington used the security afforded by the mountains to divide his army and monitor developments. One wing under Greene held position to guard Morristown while another under St. Clair moved north to aid West Point if needed. The garrison on the Hudson could presumably hold out until help arrived. Washington had afforded himself strategic flexibility in the June 1780 operations by placing his base behind a natural barrier remote from his opponent. Distance and terrain gave the Rebels time to organize a defense of the Morristown encampment if needed. Alternatively, they could economize by leaving a weak detachment to deter an enemy advance while sending the bulk of the army to protect West Point.[151]

Ultimately the second attack on June 23 pushed only as far as Springfield. Facing stiff resistance from Continentals and militia, the column under Knyphausen turned back, still eight miles short of the log-hut city near Morristown. On June 24, Crown forces pulled back to Staten Island. This ended the limited British offensive, the last significant incursion New Jersey suffered during the war.[152] Success in the Springfield campaign highlighted the importance of remotely located log-hut cities to Patriot strategy. Nestled in the New Jersey and Hudson Highlands, Washington's army stood secure from enemy attack despite its declining numbers. The commander in chief's decision to quarter the army west of the Watchungs rather than at the originally preferred Quibbletown location had paid off.

Over the course of the 1779–80 winter, the Continental Army erected a complex of well-built huts at Jockey Hollow that afforded officers and men protection from the elements during the coldest and snowiest conditions experienced during the war in the Middle States. Nathanael Greene and his staff found a locale that satisfied castrametation requirements while also placing the Continentals in a defensible, remote locale. Greene kept the army provisioned at Jockey Hollow in spite of the transportation problems its isolated location incurred. While the Patriots did frequently go hungry that winter, even in the worst conditions they never lost many men to starvation, nor did the army dissolve or disperse. Officers and veteran soldiers maintained order and cleanliness within their quarters. Doing so retained the Main Army's health and discipline for the next campaign. Troops in the Hudson Highlands did not enjoy quite as sound lodgings, but continued construction in 1780 promised to alleviate these problems the following winter.

The Morristown winter demonstrated the viability of holding the army in remote hut encampments even in the worst conditions. Moving forward, Washington's army would rely on the increasingly substantial quartering infrastructure in New Jersey and the Hudson Highlands to undergird a positional strategy in the New York region. Capt. Samuel Shaw, an aide-de-camp to Henry Knox, summed up the army's skill at building winter quarters in a December 1779 letter. He declared, "Hutting was a monstrous undertaking at Valley Forge in 1777, but it has now become an easy employment." Should the war continue for a few more years, Shaw believed hut building would become "a matter of amusement."[153] The coming winter would give the army a chance to prove correct Shaw's prediction.

CHAPTER 7

"No Longer Reason to Complain of Our Accommodations"

1780–1783

Following the engagement at Springfield, the Patriot army shifted north-ward. Washington kept his brigades in the rough terrain of the Hudson Highlands and northern New Jersey, holding to a strategy little changed from that of the previous two summers. A French expeditionary force under Lt. Gen. Jean-Baptiste Donatien de Vimeur, Comte de Rochambeau, arrived in Rhode Island in July, temporarily tipping the strategic scales in the revolutionaries' favor. Nevertheless, Washington's long-held goal of an offensive against New York continued to elude him. In September, Sir Henry Clinton conspired with Maj. Gen. Benedict Arnold, commander at West Point, to surrender that posi-tion to the British and undo the Patriot defense of the Highlands. The plot's exposure at the end of September led to Arnold's flight and the capture and execution of his British handler, Maj. John Andre.[1]

Arnold's treason shocked and dismayed the Continental officer corps and contributed to plummeting confidence for the Rebels' cause. News of Maj. Gen. Horatio Gates's crushing defeat at Camden, South Carolina, arrived in early September. Financial hardship and supply shortages continued to plague the army. Finally, the arrival of the French made little immediate impact on reversing the strategic impasse around New York. In these circumstances, Washington could do little but hold his positions and continue to deny Clinton the "key to America." Given the overall depths of Rebel morale in late 1780, whether or not the Continentals could endure yet another winter around New York appeared uncertain.

Serval issues afflicted the Main Army that made the timing of winter quarters imperative. Foremost was the wretched state of soldiers' clothing. Mismanage-ment among Patriot contractors in France delayed a shipment of ten thousand

much-needed uniforms. The Continentals consequently passed another campaign season without replacement clothes. Such a poorly clad army would face
hardship if caught in the open against the elements.[2] Good housing built as early
into the season as possible presented the best remedy for an ill-clothed soldiery.[3]

Compounding the uniform problem was an impending manpower shortage. Even more so than the previous year, Washington faced the departure of
many men due to expiring enlistments. His subordinates estimated fewer than
five thousand men would be on Continental rolls come the New Year. Such
diminished numbers would ease officers' troubles in finding suitable shelter
and food for their men but reduce the army's ability to cover the countryside
against British incursions. Throughout the summer and fall, the Continentals
had served alongside temporary levies. These six- and nine-month enlistees
had been called to augment Rebel ranks beyond the service typically given by
the militia. The presence of these men exacerbated shortages in uniforms and
equipment and promised to further strain Continental food stocks as winter
approached. On the other hand, levies increased Washington's numbers and
provided manual labor even if their combat effectiveness was negligible. They
also represented a potential body of recruits from which the army could replenish its dwindling ranks of regulars. Providing good shelter might induce these
men to enlist.

Facing these difficulties, the Rebels stood fortunate that the British garrison
in New York kept quiet through early autumn. With the New York theater in a
lull, Washington turned to the question of winter quarters at the end of October.
In a departure from the Morristown winter and a return to the method used
before Valley Forge and Middlebrook, he solicited his subordinates' input via a
council of war. On October 31, he queried whether or not to detach more forces
to the South, pondered the feasibility of an attack on New York, and posed the
familiar question of where the troops should canton for the following months.[4]

The dialogue surrounding quartering shifted from previous years. For
1780–81, the key question would be one of timing. Each of the ten respondents expressed a desire to begin constructing winter quarters earlier than in
the past. Brig. Gen. Anthony Wayne suggested that work begin immediately.
Lafayette proposed the latest date, December 1. Past years had shown that
even one month's delay could have ill effects for soldiers in building their huts.
Conversely, armies retiring early to winter quarters had suffered embarrassing
defeats as well. Thus, the generals debated the risks and rewards of keeping the
field for another month.

Most of Washington's brigadiers emphasized the benefits of an early retirement. Anthony Wayne pointed out the extreme "cold, hunger, and fatigue" the
army had encountered in erecting huts in mid-December the previous year. He

therefore wanted to get his men into quarters as quickly as possible. In particular, he sought to begin construction while temporary levies remained with the army so as to make use of their labor.[5] Jedediah Huntington worried that an early retirement to stationary positions might strain forage reserves, but given the known threat of winter weather and the army's poor clothing situation, he echoed Wayne in advocating for beginning hut construction immediately.[6] John Glover blamed the difficulties encountered the previous year on staying in the field for too long.[7] William Irvine wanted to retire quickly, "the sooner the better." So, too, did Edward Hand.[8] Of the more senior officers, Robert Howe fell into the early-retirement camp.[9]

By contrast, several of the major generals expressed greater support for prolonging the campaign. Lafayette held a more optimistic view toward the weather, which he believed would hold through the end of November. He hoped the army could stay active for that month to deny the British foraging opportunities and perhaps exploit an enemy mistake to seek a tactical advantage. Arthur St. Clair offered a compromise between the immediate-ists and Lafayette. Pointing out that a full-scale siege operation against West Point would be unlikely once winter weather set in, he suggested waiting two weeks to monitor British intentions before retiring. Since the enemy had made no major foray into the state so far, he deemed it unlikely that the situation would change in the next few weeks.[10] Lord Stirling also suggested waiting two weeks.[11]

Washington received less cogent responses regarding location. Wayne deferred to the commander in chief's judgement on the matter. Glover offered no input. Robert Howe's response summarized the various castrametation criteria familiar to veterans of earlier winter quarters: supplied with plentiful wood and forage, secure from surprise attack, easily defensible, protective of civilian populations, and convenient to wagon and cattle routes. But Howe admitted to knowing too little about the region, particularly New Jersey, to offer a suggestion of where these criteria might be met.[12]

Several commanders recognized that the army's diminished size the and infrastructure built around West Point made that locale a more attractive option than in previous winters. The various barracks, huts, and fortifications near West Point, Peekskill, and Fishkill would accommodate any force Washington would likely send to defend the region. Lafayette suggested placing the bulk of the troops near West Point, "the most important point of defense," where he supposed the time in camp could be best spent attending "to the instruction of the officers, and particularly to the forming of good noncommissioned officers and putting them upon a more respectable footing."[13] Henry Knox, Lord Stirling, and St. Clair also proposed sending the majority of the Continentals to the Hudson Highlands.[14]

In a departure from the previous two years, most of the Continental generals believed that only a minority of the army should winter in New Jersey. They disagreed on whether the previous year's campsite presented a viable option for the coming winter. Both St. Clair and Stirling believed the existing huts at Jockey Hollow would suffice to house this contingent; however, the army's weakness led several dissenting officers to push for more remote locales. Edward Hand suggested that any troops beyond those garrisoning West Point should winter ten miles west of Morristown at Black River. This would place them closer to the Delaware, easing their supply situation. Black River would add greater distance and rough terrain to impede an enemy advance, which he wanted to augment with the construction of redoubts. To Morristown's further debit, Hand believed the Continentals had depleted the region's fuel supply the previous year.[15] William Irvine also preferred a more easily supplied and defended cantonment closer to the Delaware River.[16] Knox wanted to send no more than three hundred men to New Jersey. He claimed that the army could spare no larger force and that if a regiment were to suffer a defeat in winter quarters, this presented less embarrassment than the loss of a whole brigade or division. With numbers so reduced, Knox feared that no force could resist a British foray. Indeed, he predicted that his proposal would induce the enemy to sweep through Essex, Monmouth, and Somerset Counties "and probably invade Morris." He reasoned such a turn of events stood preferable to the inverse, wintering in New Jersey and allowing the Redcoats to seize West Point. The weakened army was no longer in position to secure both places and needed to make sacrifices.[17]

While the generals disagreed over specific locations, they concurred that one or two concentrated encampments would house the army. One outsider, however, believed the 1779–80 winter had revealed the impracticality of larger camps. Pennsylvania chief executive Joseph Reed wrote to Anthony Wayne at the end of October, questioning, "Would it not be more advisable to hut in divisions in different states, where supplies can be secured, than risk the desertion and discontent of last winter?"[18] Reed felt that dispersing the army would also draw additional civilian communities into supporting the struggle. His recommendation represented a return to the distended cantonments that had garnered some support in 1778, albeit with hutting replacing billets in villages. In practice, Reed's pessimism proved unwarranted and went unheeded.

Washington's decision-making in late 1780 represented a culmination of the democratic process he had followed from Valley Forge onward. The commander in chief had grown more decisive. Only two weeks separated his council of war and his final decision on November 14.[19] As he had in the past, His Excellency struck a balance between the various suggestions he received.

Washington dismissed Knox's doubts and sent the Pennsylvania line to Morristown. The New Jersey Brigade was to move to Pompton to secure communications between Morristown and the Highlands. Agreeing with the majority of his commanders, he directed the Massachusetts brigades to West Point while the Connecticut line would take position on the opposite bank. The New Hampshire Brigade and Rhode Island Regiment likewise were to stay in the Hudson Highlands below West Point while the artillery joined Washington at his presumptive headquarters, north of the Highlands fortress at New Windsor. The remaining Continental cavalry in the northern theater under Colonels Stephen Moylan and Elisha Sheldon departed for Lancaster, Pennsylvania, and Connecticut, respectively.[20] Despite its diminished size, the Continental Army for the third consecutive year adopted a familiar strategic plan and occupied an arc of cantonments in defensible terrain outside New York.[21]

Washington's underlings also demonstrated an improved understanding of castrametation. After more than two years of positional campaigning in the same region, they recognized that a few locales best satisfied the army's quartering criteria. Further debate and reconnaissance were unlikely to find any hitherto undiscovered grounds ideal for hutting as long as strategic requirements went unchanged. Wayne, Stirling, and Knox, all of whom were Main Army veterans, perceived which locations offered the best prospects for satisfying strategic and logistical needs. Arthur St. Clair seems to have had a particularly strong grasp of the principles of castrametation, as his suggestions in both 1779–80 and 1780–81 paralleled the ultimate dispositions adopted.

The revolutionaries benefited from a summer and fall spent building up their quartering infrastructure in the Highlands. Washington noted to Maj. Gen. William Heath that some soldiers kept at building and repairing "huts, barracks, etc." even has he prepared to announce winter dispositions. New Hampshire troops near West Point worked on huts in October and early November. Henry Dearborn of the First New Hampshire proudly wrote that the brigade had on November 10 moved into huts "the best ever built in America."[22] Other soldiers labored on the more substantial barracks. Alexander McDougall wrote approvingly to William Heath in November, pointing out, "You have old and new huts and barracks to cover [a] number of troops than you have or will have till the campaign opens." Better sited than in the past, these cantonments also enjoyed better access to timber than had been common in previous winters along the Hudson.[23] After placing the bulk of the army in New Jersey for the previous two winters, the forage situation had also improved.[24] All of this portended well for the coming months.

Line officers appreciated receiving earlier notice of their winter destinations than in past years. Maj. Daniel Lyman happily reported from West Point on

This British intelligence map from 1780 reveals the extensive military infrastructure present in the Hudson Valley by 1780, which was vital to sustaining Washington's forces in the region. Beverly Robinson, "Valley of the Hudson River from Fishkill to Teller's Point" (1780). Clinton Papers, William L. Clements Library, Ann Arbor, Michigan.

November 24, "The Main Army will take up winter quarters in the vicinity."[25] Lt. Col. Ebenezer Huntington surmised the same destination, pointing out the Hudson Highlands stood as "certainly the most eligible for the remains of our army to retire to." He recognized that doing so would secure not only West Point but also the shrunken army itself.[26]

The Continentals had achieved such proficiency in hut building by late 1780 that they required less instruction in that task. Unlike any of the preceding cantonments, Washington issued no orders outlining best practices for hut construction. Nor did the commander in chief set any guidelines for arranging camp sanitation or deliver remonstrances against plundering civilians. He left day-to-day administrative direction in the hands of his subordinates. While Washington had afforded discretion to wing commanders in previous winters, he had always maintained direct control of the largest camp, which was invariably adjacent to his headquarters. In 1780–81, however, William Heath issued most of the orders for the soldiers stationed in the Highlands, despite Washington's lodging nearby at New Windsor. Given the officer corps' growing proficiency, the commander in chief entrusted his subordinates with running the camps while he turned his attention to higher-level matters.

The Continentals demonstrated their greatest progress in their work on the substantial lodgings at the West Point fortress complex. Heath's general orders on December 1 welcomed the Massachusetts and Connecticut lines to the Point, where he hoped the soldiers would soon find or make their shelter "as comfortable and agreeable as circumstances will admit." Heath placed the Second Massachusetts Brigade in the "great barracks" at West Point, while the First and Third were to hut nearby. The Fourth was to winter in barracks at nearby Fort Clinton and in adjacent unoccupied huts that were still standing. The major general left it to the brigade commanders to select specific sites for hutting, confident that they would discern locales convenient to wood and water.[27] The troops ordered to huts simply occupied previously built structures, abrogating the need to erect new cabins.[28] The brigades drew lots to determine soldiers' particular huts or barracks.[29] These readily available lodgings protected the poorly clad troops from a heavy snowstorm that rolled through the Hudson Highlands two days after their arrival.[30]

Heath took great care in arranging proper housing at West Point itself. The major general called upon the carpenters, blacksmiths, masons, and caulkers of the Massachusetts brigades to aid in construction and repair work on the barracks and fortifications.[31] Deputy quartermasters forwarded tools from the Fishkill depot to West Point to facilitate hutting and barracking.[32] Although some housing stood available for soldiers, officers lacked lodging. Heath pressured the garrison quartermaster to build, repair, and allot quarters as necessary. Benjamin Gilbert, now a captain of the Fifth Massachusetts Regiment, moved into an officers' room in the barracks in early January, where he found himself "much better accommodated than when in tents." In light of the previous winter's incendiary problems, Heath also reminded his men to take care in ministering to their fires and chimneys, the latter of which had been built in "a slight manner." While most men worked on building or repairing their quarters, small detachments collected wood, cleared roads, and prepared bridges to maintain communications in the region. To alleviate crowding at West Point, Heath also detached units as permanent garrisons for outlying works.[33]

Beyond West Point, some soldiers in New York again faced the task of building their shelters. Experience and skill meant that huts now went up with little trouble, and the Continentals improved upon their earlier record in getting under cover quickly. The Quartermaster's Department facilitated construction by stockpiling hut-building tools and contracting with local civilians for wood in early November before Washington formally announced his plans for winter.[34] Given these preparations, hutting proceeded smoothly along the Hudson. At New Windsor, Knox's men began work on December 4.[35] Artillery captain Constant Freeman described the huts built there as "much better than those of last winter."[36] Lt. William S. Pennington, a fellow gunner, praised the enlisted men for finishing their huts quickly, "being only the sixth day since we began them."[37] The Connecticut line settled into their hutting grounds across the river from West Point on December 2.[38] The Rhode Island Regiment built new

huts with little difficulty, beginning construction on December 5 and finishing ten days later.[39] Troops returned from outpost duty to find that their huts
stood complete in mid-December.[40] James Thacher reported his hut finished by
January 3. Improved organization and administration and the early retirement
to winter quarters mitigated the worst of the privations experienced in past
years. Thacher remarked, "We have now no longer reason to complain of our
accommodations; the huts are warm and comfortable, wood in abundance at
our doors, and a tolerable supply of provisions."[41]

Anthony Wayne's command in New Jersey likewise enjoyed success in securing shelter in late 1780. Washington's orders to Wayne revealed the emphasis he
now placed on reusing existing huts, or at least their wood, if possible. Only if
the previous year's huts in New Jersey were "too injured," or if the local firewood
stocks appeared depleted, was Wayne to seek out an alternative cantonment site.
The Virginian suggested nearby Mendham or Vealtown, with the former "least
liable to be beat up."[42] Following the commander in chief's instructions, on
November 14, Wayne sent Col. Thomas Craig to reconnoiter the old Jockey Hollow grounds to examine the condition of the huts, the availability of firewood,
and any potential health threats deriving from the use of the huts as hospitals
during the summer.[43] The colonel reported back five days later having found
adequate timber within one mile of the old camp and vacant huts that could
be returned to habitability with little effort.[44] On November 27, Washington
ordered Wayne to move his brigades to the old complex, where Craig's detachment was already preparing the huts for the line's arrival. Wayne was to first
get his men covered as quickly as possible, then establish patrols to the east to
curtail illegal trade and begin training the expected influx of recruits.[45]

Wayne's men transitioned to a winter footing rapidly. On December 1 the
division's officers met to establish a "plan of hutting." Two regiments were to
repair the huts occupied by elements of the Maryland line the previous winter,
while the other eight moved into the huts formerly used by Hand's brigade.[46] As
expected, by cannibalizing building materials from dilapidated structures, soldiers quickly returned huts to habitability.[47] Enlisted men met little difficulty in
repairing their quarters. Capt. Joseph McClellan reported that the rank and file
were "generally comfortable in their huts" on December 5. The men achieved
this rapid pace even with a snowstorm on December 3 that impeded work.
McClellan himself encountered more trouble. He began building his hut on
December 2, but suffered a setback two days later when a chimney he had built
"fell down at night." He moved into the structure on December 8.[48]

Given the diminished state of the army, Wayne remained apprehensive until
his men were covered. An intelligence report indicating British forces in New
York were stirring caused Wayne consternation in early December. He confided

to Brig. Gen. William Irvine that he wished the Redcoats would "remain quiet for a week or two longer, until our huts are completed and coats mended."[49] Even with distance and rough terrain promising to impede any British attack, Wayne apparently still feared for his understrength and isolated command.[50] His concern for his men's housing reveals that prudent commanders recognized shelter as a key component to health, effectiveness, and operational success. Fortunately for Wayne, the British never pushed into New Jersey.

While Washington's subordinates attended to soldiers' shelter, the commander in chief focused on their food supplies. With Nathanael Greene departed for the Southern Theater, Washington lacked an experienced senior quartermaster. The Virginian therefore exercised greater control over supply matters than in previous winters. In an attempt to avoid the early-winter crises of past years, the Continentals sought to address provisioning concerns as early as possible. Col. Ephraim Blaine, who had replaced Jeremiah Wadsworth as commissary general in early 1780, wrote to the commander in chief on November 10, 1780, explaining the preparations he had taken to "prevent the like distress the army experienced last winter." During the preceding weeks Blaine had established small magazines of beef and flour throughout the region, hoping to ensure ample stocks of food. Realizing winter weather would impede transportation, Blaine aimed to stockpile flour at Trenton before frost closed the Delaware. These supplies would keep troops in New Jersey fed. As for the army in New York, the Commissary Department had worked since August to gather salt in New York and New England to preserve meat. They also established quotas of beef to be supplied by the New England states and set up magazines along the Hudson.[51] The Continentals further augmented their winter stocks with a foraging sweep through Westchester County at the end of November that carried away significant quantities of corn, hay, and cattle.[52]

Congress continued to place the responsibility for provisioning the army on the states that hosted its detachments. A resolution issued on November 10 instructed the quartermaster general to apply to leaders of states "nearest the quarters of the army" to provide forage and help establish magazines. More distant states were also to contribute forage and assist in provisioning horses detached from the major concentrations.[53] Deputy Quartermaster Udny Hay, chiefly responsible for administering supplies in New York, optimistically reported to Washington on November 12, "There is every probability they will during the course of the winter, be tolerably supplied."[54]

Ten days later, Hay's positivity had soured. He discovered West Point had too few rations and appeared unlikely to improve its situation in the near term. Hay blamed the lack of food on currency inflation. He therefore proposed to Washington a plan for impressing wheat and flour to satisfy New York's quota, but this needed the approval of New York governor George Clinton. Hay hoped that requisitions would mostly impact illegal traders and therefore prove popular with the Whig population.[55] The commander in chief forwarded Hay's proposal to Governor Clinton. Washington shared the deputy quartermaster's concern that terrain and transportation would allow for only a limited amount of provisions to reach the West Point area from south and west. While he told Clinton that he viewed impressment as "disagreeable," he believed the threat of another winter food crisis represented an "extremity" that justified the act. The memory of the difficulties encountered at Morristown made the commander in chief "dread a repetition of the same trial." Worried that the weather would render routes along rivers and mountains impassable, he implored the governor to approve the impressment plan.[56]

While Washington waited for Clinton's response, he took further steps to limit food and forage consumption. He husbanded his meager transportation assets by ordering New England troops marching from Bergen County to West Point to hand over their wagons and animal teams to carry the Pennsylvania line's equipment as it moved southward to Morristown. As soon as Wayne's men reached camp, the Quartermaster's Department would take control of the wagons and teams to ensure adequate transportation for hauling forage and fuel through the winter. The Continentals also sought to reduce their reliance on horse teams in favor of oxen, which consumed less forage. The new quarter-master general also contributed to these economizing efforts, spending much of the fall pressuring national and state leaders to contribute more forage.[57] Finally, to keep the army as lean as possible, Washington ordered the dismissal of temporary levies after camps had been established.[58] He summed up this policy in a November 28 letter to Heath, stating, "I find we shall have occasion to divest ourselves of every mouth that we can possibly do without, and have difficulty enough to subsist afterwards."[59]

Despite these efforts, the Continentals arrived in winter quarters in early December still concerned about their supply situation. Snow had already fallen, portending another winter of poor weather. Currency was as useless as ever. And the bulk of the army now rested in mountainous terrain that was even rougher than the site of the previous year's main camp. Veteran Continentals realized by late 1780 that retirement to winter quarters frequently coincided with the worst supply shortages. Lt. Col. Ebenezer Gray of the Seventh Con-necticut Regiment wrote his brother from the Hudson Highlands in December, lamenting, "It seems it 'twas decreed in the Book of *Fates* that wherever we hut we should have short allowance." Gray recognized that the army had suffered the same conditions for the previous three winters and hoped his commanders, or Congress, would ensure that such problems did not recur.[60]

All signs seemed to point toward an even worse provision crisis soon arriving. Washington resorted to hyperbole to solicit support from his civilian hosts. On December 10, the general informed Governor Clinton that soldiers had been on short rations since their arrival in quarters, that the magazines in the region were empty, and that he had no idea when or if fresh supplies would arrive. Given these circumstances, Washington claimed, "It is impossible for me to be responsible for the important posts on this river, or even to assure myself the troops can be kept together from one day to another." This hinted at the "starve, dissolve, or disperse" fears from Valley Forge. The commander in chief beseeched Clinton to take measures to rescue the army but did "not presume to recommend the mode." He hinted that "spirited exertions, or coercive means" might be needed.[61]

Clearly, the general was not-so-subtly pressuring the governor to adopt impressment. Washington also seems to have been operating under the assumption that his supplies would soon give out rather than expressing his actual circumstances. Weather had not yet shut down transportation in early December, and soldiers' writings make little mention of severe shortages. Conditions in the Highlands seemed much better than those suffered during the Morristown winter. As at Valley Forge, some of Washington's gloomiest reports might have represented a conscious strategy of exaggeration to secure greater support from national and state governments. Regardless of Washington's intentions, his December 10 letter swayed Clinton to acquiesce to impressment. The governor responded to the commander in chief five days later, stating that "immediately on the receipt" of Washington's message, Clinton had issued an impress warrant to Udny Hay.[62]

The actual collection of provisions proceeded less smoothly than the impressment made in New Jersey in early January 1780. On December 20, Washington was "extremely unhappy" that his magazines were yet precariously stocked, though he hoped shipments would soon arrive that would temporarily alleviate this distress.[63] West Point suffered flour shortfalls in mid-December brought on by the freezing of the river. A lack of forage in the immediate vicinity prohibited the garrison from keeping cattle on hand.[64] For the New York requisition, the commander in chief operated directly through Col. Udny Hay, the Continental Army's deputy quartermaster for New York, thereby superseding Timothy Pickering. Hay's staff in New York failed to fully tabulate the supplies acquired. At the end of December, the colonel sent Washington the returns for provisions impressed, admitting that the tabulation was "a very imperfect one." Both Albany and Tryon Counties, representing most of northern New York, had not submitted returns. Hay could offer only an estimate that his men had gathered roughly two-thirds of the quota established by Congress for New York.[65]

Yet from late December onward, neither Washington's nor Hay's correspondence expressed much urgency over supplies. Hay's haphazard returns came in response to a letter in which Washington stated, "I shall be glad to hear how you are like to succeed in procuring flour." The solicitation came at the end of a brief letter discussing provisions for carpenters, hardly the conduct of the commander of an army on the verge of starvation.[66] The change in outlook likely derived from improved weather conditions. December and early January witnessed mild temperatures compared to the previous winter, without any snowfalls large enough to halt movement along the roads. Hay took advantage of ice-free navigation along the Hudson to dispatch victuals from northern magazines on January 2 and 12.[67] Lt. Henry Marble commented in a January 11 letter from the Fort Clinton barracks, "We are sometimes a little short for provisions." Despite ragged clothing, shelter and well-being were satisfactory, for Marble claimed, "Our troops are in general good health." This represented a significant improvement from the cries of starvation and impending ruin that characterized Continentals' writings form the previous January.[68]

Throughout the winter, foul weather caused only one major shortfall in rations. Washington claimed a scanty stock of flour in late January, which resulted from the freezing of the river.[69] By reducing consumption and addressing transportation problems, the Continentals again overcame these problems. On January 18, William Heath noted in his garrison orders "the many difficulties and obstructions which at present attend both land and water transportation," warning soldiers of impending shortages. Garrison commissaries and quartermasters were to take all measures necessary to ensure adequate transportation and provisions. Stores in the Fishkill magazine were to supplant cattle drives should the weather seal off the camp.[70] Heath sent out detachments of miners and sappers to keep the roads to camp open. Rather than return to huts nightly, these men were to take cover in tents, despite the bad weather, so as to not impede their important work.[71] These measures proved effective, and Heath judged prospects of provisions "favorable" in late February.[72]

Despite the improved supply situation, early 1781 brought the army closer to Washington's "dissolve or disperse" outcome than any previous winter. Food shortages did not bear the blame, but instead discontent in Rebel ranks over back pay and disputed enlistment terms. Alcohol and boredom in camp stoked these sentiments. The Pennsylvania line at Jockey Hollow exploded into open mutiny on January 1, 1781. Common soldiers paraded under arms without orders and plundered a camp magazine. Two officers were killed in the ensuing chaos, and by January 3, most of the rank and file had departed camp, marching on Pennsylvania to seek restitution from their state government. Wayne and his officers followed the mutineers, and Pennsylvania representatives met with the soldiers at Princeton to discuss terms. Ultimately, the government granted men who had served three years the right to leave the service and provided back pay. Much of the line dissolved as a result and was not reconstituted until spring.

The New Jersey Brigade at Pompton followed suit two weeks later. Washington showed no inclination to negotiate in the latter instance. He dispatched from West Point a picked force under Maj. Gen. Robert Howe of nine hundred troops drawn from the New England regiments already assembled to quell the Pennsylvania mutiny. Howe's men surprised the Jerseymen in their huts at Pompton on January 23 and executed two sergeants found guilty of inciting the men. This brought the major mutinies in the Main Army to a close.[73]

The dissolution of the Pennsylvania brigades forced Washington to adjust his winter dispositions. In late January, his right wing lay completely uncovered, with the stores and infrastructure around Morristown poorly defended. Knox's prediction that the British could easily march into northern New Jersey appeared a strong possibility. In response to the uprisings, three thousand Redcoats landed at Elizabethtown under Gen. James Robertson. Although the British endeavored only to send agents to distribute pamphlets in the New Jersey camp, Robert Howe worried that the enemy would head inland to Morristown. The major general claimed his opponents held "a great desire to burn that town." Given the conduct of Crown forces at Springfield in June 1780 and the importance Morristown had developed as a headquarters and storehouse, such fears were warranted.[74]

These weaknesses notwithstanding, Clinton held back from testing the Rebels in winter. Robertson's force withdrew quickly, and Morristown survived another potential threat. Civilians nevertheless feared that the northern areas of the state lay particularly vulnerable to enemy attacks.[75] Washington therefore ordered the bulk of the recently cowed New Jersey Brigade to the Jockey Hollow huts to protect Morristown's storehouses and escort supply trains on their way to West Point.[76] Distance and rugged terrain would afford the brigade a measure of protection, though Washington still implored its commander to maintain vigilance and stand wary of a surprise attack. He also ordered companies detached from the brigade to cover Pompton and Smith's Clove. Washington thereby preserved the crescent of posts around New York that had been the army's standard winter arrangement since late 1778.

Of course, by 1781 declining strength made this blockade a flimsy one. The New Jersey Brigade stretched from Morristown to the border with New York. In the Highlands, reorganization after January 1 left the Patriots with a reduced force. Seven brigades, all well below their stipulated size, held positions around West Point. Patriot strength in the region weakened further in February. In the middle of that month, Washington dispatched 1,200 light infantry under Lafayette to reinforce Virginia.[77] Concurrently, he directed the reconstituting Pennsylvania line to march southward once it replenished its ranks.[78] This dispersion of strength at a critical juncture bears further analysis. Although the British kept on the offensive in the South, Brig. Gen. Daniel Morgan's January victory over the British at Cowpens, South Carolina, had recently provided much-needed good news from that quarter. Why dramatically weaken the Main Army almost immediately after the mutinies? British inactivity during that episode might have convinced the commander in chief that Sir Henry Clinton was unlikely to make an offensive move in the winter. Washington might have also sought to shift more of his soldiers to a warmer climate and more active theater to dissuade further mutinous activity. The redeployments would also ease supply with the disruptive spring thaw approaching. Finally, the natural strength and man-made fortifications of the defenses in the Highlands might have assuaged any doubts Rebel commanders had of their men's ability to resist an enemy incursion. Washington planned to use the militia to augment his meager regular force if the British advanced on West Point or New Jersey.[79]

In the end, Clinton never called Washington's bluff, and *petite guerre* represented the only fighting to occur through the remainder of the winter. Despite their weakness, as in 1779–80, the Rebels sent units ranging in size from a regiment to a brigade to forward posts to deter enemy raids and foraging parties.[80] Most small-scale fighting occurred in New York. Patriot outposts skirmished with Loyalist raiders near North Castle at the end of December 1780.[81] A month later, a small operation under Lt. Col. William Hull struck Tory posts at Morrisania. At the cost of thirty casualties, Hull took fifty prisoners, destroyed a pontoon bridge, burned enemy huts and forage, and carried away their cattle. A second detachment under Col. Moses Hazen covered Hull's withdrawal with spirited resistance. Success in these actions garnered praise from Washington and helped bolster the whole army's morale in the wake of the January mutinies. Although Hull received much acclaim for his role in the engagement, Brig. Gen. Samuel Holden Parsons held overall command of the forward detachments in Westchester. The Connecticut brigadier had fulfilled similar duties successfully as outpost commander in New Jersey during the previous winter. Parsons had developed into an effective leader of detached forces covering fixed quarters.[82]

Ultimately, British forces proved a minimal threat to the cantoned revolutionaries in early 1781. More troubling for the Rebels, disease returned to undermine their strength. The large, stationary posts along the Hudson welcomed an influx of recruits replacing the three-year enlistees beginning in January. Compared to previous winters, the Highlands camps also hosted a greater number of women and children. The stationary and increasingly substantial posts seem to have offered better accommodations than earlier cantonments. This concentration of new bodies thus brought an increase in smallpox cases for the first time since Valley Forge.[83]

Drawing on lessons learned from earlier in the war, Patriot officers sought to inoculate hitherto uninfected recruits and their families upon their arrival in camp.[84] Variolation busied Continental doctors throughout early 1781. Dr. Samuel Adams, serving at the artillery park near New Windsor, recorded administering frequent inoculations in late January. On the twenty-third, he attended to some thirty soldiers and their children and then to three soldiers, one woman, and three children the following day. Unfortunately, supply shortages affected the care of inoculation patients. Effective treatment required blankets, lodging, and food for recovering patients. The sharp increase in vulnerable persons taxed the army's meager stores. Adams complained, "I am sorry to say, but [they] are too poorly provided for." He learned to his dismay that the local storehouse lay destitute of "sugar or any other stores except rice—men will not be happy." The doctor worried his disappointed patients might take their displeasure out on him; fearing the men would be "obliged to eat improper food and so the poor surgeon [would be] blamed." Compounding the situation, February began with dysentery spreading to smallpox patients. Adams nevertheless continued to perform variolation, with many of his charges described as recruits or their children. Despite poor conditions, the procedure worked largely as intended, with most patients experiencing only very light cases. On February 13, Adams declared several were nearly fully recovered. A week later, with his patients doing well, he departed for his Massachusetts home on furlough.[85]

Notwithstanding such efforts, army doctors could not keep pace with all the new uninfected bodies arriving in camp. Inevitably, vulnerable individuals contracted the virus the natural way and spread it to nearby communities. William Heath, the garrison commander at West Point, informed Washington on February 1, "I am just informed that the Small Pox is in all places in this vicinity and at the Park of Artillery, as there are Some few of the Troops who have not had it, will it not be advisable for such as incline, to have it."[86] Two days later, Washington ordered all regiments to submit returns of those soldiers who had not had smallpox.[87]

The returns revealed that more soldiers lay vulnerable than at any point since the Valley Forge winter. Heath despaired, "The number is greater than I apprehended." Fearing that the Patriots lacked the doctors, beds, and supplies necessary, the Massachusetts general opted for a strategy of isolation and quarantine. Heath hoped that if infected individuals could be quickly identified and soldiers and their families remained stationary, the army could avoid a more serious outbreak.[88] Nevertheless, by March, it became clear that early isolation efforts had failed as Heath received reports that *variola* had reached Fishkill, New Windsor, Newburgh, and other areas around West Point. The epidemic necessitated more stringent quarantine procedures. Heath's March 17 garrison orders cautioned troops who had not had the illness to "be very careful" when traveling to those areas know to have the disease. He banned visitors from contaminated locales from coming into camp.[89]

Smallpox continued to make inroads throughout the month, forcing Continental commanders to change their stance on inoculation at the end of March. On the twenty-seventh, Heath announced plans to establish a smallpox hospital across the river from West Point. He directed the New Hampshire Brigade cantoned there to vacate its huts, which would henceforth house patients undergoing inoculation. Heath estimated that the huts could accommodate 240 persons, meaning the whole army could not be inoculated at once. Instead, soldiers on outpost duty received orders to send their vulnerable soldiers back to camp immediately to receive treatment. The rest of the West Point garrison was to be variolated in April.[90]

To ensure inoculations could be administered as quickly as possible, Heath ordered "surgeons from a brigade or so many in the whole as may be necessary to inoculate and attend the patients are to go with them. The greatest care is to be taken to prevent the spread of the infection." Guards were to maintain a strict quarantine around the new smallpox hospital to prevent those recovering there from infecting their comrades or nearby civilian communities. Less helpfully, Heath also directed the construction of a smokehouse, at which anyone traveling from the hospitals was to undergo a primitive form of decontamination; such men were not to travel to the main garrison without being "first sufficiently smoked."[91] Although this was a common prophylactic practice used in the eighteenth century, it was of dubious value.[92]

James Thacher left a record of attending to variolation in April. He and his fellow doctors continued to inoculate enlisted men, officers, and their families. In Thacher's regiment, 187 people had not had the disease and therefore required treatment. He judged many of these to be too infirm to safely undergo the procedure due to the poor diet of army rations. The necessity of securing the army from the disease, however, meant that members of the Continental community in the Highlands were inoculated "without exception."[93]

The outbreak climaxed in April, when more than five hundred patients lay ill with smallpox. This group experienced mostly mild symptoms, with only four deaths recorded.[94] Yet shortages of hospital stores and food continued to trouble Continental officers. James Thacher lamented the lack of provisions to keep his charges' strength up while they recovered. Rice, sugar or molasses, and tea were reserved for those who experienced particularly bad cases, while those enjoying mild bouts subsisted on regular rations of beef and salt pork.[95] Heath found the army lacking "some hospital stores, such as sugar or molasses, and Indian meal" and appealed to the commander in chief for relief, inquiring whether hospital stores kept in reserve in Connecticut could "possibly be spared [as they] may be ordered for the relief of inoculated patients."[96]

With inadequate supplies and limited hospital space, continuing inoculations risked exposing soldiers to other ailments. Doing so might also inhibit the Continentals' ability to take the field at the start of the campaign season. Washington weighed his options and seems to have concluded that to continue variolation would create more problems than it would solve. On April 19, he announced, "considering the scarcity of Hospital stores and the advanced season," it was "proper to order a discontinuance of inoculation in the army." Instead, the commander in chief reinstated a strict quarantine, commanding that "the patients now at the small pox hospital and those who are employed to attend the sick may be prevented from straggling to their corps and all such as do not now belong to the hospital from going to it on any patients until the surgeons report that all danger of infection ceases." Anyone who developed a case would henceforth be sent immediately to the smallpox hospital, but recruits would no longer undergo inoculation upon their arrival in camp.[97]

Washington's gamble paid off; by the end of the month, the emergency appears to have subsided. The springtime flow of recruits continued, but neither Heath, nor Washington, nor any of the army doctors highlighted variolation in their subsequent writings. The establishment of smallpox hospitals and the implementation of limited inoculation and stringent quarantine met the army's needs. The Continentals had proven attentive in addressing the health issue before it became a full-blown crisis.

Beyond smallpox, officers successfully dealt with the other ailments and hygiene problems that had plagued the army in past winters. Maintaining cleanliness in the large Highlands barracks had troubled the Continentals in previous years. William Heath devoted much of his attention in early 1781 to keeping the lodgings and fortifications at West Point salubrious. In January, he ordered men to clean the various sally ports, embrasures, and firing platforms at their fortifications.[98] Prolonged stays in barracks also necessitated an increase in soap rations in late January.[99] In February, Heath forbade soldiers from splitting wood on barracks floors in order to keep them tidy.[100] During March, officers inspected barracks rooms to ensure troops' diligence in removing all filth, or else "they will meet with trouble."[101] Heath ordered a garrison-wide cleaning on March 18.[102] Beyond the Point, soldiers passed the winter in their huts secure from snow, wind, and rain. Officers continued to enforce strict regimens of cleaning huts and sweeping camp streets.[103]

April began with a refrain familiar to veterans. "As the warm season is now advancing," Heath reminded his men, extra care was to be taken to ensure cleanliness and thereby good health. Blankets were to be cleaned and all filth and dirt removed from in and around the barracks.[104] Freshly enlisted soldiers arrived at West Point throughout the spring, replenishing Continental ranks but also adding men untutored in camp routine to the Highlands quarters.[105] New levies ignored the basics of camp health and hygiene, forcing officers to undertake daily inspections of barracks rooms in May. They monitored not only cleanliness but also their men's food preparation. New men apparently failed to cook their meals properly.[106] By early May, the influx of recruits, warming temperatures, and prolonged occupation of the barracks threatened the whole garrison's well-being. Heath responded by ordering brigades to send some of their men to encamp in the field instead. The spring season permitted these soldiers to shelter in tents rather than huts.[107]

By June, it appeared that a springtime outbreak of camp fevers might strike the army as it had in 1778. Robert Howe replaced William Heath at the beginning of the month and immediately undertook an inspection of the barracks and surrounding camps. In response to his findings, the taciturn Howe admonished the garrison through his general orders. He declared that the arrival of untrained men and crowded conditions had again rendered camp "unwholesome." Howe placed the blame on his officers, however, whom he felt should have known better than to allow dirty conditions to persist. "Cleanliness is essential to the health of the men," he declared. "All officers must know this, and all officers should attend to it." Howe expected everyone in his command to be aware of hygiene's importance, but "very particularly of those whose immediate duty it is."

To put the garrison back on course to salubriousness, he established new duties for his officers and men. A fatigue party was to begin work at dawn under the direction of the adjutant general. These troops were to rake all filth together and burn it. The parties were to rotate daily until they completed their task. Within the barracks, regimental quartermasters were to increase their efforts ensure those buildings were cleaned and "kept to." Howe did not mince words, stating that he did not content himself with merely explaining his orders and would "attend to and enforce the execution of them." The following day, Howe ordered the digging of new vaults, to be repeated weekly, and issued the now familiar prohibition of soldiers easing themselves about camp. Company officers were to confine and report offenders.[108] Conditions had improved slightly by June 18, though Howe still found it necessary to repeat his instructions and threaten violators with courts-martial.[109]

Ultimately, Heath's and Howe's efforts staved off serious camp illnesses at West Point. The Continentals passed the winter without dysentery and other fevers severely impacting their capabilities. Other preparations had continued throughout the spring. Whatever the conditions of the West Point barracks, the army at large that was hutted in the Highlands avoided the camp contagions that had infected so many in June 1778. Soldiers had spent much of the spring drilling, with veterans setting the example for new troops.[110] Twice-daily exercises began at West Point in mid-April, followed in May by inspections by the new adjutant general, Edward Hand.[111]

On June 18, the army took the field once more.[112] Before breaking camp, General Howe informed his men that they would be operating alongside "the army of our illustrious ally, consisting of some of the first officers and best disciplined troops in Europe." The general recognized that his men had labored through the winter under "disadvantages and distresses" that prevented them from quite matching the French. But, "if we cannot be so well prepared as we might, at least let us as much so as we can."[113]

Indeed, the Main Army was smaller than in previous years, and veterans now stood in the ranks with a growing number of new men. Nevertheless, they had endured another winter in quarters that were as good as could be expected. When Washington embarked on the Yorktown campaign in August, a network of camps and magazines, protected by the Watchungs and Hudson Highlands, facilitated the movement of his forces. The troops Washington left behind under William Heath kept up a vigilant watch on the British in New York from their defensible position near West Point. Earlier in the year, the commander in chief had declared that the best way to deter British advances in the South was to maintain a strong force in the New York region. The strength of Continental positions along the Hudson thus enabled the Rebels to send a sizeable contingent to Virginia while still posing a credible threat along the Hudson.[114]

Following the Franco-American victory over Maj. Gen. Charles Cornwallis, Earl Cornwallis, in Virginia, the ample infrastructure standing in New Jersey and New York provided good shelter for the hard-marching Continentals. With barracks, fortresses, and huts all available, Washington essentially retired his army to secure cantonments, resembling European practices. With the best destinations for his troops well understood by late 1781, the commander in chief eschewed holding a council of war. Even before departing Virginia, Washington ordered Heath to begin making arrangements for winter quarters. Quartermasters in the Highlands prepared to distribute tools for hut building in mid-October.[115] With the direction of the war uncertain despite the recent victory, Washington hoped a successful winter would leave his men "fit for early, vigorous, and decisive action in the spring."[116]

The eventual dispositions continued to follow the previously established pattern, with Continental brigades apportioned between the Hudson and northern New Jersey. The New Jersey Brigade took position in the vicinity of Morristown, making use of the hut complex at Jockey Hollow for the third consecutive winter. The New York Brigade stood to the north, near the New Jerseyans' old cantonment at Pompton, guarding the New York–New Jersey border area. Two Connecticut brigades and two Massachusetts brigades were to canton in the Hudson Highlands, sheltering in the barracks at West Point and the various huts built during the preceding winters. Again, a light dragoon regiment guarded Connecticut.[117]

Continuing a trend set the previous year, the commander in chief also placed greater responsibility on William Heath for administering winter quarters. Washington spent much of early 1782 in Philadelphia, leaving it to his subordinate to run the camp. He brought with him the Rhode Island Regiment, which enjoyed comfortable lodgings in that city's barracks and houses.[118]

The Patriots again relied upon existing infrastructure to minimize the waste and effort of building fresh quarters. Connecticut soldiers guarding Peekskill marched to their cantonments and occupied their huts in a single day in late November.[119] The sound quality of the shelters built during the preceding winter meant many men returned from the Yorktown campaign to comfortable quarters in the Hudson Highlands without having to exert themselves in erecting new lodging.[120] This made for a satisfying end to a particularly trying journey. Contrary winds in the Chesapeake had delayed the return transit, while heavy rains in Pennsylvania added to men's miseries on their march back to the Highlands.[121] James Thacher reported in a letter to his family at the end of December that after such a taxing campaign, he hoped "to live gently" in camp.[122] Only the New York Brigade encountered difficulties. Civilians had torn down the huts at Pompton, forcing Brig. Gen. James Clinton's men to build new cabins.[123]

The Continentals passed the 1781–82 winter with comparatively few troubles. Proximity to civilians, the Yorktown contingent's southern travels, and a continuing stream of new levies demanded further attention to *variola* in early 1782.[124] In contrast to the difficulties encountered in early 1781, in 1782 the Patriots enjoyed more ample hospital stores and more hospital space afforded by the substantial military infrastructure present in the Highlands by that date. Army-wide inoculations began in January.[125] Vacant huts again provided space for recovering patients.[126] The hospitals maintained success in implementing the procedure. Nearly two thousand underwent treatment in early 1782, and

General Heath judged the patients' conditions "very favorable." The inoculations continued until May.[127]

For veterans, 1781–82 featured few adversities compared to the past. While deficiencies persisted in clothing and money, Oliver Rice pronounced himself to have spent the winter "as agreeably as possible" while residing in "a very comfortable hut." Uncharacteristically, the army had enjoyed good provisions over the winter, and Rice declared himself "favored with as much health as any person, my body is free from pain."[128] Benjamin Gilbert echoed Rice's sentiments, writing in April 1782, "Our soldiers are exceedingly well clothed and fed."[129] The two men were both in a good position to judge. Rice had served since early 1777, beginning as a sergeant and rising to the rank of lieutenant; Gilbert had been a militiaman in 1775 and risen through the Continental ranks to captain. They had served through four winters in the Highlands and had a fifth ahead of them.

The summer of 1782 passed without serious action as both Rebels and Redcoats awaited the formal announcement of peace. Diplomats took their time hammering out a treaty, however, and Continentals remained under arms in late 1782, still unsure of the conflict's outcome. They again needed winter quarters. With the war's end nearing, ease of administration and discipline took precedence over operational considerations. Therefore, the commander in chief did not detach many regulars to New Jersey or Connecticut and did not arrange his troops with a view to guarding the passes through the Highlands or contesting enemy foraging parties. He sought instead a locale that would permit most of his soldiers to be housed together to await the conclusion of hostilities. "To wait events," he wrote to Nathanael Greene, "I have concentrated the army to a point as much as possible." His force, while not numerous, appeared up for the tasks it faced in these final days. Discipline had improved over the course of the summer and fall.[130]

The huts built in the vicinity of West Point during previous winters seem to have struck Washington as insufficient to meet his goals. He therefore ordered his quartermaster to find a new site. By this point, Continental officers had honed their skills in siting their winter quarters. In mid-October 1782, Col. Timothy Pickering conducted an extensive examination of the Hudson Highlands to seek out a locale for a new log-hut city. Like Greene before him, Pickering evinced a keen eye for terrain and resources. His report to Washington described in fine detail the characteristics of various sites: in what direction huts would likely face, the availability of fresh water, the accessibility of timber, and the size of force the open ground could accommodate. Pickering also pointed out forests that might prove suitable for firewood but featured trees either too young or too large to make suitable huts. At the end of his survey, he "met with an excellent grove sufficient for hutting two brigades" near the home of John Ellison in New Windsor. A site suitable for a third brigade lay close by. These spots would become home to the Continentals' final log-hut city.[131]

Given the army's exertions over the years, the commander in chief sought to avoid undue hardship and loss for his men. Washington streamlined his command structure for administering the army, reflecting his tendency to delegate camp administration to subordinates in recent years. He appointed Maj. Gen. Horatio Gates to command the New Windsor camp and Henry Knox to head the West Point garrison. Washington wanted to avoid any health problems or disciplinary lapses with the conflict nearly over. Arranging for proper shelter consequently stood as an important task. Washington implored Knox to ensure that West Point's barracks stood ready to welcome the garrison before winter's arrival. "You know the necessity of bringing them to a certain state before the frost," he reminded Knox. The commander in chief directed carpenters to cease work on the fort's magazine and focus their efforts on the barracks, indicating that shelter had taken precedence over defense.[132]

At New Windsor the huts were to be built of a larger design than in previous years. Washington's general orders instructed his experienced soldiers to strive for "*regularity, convenience*, and even some degree of *elegance*."[133] Timothy Pickering set new dimensions: rather than the single fourteen-foot-by-sixteen-foot room that had been constant since Valley Forge, Pickering's model contained two rooms, each sixteen feet by eighteen feet, and featured a door, a chimney, and a window. The quartermaster general standardized roof pitches at forty-five degrees and demanded lathed rafters and shingles for their construction. A generous fourteen-foot-by-sixteen-foot kitchen conjoined the two wings of each hut. The size of each mess housed within a hut grew from twelve to sixteen men, who would enjoy more space, thirty-six square feet per man, rather than eighteen and a half. Officers also enjoyed larger huts at New Windsor, as well as the privilege to build separate kitchens.[134] An officer described these new structures as "double huts" that could each house half a company.[135] Only the Canadian Regiment, deployed to Pompton in New Jersey, relied on the smaller model of hut used earlier in the war.[136]

The Continentals began construction in early November, a month ahead of the pace established during the middle years of the war.[137] After retiring to mostly preexisting log-hut cantonments and barracks for two years, soldiers complained about having to make an entirely new log-hut city. Oliver Rice grumbled that the army's cantonment site sat in "a state of nature." Only by the soldiers' exertions would New York's forests be "transformed into huts."[138] The men at least enjoyed good provisions throughout construction.[139] A New Jersey officer described the work with "heavy timber" as "very fatiguing." Soldiers nevertheless made good progress. Enlisted men moved into their huts by the

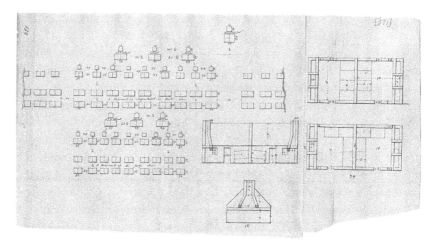

This plan for the 1782–83 New Windsor cantonment demonstrates the further improvements to camp design that Continental officers envisioned as the war drew to a close. Timothy Pickering, "Drawing of Military Quarters" (October or November 1782). Timothy Pickering Papers, Vol. 56. Ms. N-708, Massachusetts Historical Society, Boston.

middle of November, with officers occupying theirs by December 1.[140] Connecticut troops working on huts near West Point similarly put in hard work to raise these larger huts.[141] A colonel pronounced his men "as comfortable as can be expected" on December 9 in their nearly completed cabins.[142]

The Continentals also improved in building larger structures. Joseph Plumb Martin described working on new barracks at West Point in late 1782 that stood two stories high, with brick chimneys, wings at each end, and a gallery running the whole length of the front. "Large flights of steps" led to the upper floors. Martin judged the buildings large enough for two or three regiments. With the barracks standing, the veteran and his comrades "stowed ourselves away snugly in them."[143]

Overall, the 1782–83 winter evinced a full maturation in the Continental way of making quarters. In size, order, and cleanliness, the New Windsor cantonment represented the culmination of the log-hut city and the development of the army building it. With a city of sorts to retire to, the army could finally treat its winter quarters in the European fashion. Washington referred to New Windsor as a "cantonment of repose."[144] With soldiers demonstrating better order, discipline, and cleanliness than ever before, the commander in chief's orders took on a congratulatory rather than admonishing tone. He praised his men for their conduct during the summer, when a prolonged tent camp at Verplanck's Point had proceeded without "any filth or trash to be seen on the parade nor anything offensive to the sight or smell." Washington reminded his troops of this accomplishment as an example toward which to strive at their winter cantonment. The soldiers seemed to be meeting the general's lofty expectations. Washington's general orders of February 10 stated, "Every time the commander-in-chief passes through the line he finds himself very agreeably affected with a view of the present comfortable and beautiful situation of the troops." He considered it "a just testimony of applause to assert that the huts in point of convenience, regularity and elegance have equaled, if not surpassed his most sanguine expectations."[145] To William Heath, he described the army as "better covered, better clothed, and better fed than they have ever been in any former winter quarters."[146]

During the 1780–81 winter, the Continentals achieved their most successful winter quarters to date. Despite declining morale, manpower, and financial support, Washington closed the 1780 campaign season with minimal problems. By starting construction earlier and reusing existing structures, the army secured good coverings with minimal exertion. Concurrently, a mix of preemptive stockpiling and impressment mitigated supply shortages and overcame the innate difficulties the Hudson Highlands' geography imposed. Outpost commanders maintained their vigilance even as the bulk of the army enjoyed a refreshing winter removed from contact with the enemy. Within quarters, officers halted a smallpox outbreak and kept up camp cleanliness despite crowded conditions, particularly in barracks. Well-housed, adequately fed, rested, and healthy, the soldiers who marched for Yorktown contrasted greatly with the men who had gathered around Boston and New York early in the war, or even those who had departed garbage-laden Valley Forge in 1778.

For the late-war army in the Hudson Valley, the log-hut city now stood as the accepted form for winter quarters. This standardization emerged out of experience gained during the previous years. As one historian of the Continental Army has observed, rigorous training, sufficient supplies, and proficient administration brought Washington's men to their peak effectiveness in the Hudson Highlands during 1782 and 1783.[147] The built form of Patriot quarters reflected this effectiveness, with the log hut city now at the heart of an American way of castrametation. Had young George Washington, colonel of the Virginia Regiment, been able to peer thirty-five years into the future, he might have smiled at the progress made by American soldiers. They finally had good shelter.

CONCLUSION

"Something New in the Art of War"

A s the war drew to a close, Continental officers began to reflect on the log-hut city with a growing sense of pride and accomplishment. Passing through the remains of the encampment at Valley Forge in 1781, Lt. Enos Reeves credited the site with being the birthplace of the "first huts of the whole army."[1] By 1781 Reeves could look back on Valley Forge with admiration that would have seemed misplaced after the damp, disease-ridden winter of 1777–78. James Thacher praised the hut he occupied in 1782 as a "convenient and comfortable accommodation."[2] Pennsylvania troops deployed to the Southern Army expressed satisfaction with the log-hut city they built at James Island outside of Charleston in January 1783. "Officers and men all in comfortable quarters," wrote Ebenezer Denny, a veteran of Valley Forge; "James Island is a little paradise."[3] For the commander in chief, the huts represented the army's perseverance in the face of adversity. In a 1783 letter to Col. Theodorick Bland, Washington highlighted that the Continentals had spent the last six years in the field, "without any other shelter from the inclemency of weather than tents, or such houses as they could build for themselves without expense to the public."[4]

Perhaps the most striking convert to huttification was Maj. Gen. Horatio Gates. In 1777, Gates had opposed the use of rudimentary huts at Ticonderoga and beseeched Washington for tents. He had been among the log-hut city's opponents in late 1778. Yet at New Windsor he declared that the cantonment under construction promised soldiers more comfortable quarters than those that "any city in the continent would afford them." Gates also recognized the log-hut city's place in comparative context. He referred to the New Windsor encampment as something "new in the art of war."[5]

Foreign observers expressed similar judgments of the log-hut city's novelty and practicality. The Marquis de Chastellux, upon visiting Continental positions in the Hudson Highlands in 1780, declared that the Patriots, "like the

Romans in many respects, have hardly any other winter quarters than their wooden towns or barricaded camps." The Frenchman praised the Continentals for the speed and skill with which they erected their huts and highlighted the structures' chimneys and small doors for preserving warmth during the colder months.[6] At New Windsor in late 1782, Chastellux pronounced the huts then under construction there as "spacious, healthy, and well built." He again complimented the Patriots for the sound placement and quality of the shelters. The marquis also pointed out that the Rebels' skill at "putting together wood" and the absence of iron in the huts' construction allowed for much more rapid build times than would have been the case with European barracks.[7]

A February 1779 letter on the artillery park at Pluckemin that appeared in the *Pennsylvania Packet* similarly praised the Continentals' winter quarters. The author, a "foreign gentleman" under the pseudonym "Z," wrote that "the military village is superior" to others he had visited. The camp's "regularity, its appearance, and the ground on which it stands, throws over it a look of enchantment, although it is no more than the work of a few weeks." The writer pointed out that the log-hut city had "everything to recommend it" in an American environment abundant in wood. Log huts could be built quickly, using local timber cut by hand, providing an advantage over barracks made of boards, which would have required additional labor to saw and transport. The log-hut city so impressed the foreign gentleman that he claimed, "The great philosopher king of Prussia thinks it no dishonor to copy General Washington in the mode of quartering his troops." While this comment likely stretched the truth, it nevertheless indicated the novelty of the Middlebrook camp compared to how European armies wintered.[8]

The success of log huts in the War of Independence bequeathed the structure to subsequent generations of American soldiers. In 1799, the young United States raised an army amid a war scare with Revolutionary France. George Washington left retirement to nominally command, while his former aide-de-camp Alexander Hamilton, served as this "New Army's" lieutenant general. To house this force, Washington explicitly told his subordinate that "troops should be hutted in the manner they were in the late war."[9] The new army built three small log hut cantonments in Massachusetts, Virginia, and New Jersey, the latter at Green Brook, not far from the old Middlebrook camp.[10] The huts copied exactly the dimensions used from Valley Forge to Morristown.[11] Enforcing camp hygiene among recruits proved as problematic as it had during the Revolution; before the army disbanded, dysentery and smallpox broke out at Green Brook.[12] Fittingly, given the care and attention Washington had devoted to military housing since the Seven Years' War, the commander in chief died in December 1799 while still in charge of a wintering army.

Despite problems with hygiene and sickness, the method of shelter had proven sound once more. During the War of 1812, American soldiers again erected huts to protect themselves from the harsh winters along the Great Lakes.[13] Troops on the frontier in subsequent decades hutted as well, and by the mid-nineteenth century, the American way of castrametation found formal articulation in print. The *Military Dictionary*, written and published in 1861 by Col. Charles H. Scott, inspector general of the United States Army, included extensive coverage of military housing. Scott's entry for camps covered eight pages. He included several distinctions in types of camps, including definitions for barracks, tents, and cantonments. He defined huts themselves as "frequently constructed by troops retiring to winter quarters," with special distinction given as "the quarters occupied by United States troops on our frontiers." The dictionary's plan for a hut included instructions for cutting windows and doors into the structure, and the accompanying illustration bore a resemblance to its Revolutionary forebears.[14]

Eighty years after the Continental Army departed its encampments in New Jersey and New York, similar structures arose across landscapes in Maryland, Virginia, and Tennessee. The American Civil War pitted sizeable armies against each other in the densely populated eastern states. Again, American armies turned to the log-hut encampment for quarters during stationary periods. Much like the Main Army in New Jersey in 1779 and 1780, the Army of Northern Virginia's encampments of 1862 and 1863 dwarfed the cities of its host state and ranked among the largest population concentrations in the Confederacy.[15] The Confederates' opponents built even more extravagantly. During the winter of 1862–63, the Army of the Potomac erected up to 30,000 huts for its winter quarters near Falmouth, Virginia.[16] Clearly, housing remained crucial to the American military experience well after the Revolution. Historians will hopefully find the study of war and shelter in other eras and locales a fruitful field for future scholarship.

Viewing the War of Independence through the prism of shelter and its attendant problems raises the reputation of several Continental generals. Washington devoted his attention to his men's housing and health in camp throughout the war. Although he held on to impractical methods during the conflict's early years, he demonstrated flexibility in accepting new forms of housing as the conflict progressed. He tirelessly strove to make sure his men had food, cover, and security. He also relentlessly enforced discipline to prevent camp diseases. Nathanael Greene, already held in high regard as a strategist in the Southern Campaign and an administrator during his time as quartermaster general, garners further laurels for his skill in selecting and provisioning campsites. That Continental quarters were healthy and well supplied after 1778 was due in large part to the efforts of Greene and his deputies.

Other commanders, whatever their failings as generals in the field, proved themselves able camp administrators. Alexander McDougall, William Heath, and Robert Howe all tended to soldiers' needs in the difficult Hudson Highlands. Heath earned Washington's trust to hold independent command along the Hudson during the war's later years. Arthur St. Clair consistently provided sound advice in arranging winter quarters. Anthony Wayne served as huts' strongest advocate and showed an early understanding of their benefits. Samuel Holden Parsons proved himself a competent outpost commander.

Common soldiers demonstrated resilience in the face of trying conditions. Early in the war, Rebel troops endured exposure to rain, wind, and snow while campaigning with shoddy tents and shanties for cover. Their own reticence toward cleanliness and the subpar performance of their leaders exposed them to a plethora of ailments. Under better guidance during the second half of the war, enlisted men evinced greater dedication to sanitation and kept their camps remarkably clean, given their size and the duration of their use. Unlike soldiers of contemporary armies, the Continental rank and file frequently had to build their own shelters in the middle of December or later. For months on end, they occupied lodgings that soldiers of other armies would have mocked.

Strategically, the camps proved their worth. Distance and terrain made assailing Continental cantonments a risky operation. Sir Henry Clinton faced criticism during and after the war for his seemingly cautious strategy in the north during his time as commander in chief. Clinton resorted to probes, feints, and subterfuge in his efforts to draw Washington away from his Highlands bases and into open battle or to seize the Rebels' most important posts. Clinton's critics, then and now, have overlooked that the Continentals held such a seemingly unassailable position because of their ability to maintain an army in a region lacking shelter and communications. Had the Rebels dispersed into billets from Albany to Philadelphia, the Redcoats could have easily occupied northern New Jersey or taken West Point. Alternatively, had the Patriot army wintered in more open terrain, the British could have "beat up" its quarters or forced it into battle. The remotely placed huts and barracks in New Jersey and New York afforded Washington's men protection and helped maintain a strategic stalemate in the theater even when the Rebels were at a numerical disadvantage.

The Continental Army was not the only force in military history that dealt with the problem of shelter. The Patriots' encampments do, however, stand out as the most well-known winter quarters of any army. Both Valley Forge and

Jockey Hollow are preserved by the United States National Parks Service. New Windsor in New York and Redding and Somerville in New Jersey (the latter being the modern town near the ground once occupied by the Middlebrook camp) all host state parks commemorating the winter quarters built at those places. The existence of such parks testifies to the hold that the Continentals' wintertime struggles have had on popular audiences and the preservation of such history.

Cantonments played a larger role in the war than simply serving as a backdrop for the leadership and forbearance that have characterized depictions of the Valley Forge and Jockey Hollow winters. By providing shelter, streamlining discipline and supply, and keeping a sizeable army concentrated close to the enemy, hut complexes stood as distinct innovations that formed a crucial component to Continental strategy. The American log-hut city represents one of the most important and original contributions made to the art of war.

Notes

Introduction

1. Quoted in Henry Phelps Johnston, ed., *Connecticut Military Record, 1775–1748* (Hartford, CT: Adjutant General's Office, 1889), 135.
2. For the idea of the army as a city, see Wayne E. Lee, *Barbarians and Brothers: Anglo-American Warfare, 1500–1865* (New York: Oxford University Press, 2014), 197. For the idea of a Continental Community that included women and various other civilians attached to the army, see Holly A. Mayer, *Belonging to the Army: Camp Followers and Community during the American Revolution* (Columbia: University of South Carolina Press, 1999).
3. *New Jersey Gazette,* December 22, 1779.
4. Kathleen M. Brown, *Foul Bodies: Cleanliness in Early America* (New Haven, CT: Yale University Press, 2011); Caroline Cox, *A Proper Sense of Honor: Service and Sacrifice in George Washington's Army* (Chapel Hill: University of North Carolina Press, 2004).
5. Larry Gerlach, *Prologue to Independence: New Jersey and the Coming of the American Revolution* (New Brunswick, NJ: Rutgers University Press, 1976); John Gilbert McCurdy, *Quarters: The Accommodation of the British Army and the Coming of the American Revolution* (Ithaca, NY: Cornell University Press, 2019); J. Alan Rogers, "Colonial Opposition to the Quartering of British Troops during the French and Indian War," *Military Affairs* 34 (February 1970): 7–11; John J. Zimmerman, "Governor Denny and the Quartering Act of 1756," *Pennsylvania Magazine of History and Biography* 91 (July 1967): 266–81.
6. John Buchanan, *The Road to Valley Forge: How Washington Built the Army That Won the Revolution* (Hoboken, NJ: Wiley, 2004); Paul Lockhart, *The Drillmaster of Valley Forge: Baron de Steuben and the Making of the American Army* (New York: Harper, 2010); John Trussell, *Birthplace of an Army: A Study of the Valley Forge Encampment* (Philadelphia: Pennsylvania Historical Society, 1976).
7. Wayne Bodle, *The Valley Forge Winter: Civilians and Soldiers in War* (University Park: Pennsylvania State University Press, 2002).
8. The few works studying encampments include Peter Angelekos, "The Army at Middlebrook," *Proceedings of the New Jersey Historical Society* 70 (January 1952): 97–120; S. Sydney Bradford, "Hunger Menaces the Revolution, December

177

1779–January 1780," *Maryland Historical Magazine* 61 (1966): 1–23; John T. Cunningham, *The Uncertain Revolution: Washington and the Continental Army at Morristown* (West Creek, NJ: Down the Shore, 2007); Thomas Fleming, *Forgotten Victory: The Battle for New Jersey, 1780* (New York: Reader's Digest Press, 1973); Carl Prince, *Middlebrook: The American Eagle's Nest* (Somerville, NJ: Somerset, 1957); Edward S. Rutsch and Kim M. Peters, "Forty Years of Archaeological Research at Morristown National Historical Park, Morristown, New Jersey," *Historical Archaeology* 11 (1977): 15–38; John Seidel, "The Archaeology of the American Revolution: A Reappraisal and Case Study of the Continental Army Artillery Cantonment of 1778–1779, Pluckemin, New Jersey," (PhD Diss., University of Pennsylvania, 1987); Samuel Stelle Smith, *The Darkest Winter: Morristown, 1780* (Monmouth Beach, NJ: Philip Frenau, 1980); Daniel Curson, *Putnam's Revolutionary War Winter Encampment: The History and Archaeology of Putnam Memorial State Park* (Charleston, NC: History, 2011).

9. Examples of works of synthesis that have largely ignored encampments other than Valley Forge include Christopher Ward, *The War of the Revolution*, 2 vols. (New York: MacMillan, 1952); Howard H. Peckham, *The War for Independence: A Military History* (Chicago: University of Chicago Press, 1958); Don Higginbotham, *The War of American Independence: Military Attitudes, Policies, and Practice, 1763–1789* (New York: MacMillan, 1971); Robert Middlekauff, *The Glorious Cause: The American Revolution, 1763–1789* (New York: Oxford University Press, 1982).

10. Lewis Lochée, *An Essay on Castrametation* (London: T. Cadell, 1778), 1. See also the definition provided in Thomas Simes, *The Military Medley* (London: 1768).

11. Thomas Reide, *The Staff Officer's Manual* (London: T. Egerton, 1806), x–xi.

12. In this book, I use the term "Patriot" to refer to those North Americans who actively supported the cause of independence, essentially those whom previous generations of historians might have referred to as "Americans." I also use the terms "Rebels" and "Revolutionaries" to refer to these people. I use "British" and occasionally "Redcoats" for the Patriots' opponents, as well as "Hessians" when hired German soldiers are present. I reserve "Loyalist" and occasionally "Tory" for North Americans supporting the Crown. I refer to the national force of long-service soldiers fighting for independence as "Continentals," distinct from the short-term militias raised by the states, although during the war's first years, there were considerable numbers of militiamen serving alongside the Continentals in active campaigns.

13. For an overview of American adaptations of European methods, see Don Higginbotham, "The Early American Way of War: Reconnaissance and Appraisal," *William and Mary Quarterly* 3rd Series, 44 (1983): 230–73; Wayne E. Lee, "Early American Ways of War: A New Reconnaissance," *Historical Journal* 44 (March 2001): 269–89.

14. Mathew H. Spring, *With Zeal and Bayonets Only: The British Army on Campaign in North America, 1775–1783* (Norman: University of Oklahoma Press, 2010), 8.

15. Washington to Jonathan Trumbull Sr., December 17, 1780, Founders Online, https://founders.archives.gov/documents/Washington/03-01-02-0090.

16. Studies of the army's administrative development include James Kirby Martin and Mark Edward Lender, *A Respectable Army: The Military Origins of the Republic, 1763–1789* (Wheeling, IL: Harlan Davidson, 1982); Robert K. Wright, *The Continental*

Army (Washington, DC: Center of Military History, United States Army, 1986); Joseph G. Bilby and Katherine Bilby Jenkins, *Monmouth Court House: The Battle That Made the American Army* (Yardley, PA: Westholme, 2010); Joseph R. Fischer, *A Well-Executed Failure: The Sullivan Campaign against the Iroquois, July–September 1779* (Columbia: University of South Carolina Press, 1997). Few works on the environmental history of the Revolutionary War exist. See David C. Hsiung, "Food, Fuel, and the New England Environment in the War for Independence, 1775–1776," *New England Quarterly* 80 (December 2007): 614–54; Elizabeth A. Fenn, "Biological Warfare in the Eighteenth Century: Beyond Sir Jeffery Amherst," *Journal of American History* 86, no. 4 (2000): 1552–80; Fenn, *Pox Americana: The Great Smallpox Epidemic of 1775–1782* (New York: Hill and Wang, 2002). For works that intersect with the environment and American wars in general, see Lisa Brady, *War upon the Land: Military Strategy and the Transformation of Southern Landscapes during the American Civil War* (Athens: University of Georgia Press, 2012); John R. McNeill, "Woods and Warfare in World History," *Environmental History* 9, no. 3 (2004): 388–410; McNeill, *Mosquito Empires: Ecology and War in the Greater Caribbean, 1620–1914* (New York: Cambridge University Press, 2010); Kathryn Shivley Meier, *Nature's Civil War: Common Soldiers and the Environment in 1862 Virginia* (Chapel Hill: University of North Carolina Press, 2013).

Chapter 1

1. For the Military Revolution debate, see Geoffrey Parker, "The Military Revolution 1550–1650—A Myth?" *Journal of Modern History* 48 (June 1976): 195–214; R. R. Palmer, "Frederick the Great, Guibert, Bulow: From Dynastic War to National War," in *Makers of Modern Strategy: From Machiavelli to the Nuclear Age*, ed. Peter Paret (Princeton, NJ: Princeton University Press, 1986), 93.
2. Myron P. Gutmann, *War and Rural Life in the Early Modern Low Countries* (Princeton, NJ: Princeton University Press, 1980), 36–37.
3. Ibid., 61–62.
4. John A. Lynn, *The Giant of the Grand Siècle: The French Army 1610–1715* (New York: Cambridge University Press, 2008), 158; Christopher Duffy, *The Army of Frederick the Great*, 2nd ed. (London: Emperor's, 1996), 80; Duffy, *The Army of Maria Theresa: The Armed Forces of Imperial Austria, 1740–1780* (New York: Hippocrene, 1977), 139–40; J. A. Houlding, *Fit for Service: The Training of the British Army, 1715–1795* (Oxford, UK: Clarendon, 1981), 36–41, 51–57. For an overview of barracks in early modern Europe, see John Childs, "Barracks and Conscription: Civil-Military Relations in Europe from 1500," *European History Online*, August 1, 2011, accessed October 15, 2017, http://ieg-ego.eu/en/threads/alliances-and-wars/war-as-an-agent-of-transfer/john-childs-barracks-and-conscription-civil-military-relations-in-europe-from-1500#Militaryaccommodation.
5. For the role of government authority in eighteenth-century warfare, see John Brewer, *Sinews of Power: War, Money, and the English State, 1688–1783* (Cambridge, MA: Harvard University Press, 1990).
6. Lynn, *The Giant of the Grand Siècle*, 536–37.
7. Duffy, *The Military Experience in the Age of Reason, 1715–1789* (New York: Routledge, 1987), 161–62.
8. Ibid., 166.

9. Christopher Duffy, *Siege Warfare: The Fortress in the Early Modern World, 1494–1660* (New York: Routledge, 1979), 129–30.

10. Gutmann, *War and Rural Life*, 58–59.

11. Marshal d'Estrees, *Camp Topographies of the Campaign of MDCCLVII in Westphalia*, trans. James J. Mitchell (Valpariso, IN: Old Battlefield, 1996).

12. Duffy, *The Military Experience in the Age of Reason*, 185–87.

13. Gutmann, *War and Rural Life*, 58.

14. M. S. Anderson, *War and Society in Europe of the Old Regime, 1618–1789* (Guernsey, UK: Sutton, 1988),176.

15. Duffy, *Military Experience in the Age of Reason*, 185–87; Duffy, *The Army of Frederick the Great*, 220–22; Lynn, *Giant of the Grand Siècle*, 536–37.

16. André Corvisier, *Armies and Societies in Europe, 1494–1789*, trans. Abigail T. Siddall (Bloomington: Indiana University Press, 1979), 174.

17. Duffy, *The Military Experience in the Age of Reason*, 171–72.

18. Ibid.

19. Jay Luvaas, *Frederick the Great on the Art of War* (Cambridge, MA: Da Capo, 1999), 265.

20. Duffy, *The Army of Frederick the Great*, 196–97, 204–5; Luvaas, *Frederick the Great*, 278. For a comparison of Frederick's Bunzelwitz camp and Washington's position at Valley Forge, see Alex Burns, "Valley Forge vs. the Bunzelwitz Position," *Kabinettskrieg*, July 6 2016, http://kabinettskriege.blogspot.com/2016/07/valley-forge-vs-bunzelwitz-position.html.

21. Sandra L. Powers, "Studying the Art of War: Books Known to American Officers and Their French Counterparts in the Late Eighteenth Century," *Journal of Military History* 70 (July 2006): 781–814, Ewald's quote is on 791. For the overall European influence on the Continental Army, see Wright, *The Continental Army*, 3–5.

22. Lancelot, Comte Turpin de Crissé, *Essay on the Art of War*, trans. Joseph Otway (London: Strand, 1761), 554–57.

23. Ibid., 549.

24. Ibid., 551.

25. Frederick II, King of Prussia, *Military Instructions from the Late King of Prussia to His Generals*, trans. Thomas Phillips (Harrisburg, PA: Stackpole, 1960), 101–3.

26. Maurice de Saxe, *Reveries, or Memoirs Concerning the Art of War* (Edinburgh, UK: Sands, Donaldson, Murray, and Cochrane, 1759), 126–27.

27. Ibid., 82–84.

28. Ibid., 10–19.

29. Humphrey Bland, *A Treatise of Military Discipline*, 4th ed. (London: Buckley, 1740), 148–49.

30. Bennett Cuthbertson, *A System for the Complete Interior Management and Oecononmy of a Battalion of Infantry* (Bristol, UK: Rothus and Nelson, 1776), 39.

31. Ibid., 37–38.

32. Ibid., 248.

33. Frederick II, *Instructions*, 32.

34. Crissé, *Essay*, 239.

35. Timothy Pickering, *An Easy Plan of Discipline for a Militia* (Salem, MA: Samuel and Ebenezer Hall, 1775); Lewis Nicola, *A Treatise of Military Exercise, Calculated for the Use of Americans* (Philadelphia: Styner and Crist, 1776).

36. Beneton de Perrin, *Dissertation sur les Tentes* (Paris: Chez Gonichon, 1735), 1–2.

37. Guillaume Le Blond, *Essai sur la Castramétation* (Paris: Chez Carles-Antoine Jombert, 1748), ii.

38. Joseph de Fallois, *Traité de la Castramétation et de la Defense* (Paris: Chez G. J. Decker, 1771), 56.

39. Johann Dietrich Carl Pirscher, *Von der Castrametation* (Berlin: Arnold Wever, 1778).

40. Friderick Eugen Eric von Muller, *Castrametation* (Potsdam: 1776).

41. Anonymous, *Castramatatio* (Potsdam: publisher unknown, ca. 1780).

42. Francisco Antonio Freire da Fonceca Continho, *Pequeno resumo de Castrametação* (Lisbon: Na Typographia Nunesiana, 1792).

43. Lochée, *An Essay on Castrametation*, 33–49.

44. Ibid., 50–78.

45. John Pringle, *Observations on Diseases of the Army, in Camp, and in Garrison* (London: Strand, 1752.)

46. Cox, *A Proper Sense of Honor*, 126–27.

47. Fenn, "Biological Warfare," 1565–66; Cox, *A Proper Sense of Honor*, 119–25.

48. Stephen C. Eames, *Rustic Warriors: Warfare and the Provincial Soldier on the New England Frontier, 1689–1748* (New York: New York University Press, 2011), 51–68; Wright, *The Continental Army*, 5–8. For the British role in the military buildup in North America after 1754 in general, see Guy Chet, *Conquering the American Wilderness: The Triumph of European Warfare in the Colonial Northeast* (Amherst: University of Massachusetts Press, 2003).

49. McCurdy, *Quarters*, 50–88.

50. Quoted in Jack P. Greene, "The South Carolina Quartering Dispute, 1757–1758," *South Carolina Historical Magazine* 60 (October 1959): 197.

51. Matthew C. Ward, "The British Army and Epidemic Disease among the Ohio Indians," in *The Sixty Years War for the Great Lakes, 1754–1814*, ed. David Curtis Skaggs and Larry L. Nelson (East Lansing: Michigan State University Press, 2001), 68–69. For British forts on the frontier in general, see Michael N. McConnell, *Army and Empire: British Soldiers on the American Frontier, 1758–1775* (Lincoln: University of Nebraska Press, 2004).

52. Washington to John Forbes, April 23, 1758, in *The Papers of George Washington: Colonial Series*, 10 vols., ed. W. W. Abbot (Charlottesville: University of Virginia Press, 1985–1995), 5:138–39.

53. Washington to Henry Bouquet, July 3, 1758, and Bouquet to Washington, July 27, 1758, both in ibid., 5:256–59, 344–46.

54. Washington to Fauquier, September 28, 1758, in ibid., 6:52–53.

55 Washington to Fauquier, November 20, December 2, and December 9, 1758, all in ibid., 6:158–60, 161–64, 165–66.

56. Orders, July 6–8, 1756, in ibid., 3:238–42.

57. Washington to Charles Smith, June 24, 1758, in ibid., 5:238–39.

58. Orderly Book, September 21, 1758, in ibid., 6:31–32.

59. William Seward Webb, ed., *General Orders of 1757, Issued by the Earl of Loudoun and Phineas Lyman in the Campaign against the French* (New York: Dodd, Mead, 1899), 32.

60. Ibid., 132.

61. Benjamin Glasier, "French and Indian War Diary of Benjamin Glasier of Ipswich," *Essex Institute Historical Collections* 86 (1950): 81.

62. Archelaus Fuller, "Journal of Colonel Archelaus Fuller of Middletown," *Essex Institute Historical Collections* 46 (1910): 220.

63. Ralph Button to Loudoun, August 27, 1756, quoted in Fred Anderson, *A People's Army: Massachusetts Soldiers and Society in the Seven Years' War* (Chapel Hill: University of North Carolina Press, 1984), 95–96; Cox, *A Proper Sense of Honor*, 132–33.

64. David Holden Diary, in *Three Military Diaries Kept by Groton Soldiers in Different Wars*, ed. Samuel A. Green (Cambridge, MA: John Wilson and Son, 1901), 69.

65. Charles L. Fisher, "The Archaeology of Provincial Officers' Huts at Crown Point State Historic Site," *Northeast Historical Archaeology* 24 (1995): 78.

66. Anderson, *A People's Army*, 92–93.

67. Douglas R. Cubbison, *All Canada in the Hands of the British: General Jeffery Amherst and the 1760 Campaign to Conquer New France* (Norman: University of Oklahoma Press, 2014), 92–94.

68. Ibid., 141–42.

69. Ibid., 26–29.

Chapter 2

1. Hsiung, "Food, Fuel, and the New England Environment," 615.

2. Phineas Ingalls Diary, May 24–25, July 15, 1775, Massachusetts Historical Society, Boston, Massachusetts, hereafter MHS.

3. Joseph to Sarah Hodgkins, June 8, 1775, quoted in Herbert T. Wade and Robert A. Lively, *This Glorious Cause: The Adventures of Two Company Officers in Washington's Army* (Princeton, NJ: Princeton University Press, 1958), 24.

4. Isaac Greenwood, ed., *The Revolutionary Services of John Greenwood of Boston and New York, 1775–1783* (New York: De Vinne, 1922), 42–43.

5. William Emerson to Mary Emerson, July 17, 1775, quoted in Allen French, *The First Year of the American Revolution* (Boston: Houghton Mifflin, 1934), 300.

6. Benjamin Craft, "Craft's Journal of the Siege of Boston," ed. S. P. Fowler, *Historical Collections of the Essex Institute* 3 (1861): 55, 134.

7. Samuel Richards, *Diary of Samuel Richards, Captain of Connecticut Line, War of the Revolution, 1775–1781* (Philadelphia: Leeds and Biddle, 1909), 19.

8. Notes for Letter, July 10, 1775, in *The Papers of George Washington: Revolutionary War Series*, 25 vols. to date, ed. W. W. Abbot et al. (Charlottesville: University of Virginia Press, 1987–), 1:84–85, hereafter cited as *PGWRWS*.

9. Washington to Hancock, July 11, 1775, in ibid., 1:84.

10. Washington to Hancock, July 21, 1775, in ibid., 1:136–37.

11. Massachusetts Congress to Washington, July 6, 1775, quoted in Charles Royster, *A Revolutionary People at War: The Continental Army and American Character, 1775–1783* (Chapel Hill: University of North Carolina Press, 1979), 59.

12. Royster, *Revolutionary People at War*, 58–62; Brown, *Foul Bodies*, 169; Cox, *A Proper Sense of Honor*, 138–42.

13. Nathanael Greene to Jacob Greene, June 28, 1775, in *The Papers of Nathanael Greene*, 13 vols., ed. Richard K. Showman, Dennis R. Conrad, and Roger N. Parks (Chapel Hill: University of North Carolina Press, 1976–2005), 1:92–93, hereafter cited as *Greene Papers*.

14. Royster, *A Revolutionary People at War*, 82–84.
15. General Orders, July 17, 1775, in *PGWRWS*, 1:114–15.
16. General Orders, August 14, 1775, in *Greene Papers*, 1:108; General Orders, November 22, 1775, and December 7, 1775, both in *PGWRWS*, 2:415, 503.
17. Hsiung, "Food, Fuel," 619; Wright, *The Continental Army*, 29–36.
18. For the impact of weather on the health and morale of an army, see, Meier, *Nature's Civil War*, 35–64.
19. Craft, "Craft's Journal of the Siege of Boston," 51, 55, 57.
20. Phineas Ingalls Diary, August 2–6, 1775, MHS.
21. Craft, "Craft's Journal of the Siege of Boston," 135.
22. Asa Andrews to Josiah Williard, August 6, 1776, American Revolution Collection, Box 11, Folder B, Connecticut Historical Society, Hartford, CT, hereafter cited as CHS.
23. See entries for "lousy weather," August 30–September 4, 1775, in James Stevens, "The Revolutionary Journal of James Stevens of Andover Mass.," *Historical Collections of the Essex Institute* 48 (1912): 55.
24. Craft, "Craft's Journal of the Siege of Boston," 51, 55, 136–39.
25. Benjamin Boardman, "Diary of Rev. Benjamin Boardman," *Collections of the Massachusetts Historical Society, Second Series* 10 (1895–96): 402, 404, 408.
26. Stevens, "The Revolutionary Journal," 54.
27. Richards, *Diary of Samuel Richards*, 21.
28. Thomas Cushman Diary, entries for October and November 1775, MHS.
29. Stevens, "The Revolutionary Journal," 57–61.
30. Daniel McCurtin, "Journal of the Siege of Boston," in *Papers Chiefly Related to the Maryland Line*, ed. Thomas Blach (Philadelphia: T. K. and P. G. Collins, 1857), 15.
31. Greenwood, *The Revolutionary Services*, 43.
32. Nathaniel Morgan, "Journal of Ensign Nathaniel Morgan, April 21 to December 11, 1775," *Collections of the Connecticut Historical Society* 7 (1899): 105.
33. Craft, "Craft's Journal of the Siege of Boston," 139.
34. Thomas Cushman Diary, October 25, 1775, MHS.
35. McCurtin, "Journal," 29.
36. Washington to Hancock, August 4, 1775, in *PGWRWS*, 1:225.
37. General Orders, August 15, 1776, in ibid., 1:309.
38. Circular to General Officers, September 8, 1775, in ibid., 1:433–35.
39. Council of War, September 11, 1775, in ibid., 1:450–51. Present at this council were Major Generals Artemas Ward, Charles Lee, and Israel Putnam, as well as Brigadier Generals William Heath, John Thomas, John Sullivan, Joseph Spencer, and Nathanael Greene.
40. Hancock to Washington, September 26, 1775, in ibid., 1:49.
41. Estimate of Quarter Master Expenses, October 5, 1775, and Estimate of Commissary Expenses, October 7, 1775, both in *PGWRWS*, 2:151, 150; Erna Risch, *Supplying Washington's Army* (Washington, DC: Center of Military History, United States Army, 1981), 141. Payment for labor in building barracks is mentioned in Loammi Baldwin to Mary Baldwin, December 31, 1775, Loammi Baldwin Papers, Harvard University Library, Cambridge, MA, hereafter cited as HUL.
42. Stevens, "Revolutionary Journal," 58–60.
43. Ibid., 61–62.

44. Ibid., 65–66.
45. Simeon Lymon, "Journal of Simeon Lymon," *Collections of the Connecticut Historical Society* 7 (1899): 120.
46. Ibid., 121.
47. Ibid., 122–23.
48. Ibid., 124, 126, 131.
49. Sara Martin et al., *The Papers of John Adams*, 20 vols. to date (Cambridge, MA: Harvard University Press, 1977–), 3:280–85.
50. Washington to William Ramsay, November 10–16, 1775, in *PGWRWS*, 2:344.
51. Washington to Joseph Reed, December 25, 1775, in ibid., 2:606–7.
52. Greene to Samuel Ward Sr., December 18, 1775, in *Greene Papers*, 1:165.
53. General Orders, January 24, 1776, in *PGWRWS*, 3:176.
54. James Thacher, *A Military Journal during the American Revolutionary War, from 1775 to 1783; Describing Interesting Events and Transactions of this Period; with Numerous Historical Sketches of Several General Officers* (Boston: Cottons & Barnard, 1827), 46.
55. Richards, *Diary of Samuel Richards*, 21.
56. An account of the barracks improved by the Continental troops, undated but likely January 1776, in Peter Force, *American Archives*, 4th series, 9 vols. (Washington, DC: Published under Authority of an Act of Congress, 1837–1853), 4:844; McCurtin, "Journal," 26, 35. Regimental dispersions like Huntington's were common. Col. Loammi Baldwin's unit was spread between Chelsea and Cambridge in January 1776. See Loammi Baldwin to Mary Baldwin, January 12, 1776, Loammi Baldwin Papers, HUL.
57. Joseph to Sarah Hodgkins, October 6, 1775, quoted in Wade and Lively, *This Glorious Cause*, 41.
58. Ibid., 42.
59. General Orders, November 22, 1775, in *PGWRWS*, 2:415–17.
60. General Orders, January 3, 1776, in ibid., 3:13.
61. Reed to Washington, March 7, 1776, in ibid., 3:429.
62. Worthington C. Ford et al., eds., *Journals of the Continental Congress*, 34 vols. (Washington, DC: United States Government Printing Office, 1904–37), 4:102.
63. Washington to Reed, February 10, 1776, and Reed to Washington, March 15, 1776, both in *PGWRWS*, 3:287, 477.
64. Washington to the Massachusetts Council, August 29, 1775, in *PGWRWS*, 1:376.
65. *Massachusetts House of Representatives Journal*, July–November 1775 session, 229–30, quoted in *PGWRWS*, 2:119n1.
66. Greene to Samuel Ward Sr., December 31, 1775, in *Greene Papers*, 1:173.
67. Hsiung, "Food, Fuel," 643–51.
68. General Orders, January 24, 1776, in *PGWRWS*, 3:176.
69. Cox, *Proper Sense of Honor*, 139.
70. Ann M. Becker, "Smallpox in Washington's Army: Strategic Implications of the Disease in the American Revolutionary War," *Journal of Military History* 68 (April 2004): 387–89.
71. Amos Clark to Sarah Clark, July 31, 1775, Andre de Coppet Collection, Box 3, Folder 6, Princeton University Firestone Library, Princeton, NJ.
72. General Orders, July 4, 1775, in *PGWRWS*, 1:55.

73. Washington to Hancock, July 21, 1775, in ibid., 1:140.
74. William Sever to Washington, December 11, 1775, in ibid., 2:535.
75. David Avery Diary, December 21, 1775, and January 6, 1776, CHS.
76. Becker, "Smallpox in Washington's Army," 395.
77. Ibid., 384.
78. John Morgan to Washington, December 12, 1775, in *PGWRWS*, 2:541.
79. Thacher, *Military Journal*, 40.
80. Becker, "Smallpox in Washington's Army," 392.
81. Craft, "Craft's Journal of the Siege of Boston," 52–55, 171; Stevens, "Revolutionary Journal," 48; Phineas Ingalls Diary, November 17, 1775, MHS.
82. Edward G. Lengel, *Washington: A Military Life* (New York: Random House, 2005), 116.
83. Wright, *The Continental Army*, 55–56.
84. Lee to Washington, February 29, 1776, in *PGWRWS*, 2:390.
85. William Thompson to Washington, March 28, 1776, in ibid., 3:558.
86. Washington to Thomas Mifflin, March 24, 1776, in ibid., 3:520.
87. Solomon Nash, *Journal of Solomon Nash, a Soldier of the Revolution*, ed. Charles I. Bushnell (New York: privately printed, 1861), 12.
88. General Orders, April 25, April 29, April 30, May 11, and May 20, 1776, in *PGWRWS*, 4:123, 162, 174, 274, 343–44; Richards, *Diary of Samuel Richards*, 30; Loammi Baldwin to Mary Baldwin, May 21, 1776, Loammi Baldwin Papers, HUL.
89. Washington to Hancock, June 8, 1776, in *PGWRWS*, 4:463.
90. Philip Vickers Fithian, *Journal, 1775–1776: Written on the Virginia-Pennsylvania Frontier and in the Army around New York*, ed. Robert Greenhalgh Albion and Leonidas Dodson (Princeton, NJ: Princeton University Press, 1934), 187–88.
91. Loammi Baldwin to Mary Baldwin, July 4–5, 1776, Loammi Baldwin Papers, HUL.
92. David Hackett Fischer, *Washington's Crossing* (New York: Oxford University Press, 2004), 86–87.
93. Nash, *Journal*, 26.
94. Edward Morgan to Hannah Morgan, August 9, 1776, American Revolution Collection, Box 11, Folder C, CHS.
95. Amos Clark to Sarah Clark. August 5, 1776, Andre de Coppet Collection, Box 4, Folder 6, Princeton University Firestone Library.
96. Epaphroditus Champion Pension, S. 16711 Roll 0510, Revolutionary War Pension Applications, National Archives and Records Administration, Washington, DC, hereafter cited as RWP.
97. Fithian, *Journal*, 190.
98. Arthur Bowler, *Logistics and the Failure of the British army in America, 1775–1783* (Princeton, NJ: Princeton University Press, 1975), 147–48.
99. David Hackett Fischer, *Washington's Crossing* (New York: Oxford University Press, 2003), 87.
100. Nash, *Journal*, 29.
101. General Orders, August 30, 1776, in *PGWRWS*, 6:163.
102. Washington to Hancock, September 8, 1776, in ibid., 6:249–52.
103. Washington to Hancock, September 8, 1776, in ibid., 6:249–52. The Patriots chose their winter quarters site wisely; British forces would erect huts in the same vicinity in late 1779. See Reginald Pelham Bolton, "The Military Hut-Camp of the War

of the Revolution on the Dyckman Farm, Manhattan," *New York Historical Society Quarterly* 2 (1918, 1919): 89–97, 130–36.

104. Tench Tilghman to Stephen Moylan, September 9, 1776, in *PGWRWS*, 6:252–53.
105. Washington to Schuyler, September 12, 1776, and Schuyler to Washington, October 6, 1776, both in ibid., 6:297, 492.
106. General Orders, October 9, 1776, in ibid., 6:514.
107. General Orders, September 24, 1776, in ibid., 6:385.
108. Hugh Hughes Letterbook, September 12, 1776, quoted in Risch, *Supplying Washington's Army*, 143.
109. General Orders, September 21, 1776, in *PGWRWS*, 6:359.
110. Washington to Glover, September 18, 1776, ibid., 6:330.
111. Loammi Baldwin to Mary Baldwin, October 2, 1776, Loammi Baldwin Papers, HUL.
112. Robert Hanson Harrison to William Heath, September 30, 1776, quoted in *PGWRWS* 6:436–37.
113. Fithian, *Journal*, 236.
114. Richards, *Diary of Samuel Richards*, 42.
115. Edward Rogers to Hannah Rogers, September 17, 1776, American Revolution Collection, Box 11, Folder C, CHS; Rogers was not alone in the loss of his belongings. See David King to Samuel Boardman, September 15, 1776, Thomas Addis Emmet Collection, New York Public Library, New York, hereafter NYPL.
116. Loammi Baldwin to Mary Baldwin, September 28, 1776, Loammi Baldwin Papers, HUL.
117. General Orders, September 20, 1776, and September 25, 1776, both in *PGWRWS*, 6:347–50, 393.
118. Washington to Hancock, September 25, 1776, in ibid., 6:396.
119. General Orders, September 28, 1776, in ibid., 6:418.
120. Zacchaeus Towne Diary, September 25, 1776, Rutgers University Alexander Library, New Brunswick, NJ.
121. Fithian, *Journal*, 237.
122. Edward Rogers to Hannah Rogers, October 2, 1776, Revolutionary War Collection, Box 11, Folder B, CHS.
123. Loammi Baldwin to Mary Baldwin, October 1, 1776, Loammi Baldwin Papers, HUL.
124. Loammi Baldwin to Mary Baldwin, October 12, 1776, ibid.
125. Loammi Baldwin to Mary Baldwin, October 9, 1776, ibid.
126. Loammi Baldwin to Mary Baldwin, October 23, 1776, ibid.
127. Loammi Baldwin to Mary Baldwin, October 31, 1776, ibid.
128. Fithian, *Journal*, 241.
129. James McMichael, "Diary of Lieutenant James McMichael, of the Pennsylvania Line, 1776–1778," *Pennsylvania Magazine of History and Biography* 16 (July 1892): 136.
130. Robert Hanson Harrison to John Hancock, October 20, 1776, in *PGWRWS*, 6:592.
131. General Orders, November 5, 1776, in ibid., 7:85; Risch, *Supplying Washington's Army*, 149.
132. Loammi Baldwin to Mary Baldwin, October 23, 1776, Loammi Baldwin Papers, HUL.

133. McMichael, "Diary," 138.

134. Loammi Baldwin to Samuel Blodget, November 15, 1776, Loammi Baldwin Papers, HUL.

135. Greene to Washington, October 24, 1776, in *PGWRWS*, 7:23. For the British campaign in New Jersey, see Arthur Leftkowitz, *The Long Retreat: The Calamitous Defense of New Jersey* (New Brunswick, NJ: Rutgers University Press, 1999).

136. Charles Lee to the Governor of Rhode Island, November 14, 1776, in *The Lee Papers*, 4 vols., ed. Henry Edward Bunbury (New York: New York Historical Society, 1872), 2:278.

137. Fischer, *Washington's Crossing*, 106–7.

138. Washington to Greene, November 7, 1776, in *PGWRWS*, 7:108.

139. Washington to William Livingston, November 7, 1776, in ibid., 7:111.

140. McMichael, "Diary," 138–39.

141. Joseph White Diary, 11, in Joseph White Pension, W. 11805, Roll 2556, RWP.

142. Washington to Lee, November 24, 1776, in *PGWRWS*, 7:209–10.

143. Charles Lee to Joseph Reed, November 24, 1776, in Bunbury, *Lee Papers*, 2:305–6.

144. Louise Rau, ed., "Sergeant John Smith's Diary of 1776," *Mississippi Valley Historical Review* 20 (September 1933): 262–63.

145. Ibid.

146. Loammi Baldwin to Mary Baldwin, December 21, 1776, Loammi Baldwin Papers, HUL.

147. Fischer, *Washington's Crossing*, 185–89.

148. Orders to Brigadier Generals Stirling, Mercer, Stephen, and La Rochefermoy, December 12, 1776, in *PGWRWS*, 7:307.

149. Stirling to Washington, December 12, 1776, in ibid., 319.

150. Jared C. Lobdell, ed., "The Revolutionary War Journal of Sergeant Thomas McCarty," *Proceedings of the New Jersey Historical Society* 82 (January 1964): 39.

151. John C. Dann, *The Revolution Remembered: Eyewitness Accounts of the War of Independence* (Chicago: University of Chicago Press, 1980), 394.

152. Joseph White Diary, 11-1, Joseph White Pension, RWP.

153. Isaac Glynn, "A Soldier's Story, or A Journal of Soldier in the Revolutionary War," 3, American Antiquary Society, Worcester, MA, hereafter cited as Glynn Narrative.

154. McMichael, "Diary," 140.

155. Fischer, *Washington's Crossing*, 234–345.

Chapter 3

1. Wright, *The Continental Army*, 91–98.

2. Charles A. Stansfield Jr., *A Geography of New Jersey: The City in the Garden State*, 2nd ed. (New Brunswick, NJ: Rutgers University Press, 1988), 12–21; Richard W. Hunter and Ian C. G. Burrow, "The Historical Geography and Archaeology of the Revolutionary War in New Jersey," in *New Jersey in the American Revolution*, ed. Barbara J. Mitnick (New Brunswick, NJ: Rutgers University Press, 2005), 165–94.

3. Eugene J. Palka and Francis A. Galgano, *The Historical Geography of the Hudson Highlands*, 2nd ed. (West Point, NY: United States Military Academy, 2006), 1–15.

4. Thomas Mifflin to William Duer, October 26, 1776, in Force, *American Archives, 5th Series*, 2:1254.

5. Greene to Washington, November 5, 1776, in *PGWRWS*, 7:87.
6. Washington to Heath, November 12, 1776, and Heath to Washington, November 18, 1776, both in ibid., 7:147.
7. Charles Lee to Heath, November 20, 1776, and Heath to Lee, November 21, 1776, both in Bunbury, *The Lee Papers*, 2:290, 291.
8. Thomas Rodney, "Diary of Captain Thomas Rodney 1776–177," ed. Caesar A. Rodney, *Papers of the Historical Society of Delaware* 8 (1888): 38, 39.
9. McMichael, "Diary," 141.
10. Michael Cecere, ed., *They Behaved like Soldiers: Captain John Chilton and the Third Virginia Regiment, 1775–1778* (Bowie, MD: Heritage, 2004), 114.
11. John Cadwalader to Pennsylvania Council, January 5, 1777, Ferdinand Dreer Autograph Collection, Historical Society of Pennsylvania, Philadelphia, PA, hereafter cited as HSP.
12. Washington to Hancock, January 5, 1777, in *PGWRWS*, 7:523.
13. Washington to Hancock, January 7, 1777, in ibid., 8:9.
14. Thomas Rodney to Caesar Rodney, January 14, 1777, in *Letters to and from Caesar Rodney*, ed. George Herbert Ryden (Philadelphia: University of Pennsylvania Press, 1933), 154–55; Rodney, "Diary," 38.
15. James Read to Susanna Read, January 8, 1777, Andre de Coppet Collection, Box 28, Folder 6, Princeton University Firestone Library.
16. James Read to Susanna Read, January 14, 1777, ibid.
17. Ashbel Green, *The Life of Ashbel Green* (New York: R. Carter, 1849), 90.
18. Cecere, *They Behaved like Soldiers*, 114.
19. McMichael, "Diary," 142.
20. Fischer, *Washington's Crossing*, 352–55.
21. McMichael, "Diary," 11.
22. Ibid.
23. Ibid.
24. Lobdell, "The Revolutionary War Journal," 44–45.
25. Joseph White Diary, 29, Joseph White Pension, W. 11805, Roll 2556, RWP.
26. Zacchaeus Towne Diary, January 19–February 23, Rutgers University Alexander Library.
27. General Orders, January 22, 1777, Josiah Whiting Orderly Book, American Antiquarian Society, Worcester, MA, hereafter cited as AAS.
28. General Orders, February 9 and February 12, 1777, ibid.
29. General Orders, February 17 and February 28, 1777, ibid.
30. Washington to Heath, February 3, 1777, *PGWRWS*, 8:229–31.
31. Heath to Washington, February 6, 1777, ibid., 8:259–61.
32. Fischer, *Washington's Crossing*, 350–51.
33. S. Sydney Bradford, ed., "A British Officer's Revolutionary War Journal, 1776–1778," *Maryland Historical Magazine* 56 (1961): 167.
34. J. E. Tyler, ed., "The Operations in New Jersey: An English Officer Describes the Events of December 1776," *Proceedings of the New Jersey Historical Society* 70 (1952): 136.
35. Washington to Schuyler, February 23, 1777, *PGWRWS*, 9:433–34.
36. David Avery Diary, Entries for June, July, and August 1776, CHS; Becker, "Smallpox in Washington's Army," 402–14.

37. William Shippen to Washington, January 25, 1777, in *PGWRWS*, 8:156.
38. Charles H. Lesser, *Sinews of Independence: Monthly Strength Reports of the Continental Army* (Chicago: University of Chicago Press, 1976), xxix–xxx. Lesser records 34.9 percent sick for December 1776. Records are missing for the first three months of 1777, but returns for April showed only 21.7 percent sick.
39. Fenn, *Pox Americana*, 92–93.
40. Washington to Robert Hanson Harrison, January 20; Washington to John Cochran, January 20, 1777; William Shippen to Washington, January 25, 1777, all in *PGWRWS*, 8:112, 116, 156.
41. Washington to Gates, January 28, 1777; Washington to Shippen, January 28, 1778; Cochrane and Shippen to Washington, January 30, 1777, all in ibid., 8:172, 174, 208.
42. For the presence of smallpox among New England troops, see Schuyler to Washington, February 5, 1777, in ibid., 8:243.
43. Washington to Gates, February 5–6, 1777, in ibid., 8:248.
44. Washington to Hancock, February 5, 1777, in ibid., 8:249–53.
45. Becker, "Smallpox in Washington's Army," 424.
46. Continental Congress Medical Committee to Washington, February 13, 1777, in *PGWRWS*, 8:323; Hugh Thrusfield, "Smallpox in the American War of Independence," *Annals of Medical History* 3 (1940): 316–17.
47. Green, *The Life of Ashbel Green*, 91–93.
48. Cecere, *They Behaved like Soldiers*, 114.
49. Parsons to Washington, April 15, 1777, in *PGWRWS*, 9:172.
50. Washington to George Baylor, March 28, 1777, in ibid., 9:1.
51. Washington to Brigadier Generals Samuel Holden Parsons, Enoch Poor, and James Mitchell Varnum, March 29, 1777, and Washington to Jonathan Trumbull, March 29, 1777, both in ibid., 9:19, 21–22.
52. Varnum to Washington, April 4, 1777, in ibid., 9:41–42.
53. Washington to Nicholas Cooke, April 3, 1777, and Washington to Varnum, April 4, 1777, both in ibid., 9:52–53, 57.
54. Varnum to Washington, April 13, 1777, in ibid., 9:153–55.
55. Washington to Samuel Blachley Webb, April 7, 1777, in ibid., 9:84.
56. Executive Committee to John Hancock, February 22, 1777, in *Letters of Delegates to Congress, 1774–1789*, 26 vols., ed. Paul H. Smith (Washington, DC: Library of Congress, 1976–2000), 6:343. See also William Whipple to Josiah Bartlett, February 22, 1777, in ibid., 6:347–48.
57. Washington to Jonathan Trumbull, March 6, 1777, in *PGWRWS*, 8:531–32; General Orders, March 11, 1777, Whiting Orderly Book, AAS.
58. Return of American forces in New Jersey, March 15, 1777, in *PGWRWS*, 8:576.
59. Thomas Davis to John Page, April 26, 1777, Andre de Coppet Collection, Box 4 Folder 9, Princeton University Firestone Library.
60. Jonathan Trumbull to Washington, April 16, 1777, in *PGWRWS*, 9:183.
61. Washington to Parsons, June 17, 1777, in ibid., 10:62.
62. Ibid., 10:62–63.
63. Jeremiah Greenman, *Diary of a Common Soldier in the American Revolution, 1775–1783: An Annotated Edition to the Military Journal of Jeremiah Greenman*, ed. Robert Bray and Paul Bushman (DeKalb: Northern Illinois University Press, 1978), 72.

64. General Orders, April 1 and April 10, 1777, both in *PGWRWS*, 9:109, 224.
65. Division Orders, May 15, 1777, and Regimental Orders, May 19, 1777, both in William Heth, "Orderly Book of Major William Heth of the Third Virginia Regiment, May 15–July 1, 1777," *Virginia Historical Society Collections* 2 (1892): 332, 333.
66. General Orders, May 26, 1777, in *The Journal and Order Book of Captain Robert Kirkwood of the Delaware Regiment of the Continental Line*, ed. Joseph Brown Turner (Wilmington: The Historical Society of Delaware, 1910), 69; General Orders, April 1, 1777, in *PGWRWS*, 9:123–24.
67. Greenman, *Diary*, 73.
68. Washington to Hancock, May 21, 1777, in *PGWRWS*, 9:492–93.
69. General Orders, May 22, 1777, ibid., 9:495–96.
70. Circular to Brigade Commanders, May 20, 1777, in ibid., 9:483–84.
71. Washington to Heath, March 13, 1777, in ibid., 8:564–65.
72. Alexander McDougall to Washington, March 29, 1777, in ibid., 9:14–17.
73. Washington to Hugh Hughes, May 15, 1777, in ibid., 9:431.
74. Samuel Holden Parsons to Washington, June 12, 1777, and Washington to Parsons, June 17, 1777, both in ibid., 10:15–16, 62.
75. Greene to Washington, May 24, 1777, in ibid., 9:516–17.
76. Greene to Washington, May 25, 1777, in *Greene Papers*, 2:92–93.
77. Mifflin to Washington, May 27, 1777, in *PGWRWS*, 9:543.
78. Washington to Mifflin, May 31, 1777, in ibid., 9:574.
79. Michael Barbieri, "Winter Soldiering in the Champlain Valley," *Journal of the American Revolution*, October 19, 2015, retrieved December 16, 2016, https://allthingsliberty.com/2015/10/winter-soldiering-in-the-lake-champlain-valley/.
80. Gates to Washington, May 13, 1777, in *PGWRWS*, 9:410–11.
81. Gates to Washington, May 24, 1777, in ibid., 9:514.
82. Washington to Gates, May 15, 1777, in ibid., 9:429.
83. Board of War to Horatio Gates, June 4, 1777, in Smith, *Letters of the Delegates of Congress*, 7:168.
84. Elbridge Gerry to Thomas Gerry, June 15, 1777, in ibid., 7:201.
85. Greene to Washington, May 25, 1777, in *PGWRWS*, 9:524–25.
86. Ibid.
87. General Orders, May 30, 1777; in ibid., 9:559–60.
88. General Orders, June 9, 1777, in ibid., 9:652.
89. General Orders, June 3, 1777, in ibid., 9:597.
90. General Orders, June 1, 1777, and June 4, 1777, in ibid., 9:588–89, 602–3.
91. Regimental Orders, May 27, 1777, in Heth, "Orderly Book," 342.
92. General Orders, June 16, 1777, in *PGWRWS*, 10:47–48.
93. General Orders, June 17, 1777, in ibid., 10:58 59.
94. General Orders, May 26, 1777, and Greene to Washington, May 27, 1777, both in *Greene Papers*, 2:94, 93–98.
95. General Orders, May 29, 1777, in *PGWRWS*, 9:551–52.
96. General Orders, June 1, 1777, in ibid., 9:577.
97. Regimental Orders, June 27, 1777, in Heth, "Orderly Book," 370.
98. General Orders, June 1, 1777, in *PGWRWS*, 9:578–79.
99. General Orders, June 4, 1777, in ibid., 9:602–3.
100. General Orders, June 9, 1777 in ibid., 9:652.

101. General Orders, May 31, 1777, in ibid., 9:567–69.
102. Washington to Arnold, June 17, 1777, in *PGWRWS*, 10:58–59.
103. Journal of the Proceedings of the Army under the Command of Sir William Howe in the Year 1777, HUL.
104. Brigade Orders, June 18, 1777, in Turner, *Journal and Order Book*, 86; General Orders, June 26, 1777, in *PGWRWS*, 10:90.
105. For a strategic overview, see Washington to Hancock, June 20, 1777, and Washington to Hancock, June 22, 1777, both in *PGWRWS*, 10:84–86, 104–5.
106. Washington to John Augustine Washington, June 29, 1777, in ibid., 10:149.
107. General Orders, July 2, 1777, in ibid., 10:166–67.
108. For an overview of the June campaign, see Ward, *War of the Revolution*, 1:325–38.
109. Greene to John Adams, May 28, 1777, in *Greene Papers*, 2:98–99.
110. General Orders, June 7, 1777, in *PGWRWS*, 9:630–31.
111. Hancock to Washington, June 24, 1777, in ibid., 9:118–19.

Chapter 4

1. Bodle, *The Valley Forge Winter*, 31–54.
2. General Orders, November 30, 1777, in *PGWRWS*, 12:444–45. Responding to Washington's query were John Armstrong, Louis Duportail, Nathanael Greene, William Irvine, Johann de Kalb, Henry Knox, the Marquis de Lafayette, William Maxwell, Peter Muhlenberg, Enoch Poor, Casimir Pulaski, Charles Scott, William Smallwood, Lord Stirling, John Sullivan, James Varnum, Anthony Wayne, George Weedon, and William Woodford. Henry Emanuel Lutterloh, John Cadwalader, and Joseph Reed also offered their input.
3. Benjamin H. Newcomb, "Washington's Generals and the Decision to Camp at Valley Forge," *Pennsylvania Magazine of History and Biography* 117 (October 1993): 313.
4. Wayne K. Bodle, "Generals and 'Gentlemen': Pennsylvania Politics and the Decision for Valley Forge," *Pennsylvania History: A Journal of Mid-Atlantic Studies* 62 (Winter 1995): 60–64.
5. Washington to Joseph Reed, December 2, 1777, in *PGWRWS*, 12:500.
6. Newcomb, "Washington's Generals," 319–21.
7. Reed to Washington, December 1, 1777, in *PGWRWS*, 12:477–81.
8. Cadwalader to Washington, December 3, 1777, in ibid., 12:507–10.
9. Greene to Washington, December 1, 1777, in ibid., 12:459–63.
10. Lutterloh to Washington, December 1, 1777, in ibid., 12:473–74.
11. Knox to Washington, December 1, 1777, in ibid., 12:465–66.
12. Sullivan to Washington, December 1, 1777, in ibid., 12:485–87.
13. John Laurens to Henry Laurens, December 3, 1777, in *The Army Correspondence of Colonel John Laurens in the Years 1777–1778*, ed. W. M. Gilmore Simms (New York: Bradford Club, 1867), 91–92.
14. Stirling to Washington, December 1, 1777, in *PGWRWS*, 12:483–85.
15. John Laurens to Henry Laurens, December 3, 1777, in Simms, *The Army Correspondence of John Laurens*, 92.
16. John Laurens to Henry Laurens, December 15, 1777, in ibid., 94.
17. Armstrong to Washington, December 1, 1777, in *PGWRWS*, 12:536–38.
18. Lafayette to Washington, December 1, 1777, in ibid., 12:466–68.

19. Sullivan to Washington, December 1, 1777, in ibid., 12:485.
20. Smallwood to Washington, December 1, 1777, in ibid., 12:482–83.
21. General Orders, December 17, 1777, in ibid., 12:620–21.
22. General Orders, December 18, 1777, in ibid., 12:626–28.
23. Ibid.
24. Ibid.
25. Jonathan Libby Narrative, Abigail Libby Pension, W. 24557, Roll 1561, RWP.
26. Jonathan Todd to Timothy Todd, December 25–26, 1777, Jonathan Todd Pension Application, RWP.
27. For African American participation in the war, see Benjamin Quarles, *The Negro in the American Revolution* (Chapel Hill: University of North Carolina Press, 1961); Judith L. Van Buskirk, *Standing in Their Own Light: African American Patriots in the American Revolution* (Norman: University of Oklahoma Press, 2017); Charles Patrick Neimeyer, *America Goes to War: A Social History of the Continental Army* (New York: New York University Press, 1996), 65–85.
28. Nancy K. Loane, *Following the Drum: Women at the Valley Forge Encampment* (Washington, DC: Potomac, 2009), 113–126; Mayer, *Belonging to the Army*, 122–53.
29. Ebenezer Wild, *The Journal of Ebenezer Wild*, ed. James M. Bugabee (Cambridge, MA: John Wilson and Son, 1891), 31.
30. Samuel Armstrong, "From Saratoga to Valley Forge: The Diary of Lieutenant Samuel Armstrong," ed. Joseph Lee Boyle, *Pennsylvania Magazine of History and Biography* 121 (July 1997): 261.
31. Benjamin Farnum Diary, December 30, 1777, MHS.
32. Edward P. Hoyt, ed., "A Revolutionary Diary of Captain Paul Brigham, November 19, 1777–September 4, 1778," *Vermont History* 34 (January 1966): 8.
33. Greenman, *Diary of a Common Soldier*, 109.
34. Ebenezer Crosby to anonymous recipient, April 14, 1778, quoted in Jacqueline Thibaut, *In the True Rustic Order: Material Aspects of the Valley Forge Encampment, 1777–1778* (Washington, DC: National Parks Service, 1980), 58.
35. William Gifford to Benjamin Holme, January 24, 1778, in *Writings from the Valley Forge Encampment of the Continental Army*, 7 vols., ed. Joseph Lee Boyle (Bowie, MD: Heritage, 2000–12), 2:31.
36. Edward White to Benjamin White, January 2, 1778, in ibid., 6:6.
37. Richard Wheeler to Thomas Wheeler, January 25, 1778, Lloyd W. Smith Collection, Morristown National Historical Park, Morristown, NJ.
38. Bauermeister to von Jungkenn, January 20, 1778, and Bauermesiter to von Jungkenn, June 15, 1778, both in *Letters from Major Bauermeister to Colonel von Jungkenn Written During the Philadelphia Campaign, 1777–1778*, ed. Bernhard A. Uhlendorf and Edna Vosper (Philadelphia: Historical Society of Pennsylvania, 1935), 42, 62.
39. Friedrich von Muenchhausen, *At General Howe's Side, 1776–1778*, ed. Samuel Stelle Smith, trans. Ernst Kipping (Monmouth Beach, NJ: Philip Freneau, 1974), 46.
40. Henry Sewall Diary, January 6, 1778, MHS.
41. Ebenezer David to unknown, December 22, 1777, in Ebenezer David, *A Rhode Island Chaplain in the Revolutionary War*, ed. Jeannette D. Black and William Green Roekler (Providence: Rhode Island Historical Society, 1949), 74–75.
42. Quoted in Thibaut, *In the True Rustic Order*, 36.

43. Muenchhausen, *At General Howe's Side*, 47.

44. Thomas Paine, "Military Operations near Philadelphia in the Campaign of 1777–1778. Described in a Letter from Thomas Paine to Dr. Franklin," *Pennsylvania Magazine of History and Biography* 2 (1878): 294.

45. Elias Boudinot to Hannah S. Boudinot, December 22, 1777, Thomas Addison Emmet Collection, NYPL.

46. Quoted in Trussell, *Birthplace of an Army*, 21.

47. Samuel Shaw, *The Journals of Major Samuel Shaw*, ed. Josiah Quincy (Boston: Crosby and Nichols, 1847), 52.

48. Enoch Poor to Thomas Odiorn, December 17, 1777, Dreer Autograph Collection, HSP.

49. George Weedon to Patrick Henry, January 4, 1778, in Boyle, *Writings from the Valley Forge Encampment*, 7:19.

50. Henry Beekman Livingston to Robert R. Livingston, December 24, 1777, in ibid., 2:2.

51. Jedidiah Huntington to Jonathan Trumbull, December 14, 1777, in *Collections of the Massachusetts Historical Society*, 7th series, 10 vols., ed. Charles C. Smith et al. (Boston: Massachusetts Historical Society, 1901–15), 2:204–7.

52. Jedidiah to Joshua Huntington, December 20, 1777, in *Collections of the Connecticut Historical Society*, 31 vols., ed. Albert C. Bates et al. (Hartford, Connecticut Historical Society, 1860–1967), 20:386.

53. Jedidiah Huntington to Andrew Huntington, December 20, 1777, in ibid., 20:389.

54. Lochée, *An Essay on Castrametation*, 6.

55. Timothy Pickering to Rebecca Pickering, December 30, 1777, Pickering Papers, MHS.

56. John Laurens to Henry Laurens, January 1, 1778, in Simms, *Correspondence of John Laurens*, 100.

57. Jedidiah Huntington to Jonathan Trumbull, January 13, 1778, in Bates et al., *Collections of the Massachusetts Historical Society*, 2:213.

58. Jonathan Todd to Timothy Todd, January 19, 1778, Jonathan Todd Pension Application, RWP.

59. Thibaut, *True Rustic Order*, 61–62.

60. Armstrong, "From Saratoga to Valley Forge," 264.

61. Mark A. Brier, "Tolerably Comfortable: A Field Trial of a Recreated Soldier Cabin at Valley Forge," Valley Forge National Historical Park, Valley Forge, PA.

62. Michael Parrington, Helen Schenck, and Jacqueline Thibaut, "The Material World of the Revolutionary Soldier," in *Images of the Recent Past: Readings in Historical Archaeology*, ed. Charles E. Olsen Jr. (Lanham, MD: Rowman Altamaria, 1996), 118.

63. Washington to William Heath, December 17, 1777, and Washington to Continental Congress Camp Committee, January 29, 1778, both in *PGWRWS*, 12:623–24, 13:376–409.

64. General Orders, January 9, 1777, in ibid., 13:185–86.

65. Jonathan Todd to Timothy Todd, January 19, 1778, Jonathan Todd Pension Application, RWP.

66. Circular to the States, December 29, 1777, in *PGWRWS*, 13:36–39.

67. Washington to William Heath, December 17, 1777, and Washington to Continental Congress Camp Committee, January 29, 1778, both in ibid., 12:623–24, 13:376–409.

68. General Orders, January 6, 1778, in ibid., 13:158–60.

69. Jonathan Todd to Timothy Todd, January 19, 1778, Jonathan Todd Pension Application, RWP.

70. Jonathan Libby Narrative, Abigail Libby Pension, W. 24557, Roll 1561, RWP.

71. Benjamin Farnum Diary, January 23, 1778, MHS.

72. Francis Barber to Elias Dayton, January 22, 1778, Jared Sparks Collection, HUL.

73. Risch, *Supplying Washington's Army*, 38–45, 210–21.

74. Jaqueline Thibaut, *Logistics, Supply, and the Continental Army at Valley Forge* (Washington DC: National Parks Service, 1980), 112.

75. John Shy, "Logistical Crisis and the American Revolution: A Hypothesis," in *Feeding Mars: Logistics in Western Warfare from the Middle Ages to the Present*, ed. John A. Lynn (Boulder, CO: Westview, 1993), 161–79; Bodle, *Valley Forge Winter*, 103, 125.

76. Varnum to Greene, February 12, 1778, in *Greene Papers*, 2:280.

77. Thibaut, *Logistics, Supply*, 113–14.

78. Washington to Henry Laurens, December 23, 1777, in *PGWRWS*, 12:683.

79. Bodle, *Valley Forge Winter*, 112–15.

80. Thibaut, *Logistics, Supply*, 121–22, 135–36, 162–64, 176; Ricardo A. Herrera, "Foraging and Combat Operations at Valley Forge, February–March, 1778," *Army History* 79 (Spring 2011): 9.

81. Bodle, *The Valley Forge Winter*, 140–41, 136–37, 208–9; Thibaut, *Logistics, Supply*, 115–16.

82. Herrera, "Foraging and Combat Operations," 12–15.

83. Ibid., 15–24.

84. Bodle, *The Valley Forge Winter*, 208.

85. William Heath to Washington, January 6, 1777, and Thomas Nelson to Washington, January 20, 1778, both in *PGWRWS*, 13:162–64, 298–99.

86. Brigade Orders, February 18, 1778, in George Weedon, *Valley Forge Orderly Book of General George Weedon of the Continental Army* (New York: Dodd, Mead, 1902), 237; Brigade Orders, March 2, 1778, Malcolm's Regiment Orderly Book, New York Historical Society, New York, hereafter NYHS.

87. General Orders, March 18, 1778, in ibid., 14:215n1.

88. General Orders, April 17, 1778, in ibid., 14:535–36.

89. Washington to William Woodford, March 28, 1778, in ibid., 14:346–47.

90. Washington to Lachlan McIntosh, April 3, 1778; Washington to David Mason, April 4, 1778; Washington to Alexander McDougall, April 8, 1778; and Washington to Theodorick Bland, April 18, 1778, all in ibid., 14:393, 406–7n2, 426–27, 545–46; Fenn, *Pox Americana*, 198–202.

91. Jonathan Britton affidavit, Beulah Britton Pension, W 35, 281, 300033, M804, Roll 0345, RWP.

92. Regimental Orders, March 14, 1778, Isaac Sherman's Second Connecticut Regiment Orderly Book, CHS.

93. Trussell, *Birthplace of an Army*, 49–51.

94. Bodle, *Valley Forge Winter*, 200–202.

95. Ezra Seldon to Samuel Mather, May 15, 1778, in Henry Phelps Johnston, *Yale and Her Honor Roll in the American Revolution: Including Original Letters, Records of Service, Biographical Sketches* (New York: Putnam and Sons, 1888), 88.

96. Fenn, *Pox Americana*, 98–99; Washington to Gates, May 29, 1778, in *PGWRWS*, 15:254.

97. Stephen R. Taaffe, *Washington's Revolutionary Generals* (Norman: University of Oklahoma Press, 2019), 137–72.

98. Regimental Orders, March 14, 1778, in Isaac Sherman's Second Connecticut Regiment Orderly Book, CHS.

99. Regimental Orders, March 30, 1778, in ibid.

100. General Orders, April 14, 1778, in *PGWRWS*, 16:508.

101. Thibaut, *In the True Rustic Order*, 58.

102. Trussell, *Birthplace of an Army*, 40–41.

103. John Laurens to Henry Laurens, March 9, 1778, in Simms, *The Army Correspondence*, 135.

104. Anthony Wayne, "Letter to Richard Peters, May 13, 1778," *Pennsylvania Magazine of History and Biography* 31 (1907): 240–41.

105. Jonathan Libby Narrative, Abigail Libby Pension, W. 24557, Roll 1561, RWP.

106. Greenman, *Diary*, 119.

107. Hoyt, "A Revolutionary Diary," 23–24.

108. Joseph Clark, "Diary of Joseph Clark, Attached to the Continental Army from May 1778 to November 1779," *Proceedings of the New Jersey Historical Society* 7 (1853–54): 105.

109. Washington to Greene, June 8, 1778, and General Orders, June 9, 1778, both in *PGWRWS*, 15:351–52, 357–58.

110. Diarca Allen Pension, S. 12917, Roll 0035, M804, RWP.

111. William Johnston to "Baldy," June 15, 1778, William Johnston Papers, Library of Congress, Washington, DC.

112. Lesser, *Sinews of Independence*, xxxi.

113. Trussell, *The Birthplace of an Army*, 42.

114. Lesser, *Sinews of Independence*, xxxi.

115. For the Monmouth campaign, see Mark Edward Lender and Gary Wheeler Stone, *Fatal Sunday: George Washington, the Monmouth Campaign, and the Politics of Battle* (Norman: University of Oklahoma Press, 2017).

Chapter 5

1. R. Sill to Stephen R. Bradley, July 27, 1778, in Stephen R. Bradley, *Stephen R. Bradley: Letters of a Revolutionary War Patriot and Vermont Senator*, ed. Dorr Bradley Carpenter (Jefferson, NC: McFarland, 2009), 51; General Orders, July 22, 1778, in *PGWRWS*, 16:121–23; Higginbotham, *The War of American Independence*, 390.

2. Middlekauff, *The Glorious Cause*, 382–83.

3. For the changing character of the northern war after 1778, see Mark Kwasny, *Washington's Partisan War* (Kent, OH: Kent State Press, 1996), 225; Todd Braisted, *Grand Forage 1778: The Battleground around New York City* (Yardley PA: Westholme, 2016).

4. Charles E. Miller Jr., Donald V. Lockey, and Joseph Visconti Jr., *Highlands Fortress: The Fortification of West Point during the American Revolution* (West Point, NY: United States Military Academy, 1988), 87–116.

5. General Orders, September 15, 1778, and Washington to Henry Laurens, September 23, 1778, both in *PGWRWS*,17:1–4, 92–94.

6. George Washington, "Circular to Seven General Officers," October 14, 1778, in ibid., 17:373.

7. Council of War, October 16, 1778, in ibid., 17:399.

8. Gates to Washington, October 19, 1778, in ibid., 17:460.

9. Maxwell to Washington, October 21, 1778, in ibid., 17:506–11.

10. Lord Stirling to Washington, October 26, 1778, in ibid., 17:592–93.

11. Greene to Washington, October 1, 1778, in *Greene Papers*, 3:5.

12. De Kalb to Washington, October 18, 1778, in *PGWRWS*, 17:452.

13. Von Steuben to Washington, October18, 1779, in ibid., 17:450.

14. Knox to Washington, October 19, 1778, in ibid., 17:465–67.

15. Muhlenberg to Washington, October 16, 1778; Parsons to Washington, October 17, 1778; Smallwood to Washington, October 17, 1778; Hand to Washington, October 18, 1778; Wayne to Washington, October 18, 1778, all in ibid., 17:408–9, 424–25,428–29, 439–40, 452–53.

16. Muhlenberg to Washington, October 16, 1778; Parsons to Washington, October 17, 1778; Smallwood to Washington, October 17, 1778; Hand to Washington, October 18, 1778; von Steuben to Washington, October 18, 1779; de Kalb to Washington, October 19, 1779, all in ibid., 17:408–9, 424–25, 428–29, 439–40, 450, 463–65.

17. McDougall to George Clinton, November 5, 1778, in *The Public Papers of George Clinton, First Governor of New York*, ed. Hugh Hastings, 10 vols. (New York: Wynkoop, Hallenbeck, and Crawford, 1899–1914), 4:248, hereafter cited as *Clinton Papers*.

18. Nixon to Washington, October 19, 1778, in *PGWRWS*, 17:468–69.

19. Knox to Washington, October 19, 1778, in ibid., 17:465–67.

20. Stirling to Washington, October 26, 1778, in ibid., 17:592–93; Paul David Nelson, *The Life of William Alexander, Lord Stirling* (Tuscaloosa: University of Alabama Press, 1987), 137.

21. Greene to Washington, October 18, 1778, in *Greene Papers*, 3:13.

22. Greene to McDougall, November 8, 1778, in ibid., 3:48.

23. Washington to Greene, October 29, 1778, in ibid., 3:32.

24. McDougall to George Clinton, November 5, 1778, in Hastings, *Clinton Papers*, 4:248.

25. Greene to Washington, October 18, 1778, in *Greene Papers*, 3:13.

26. Burnside to Maj. Peter Gordon, November 8, 1779; Burnside to Moore Furman, November 13, 1778; Burnside to Charles Stewart, November 15, 1778, all in James Burnside Letterbook, HSP.

27. Washington to Putnam, November 25, 1778, in *The Writings of George Washington from the Original Manuscript Sources, 1745–1799*, 39 vols., ed. John C. Fitzpatrick (Washington, DC: US Government Printing Office, 1931–54), 13:324.

28. Washington to Congress, November 27, 1778, in ibid., 13:352.

29. Greene to Washington. October 24, 1778, in *Greene Papers*, 3:13.

30. Greene to Washington, October 18, 1778, in *PGWRWS*, 17:436.

31. McDougall to Washington, December 9, 1778, in *PGWRWS*, 18:387–89.

32. Washington to Thomas Clark, November 18, 1778, in ibid., 18:188.

33. Washington to Congress, November 27, 1778, in Fitzpatrick, *The Writings of George Washington*, 13:350–52; Washington to Greene, December 4, 1778, in *Greene Papers*, 3:32; Lesser, *Sinews of Independence*, 100–101.

34. Washington to Congress, November 27, 1778, in Fitzpatrick, *The Writings of George Washington*, 13:350–52.
35. Washington to the Board of War, December 20, 1778, in ibid., 13:437–38.
36. Livingston to Washington, November 7, 1778; Washington to Livingston, November 24, 1778; Livingston to Washington, December 15, 1778; Washington to Livingston, December 16, 1778; Livingston to Washington, December 21, 1778, all in *The Papers of William Livingston*, 5 vols., ed. Carl E. Prince et al., (Trenton: New Jersey Historical Commission, 1980), 474–75, 490, 512, 513–14, 518.
37. J. F. Clark to Richard Varick, November 12, 1779, Richard Varick Papers, NYHS; Jedediah Huntington to Alexander McDougall, November 15, 1778, Jared Sparks Collection, HUL.
38. John Laurens to Henry Laurens, October 23, 1778, in *The Papers of Henry Laurens*, 16 vols., ed. David R. Chestnut et al. (Columbia: University of South Carolina Press, 1968–2004), 14:445.
39. Walter Finney to William McPherson, November 21, 1778, McPherson Collection, Library of Congress, Washington, DC.
40. Henry Dearborn, *Revolutionary War Journals of Henry Dearborn, 1775–1783*, ed. Lloyd Brown and Howard Peckham (New York: Da Capo, 1939), 140.
41. Route and Order of March for the Troops from Fredericksburg to Middlebrook, November 28, 1778, Anthony Wayne Papers, HSP.
42. Greene to Washington, November 30, 1778, in *Greene Papers*, 3:91.
43. Robert H. Harrison to Greene, December 5, 1778, in ibid., 3:105.
44. *New Jersey Gazette*, October 20, 1779.
45. Washington to Putnam, November 25, 1778, in Fitzpatrick, *The Writings of George Washington*, 13:324.
46. General Orders, December 14, 1778, in ibid., 13:395.
47. "Hutting Tools Furnished for a Regiment," December 1779, Timothy Pickering Papers, MHS.
48. For the establishment of magazines in New Jersey, see Thibaut, *Logistics, Supply*, 207.
49. Jacob Weiss to Udny Hay, November 30, 1778; Jacob Weiss to James Abeel, December 2, 1778; Jacob Weiss to James Abeel, December 16, 1778, all in Jacob Weiss, *Jacob Weiss Letterbook*, ed. Melville J. Boyer (Allentown, PA: Lehigh County Historical Society, 1956), 48, 49, 52–53.
50. Jacob Weiss to James Abeel, December 23, 1778, in ibid., 55–56.
51. Cornelius Ten Broeck to James Abeel, December 29, 1778, in ibid., 56.
52. Shaw, *The Journals of Major Samuel Shaw*, 52.
53. Elijah Fisher, *Elijah Fisher's Journal while in the War for Independence and Continued Two Years after He Came to Maine, 1775–1784* (Augusta, ME: Badger and Manley, 1880), 11; Wayne to Joseph Reed, December 28, 1778, Anthony Wayne Papers, HSP.
54. Josiah Harmar Diary, January 1, 1779, Lyman Draper Manuscript Collection, Wisconsin Historical Society, Madison, WI; Walter Finney, "The Walter Finney Diary," ed. Joseph Lee Boyle, *New Jersey History* 121 (2003): 45.
55. Stirling to Washington, December 28, 1778, in *PGWRWS*, 18:523.
56. John Eccleston to Charles Eccleston, February 1, 1779, John Eccleston Letters, Rutgers University Alexander Library.
57. Washington to McDougall, November 24, 1778, in *PGWRWS*, 18:281–82.

58. McDougall to Washington, December 5, 1778, in ibid., 18:370–71.
59. McDougall to George Clinton, December 2, 1778, and Clinton to McDougall, December 15, 1778, both in Hastings, *Clinton Papers*, 4:346–47, 383–85; McDougall to Israel Putnam, December 3, 1778, Alexander McDougall Papers, NYHS.
60. General Orders, December 25, 1778, Alexander McDougall Headquarters Orderly Book, NYHS.
61. General Orders, December 28, 1778, ibid.
62. McDougall to Clinton, December 31, 1778, in Hastings, *Clinton Papers*, 438–40.
63. Zebulon Vaughan, "The Journal of Private Zebulon Vaughan, Revolutionary Soldier, 1777–1780," ed. Virginia Steel Wood, *Daughters of the American Revolution Magazine* (February 1979): 113.
64. Palka and Galango, *The Historical Military Geography of the Hudson Highlands*, 4–12; Miller et al., *Highlands Fortress*, 92, 133.
65. McDougall to Paterson, December 7, 1778, and McDougall to Jean-Baptiste Gouvion, December 17, 1778, both in Alexander McDougall Papers, NYHS.
66. Estimate of Barrack Room at West Point, January 1778, ibid.
67. Henry Sewall Diary, December 11 and December 12, 1778, MHS.
68. Paterson to McDougall, December 8, 1778, Alexander McDougall Papers, NYHS.
69. David A. Poirier, "Camp Reading: Logistics of a Revolutionary War Winter Encampment," *Northeast Historical Archaeology* 5 (1976): 50–52.
70. Huntington to Washington, November 20, 1779, in *PGWRWS*, 18:226–27.
71. Dearborn, *Revolutionary War Journals*, 140, 142, 150; Thomas Blake Journal, in Frederic Kidder, *History of the First New Hampshire Regiment in the War of the Revolution* (Albany, NY: J. Munsell, 1868), 46.
72. James Kirby Martin, ed., *Ordinary Courage: The Revolutionary War Adventures of Joseph Plumb Martin* (St. James, NY: Brandywine, 1993), 88–89; Richards, *Diary*, 61.
73. Division Orders, January 4, 1779, David Smith's Orderly Book, CHS.
74. Martin, *Ordinary Courage*, 91–92.
75. Lewis Woodruff to Richard Varick, January 10, 1779, Richard Varick Papers, NYHS.
76. Regimental Orders, First Pennsylvania Regiment, December 16, 1778, in *Pennsylvania Archives, Second Series*, 19 vols., ed. John B. Linn and William Henry Egle (Harrisburg: Pennsylvania State Archives, 1874–1890), 11:393; General Orders for January 4 and January 10, Jacob Brower's Sixth Pennsylvania Regiment Orderly Book, Society of the Cincinnati, Washington, DC; Charles S. Hall, ed., *Life and Letters of Samuel Holden Parsons: Major-General in the Continental Army and Chief Judge of the Northwestern Territory, 1737–1789* (Binghamton, NY: Otsenigo, 1905), 204.
77. Thacher, *A Military Journal*, 155–56.
78. Josiah Harmar to Francis Johnston, December 23, 1778, in Josiah Harmar Letterbook, William L. Clements Library, Ann Arbor, MI.
79. Alexander McDougall, Orders to Jackson's Regiment, December 13, 1778, in Hastings, *Clinton Papers*, 4:378–80.
80. General Orders, December 29, 1778, Alexander McDougall Headquarters Orderly Book, NYHS.

81. Brigade Orders, December 4, 1778, David Smith Orderly Book, CHS.

82. Hall, *Life and Letters*, 204.

83. John Hawkins Diary, January 1779, HSP.

84. Daniel Curson, "Archaeology of an Enlisted Man's Hut at Putnam Memorial State Park," *Bulletin of the Archaeological Society of Connecticut* 63 (2001): 56–58; Poirier, "Camp Reading," 44.

85. General Orders, December 24, 1778, in Fitzpatrick, *The Writings of George Washington*, 13:453.

86. General Orders, January 4, 1779, Jacob Brower's Sixth Pennsylvania Regiment Orderly Book, Society of the Cincinnati.

87. Alexander McDougall, Orders to Jackson's Regiment, December 13, 1778, in Hastings, *Clinton Papers*, 4:378–80.

88. General Orders, December 4, 1778, Alexander McDougall Headquarters Orderly Book, NYHS.

89. Stirling to Washington, December 28, 1778, in *PGWRWS*, 18:523.

90. John L. Seidel, "Archaeological Research at the 1778–1779 Winter Cantonment of the Continental Artillery, Pluckemin, New Jersey," *Northeast Historical Archaeology* 12 (1983): 7–9.

91. Oliver Rice to Jonathan Rice, January 26, 1779, Sol Feinstone Collection, David Library of the American Revolution, Washington Crossing, PA, hereafter DLAR.

92. Division Orders, March 22, 1779, Eighth Massachusetts Regiment Orderly Books, Huntington Library, San Marino, CA, hereafter HL.

93. McDougall to Washington, January 25, 1779, *PGWRWS*, 19:70–72.

94. Risch, *Supplying Washington's Army*, 223–26.

95. Stirling to Washington, January 3, 1779, in *PGWRWS*, 18:561.

96. James Parker Diary, February 14, 1779, Rutgers University Alexander Library.

97. Smallwood to Mordecai Gist, January 17, 1779, Mordecai Gist Papers, Maryland Historical Society, Baltimore, MD.

98. Hall, *Life and Letters*, 205; Martin, *Ordinary Courage*, 88–89.

99. Peter Colt to Horatio Gates, February 12, 1779, in Johnston, *Yale and Her Honor Roll*, 96.

100. Division Orders, December 25, 1778, David Smith's Orderly Book, CHS; Lewis Woodruff to Richard Varick, January 8, 1779, Richard Varick Papers, NYHS.

101. Division Orders, February 16 and April 11, and After Orders, April 13, 1779, Eighth Massachusetts Regiment Orderly Books, HL.

102. Henry Clinton, *The American Rebellion: Sir Henry Clinton's Narrative of His Campaigns, 1775–1782, with an Appendix of Original Documents*, ed. William B. Wilcox (New Haven, CT: Yale University Press, 1954), 122.

103. Johann Ewald, *Diary of the American War: A Hessian Journal*, ed. and trans. Joseph P. Trustin (New Haven, CT: Yale University Press, 1979), 156.

104. Maxwell to Washington, February 25, 1779, *PGWRWS*, 18:262–63.

105. John Combs to Israel Shreve, undated but likely early 1779, Israel Shreve Papers, University of Houston Library, Houston, TX.

106. Shreve to Washington, March 22, 1779, in *PGWRWS*, 19:571.

107. Maxwell to Washington, March 31, 1779, in ibid., 19:670.

108. Kwasny, *Washington's Partisan War*, 233–35.

109. Parsons to McDougall, December 7, 1778, Alexander McDougall Papers, NYHS; Parsons to McDougall, December 27, 1778, in Hall, *Life and Letters*, 206.

110. McDougall to Washington, February 4, 1779, *PGWRWS*, 19:125–26.

111. McDougall to Burr, January 15, 1779, in *Some Papers of Aaron Burr*, ed. Worthington Chauncy Ford (Worcester, MA: American Antiquarian Society, 1920), 44–45.

112. Kwasny, *Washington's Partisan War*, 233–35.

113. Henry Rutgers to Richard Varick, April 10, 1779, Richard Varick Papers, NYHS.

114. Division Orders, February 12, 1779, Second Pennsylvania Regiment Orderly Book, American Philosophical Society, Philadelphia, PA.

115. Division Orders, February 21, 1779, and Regimental Orders, February 25, 1779, Eighth Massachusetts Regiment Orderly Books, HL.

116. General Orders, First Pennsylvania Regiment, April 5, 1779, in *Pennsylvania Archives*, 11:431.

117. Brigade Orders, First Pennsylvania Regiment, April 8, 1779, in ibid., 11:433.

118. Brigade Orders, April 29, 1779, Second Pennsylvania Regiment Orderly Book, American Philosophical Society.

119. General Orders, April 11, 1779, in Fitzpatrick, *The Writings of George Washington*, 14:367–68.

120. Washington to James Clinton, January 19, 1779, and Washington to Malachi Treat, January 19, 1779, both in *PGWRWS*, 19:26–27, 35; Meier, *Nature's Civil War*, 99–125.

121. Brigade Orders, April 1, 1779, William Smallwood's Orderly Book, HSP.

122. General Orders, April 17, 1779, in *PGWRWS*, 20:96.

123. See, for example, Putnam to Washington, May 7, 1779, and Washington to McDougall, June 11, 1779, both in *PGWRWS*, 20:368; 21:34; James Parker Diary, March 24 and March 25, 1779, Rutgers University Alexander Library.

124. Biddle to Washington, May 27, 1779, and Washington to Biddle, May 29, 1779, both in *PGWRWS*, 20:646, 668.

125. Greene to Biddle, July 28, 1779, in *Greene Papers*, 4:273.

126. Washington to Lafayette, March 8, 1779, in Fitzpatrick, *The Writings of George Washington*, 14:220.

127. Samuel Adams to Sally Adams, May 6, 1779, Sol Feinstone Collection, DLAR.

128. Jedediah Huntington to Jabez Huntington, March 15, 1779, in Bates et al., *Collections of the Connecticut Historical Society*, 20:427.

129. Elijah Porter Journal, Spring 1779, CHS.

130. David Avery Diary, March 27, 1779, CHS.

131. Enos Hitchcock, *Diary Enos Hitchcock, D.D., Chaplain of the Revolutionary Army*, ed. William B. Weeden (Providence: Rhode Island Historical Society, 1899), 164.

132. Henry Sewall to Richard Varick, May 30, 1779, Ferdinand Dreer Autograph Collection, HSP.

133. Lesser, *Sinews of Independence*, xxxi.

134. Thacher, *Journal*, 156.

135. Wayne to Washington, January 20, 1779, in *PGWRWS*, 19:47.

136. Washington to Wayne, February 16, 1779, in ibid., 23:220.

137. Wayne to Washington, January 20, 1779, in ibid., 23:47.
138. Greene to Washington, January 5, 1779, in ibid., 18:570.

Chapter 6

1. Ward, *War of the Revolution*, 2:616–28, 638–45.
2. Washington to Duportail, September 22, 1779, and Duportail to Washington, September 24, 1779, both in *PGWRWS*, 22:474, 486–88.
3. Nathanael Greene to Moore Furman, September 17, 1779, and Greene to Nehemiah Hubbard, September 17, 1779, both in *Greene Papers*, 4:393.
4. Order of Cantonment, November, 1779, *PGWRWS*, 23:499–501; Nathanael Greene to Moore Furman, September 17, 1779, in *Greene Papers*, 4:393.
5. Greene to Moore Furman, September 17, 1779, and Greene to Clement Biddle, October 18, 1779, both in *Greene Papers* 4:393, 473–74.
6. William Woodford to Lord Stirling, October 28, 1779, Ferdinand Dreer Autograph Collection, HSP.
7. Biddle to Greene, October 30, 1779, in *Greene Papers*, 4:522–24; Henry Remsen to George Clinton, October 29, 1779, Thomas Addis Emmet Collection, NYPL; John Graves Simcoe, *A Journal of the Operations of the Queen's Rangers from the End of the Year 1777 to the Conclusion of the Late American War* (Exeter, UK: privately printed, 1789), 71–78.
8. Furman to Greene, October 29, 1779; Biddle to Greene, October 30, 1779; James Caldwell to Greene, October 27, 1779, all in *Greene Papers*, 4:519, 522–23, 504–5.
9. Arthur St. Clair to Washington, November 2, 1779, in *The St. Clair Papers: The Life and Public Services of Arthur St. Clair*, 2 vols., ed. William Henry Smith (Cincinnati: Robert Clark and Company, 1881), 1:489–92.
10. Greene to Furman, November 3, 1779, in *Greene Papers*, 5:9.
11. Greene to James Abeel, November 4, 1779, in ibid., 5:12–13.
12. Paul G. E. Clemens and Peter O. Wacker, *Land Use in Early New Jersey: A Historical Geography* (New Brunswick, NJ: Rutgers University Press, 1995), 55.
13. Greene to Washington, November 20, 1779, in *Greene Papers*, 5:102–4.
14. Clemens and Wacker, *Land Use*, 71.
15. Biddle to Greene, November 6, 1779, and Lord Stirling to Greene, November 9, 1779, both in *Greene Papers*, 5:22, 44.
16. Abeel to Greene, November 17, 1779, in ibid., 5:91.
17. Greene to Washington, November 20, 1779, in ibid., 5:102–4.
18. Greene to Washington, November 14, 1779, in *PGWRWS*, 23:264.
19. Washington to McDougall, November 14, 1779, in ibid., 23:260.
20. Greene to Washington, November 17, 1779, in ibid., 23:312.
21. Washington to Hamilton and Duportail, November 11, 1779, and Washington to Samuel Huntington, November 14, 1779, both in ibid., 23:239–42, 275–77.
22. Greene to Washington, November 23, 1779, in ibid., 23:406–7.
23. Greene to Washington, November 27, 1779, in ibid., 23:444–45.
24. Greene to John Cox, November 27, 1779, in *Greene Papers*, 5:122–23.
25. Greene to Washington, November 27, 1779, in *PGWRWS*, 23:444–45.
26. Washington to Greene, November 30, 1779, and Greene to Washington, November 27, 1779, both in ibid., 23:490.

27. Washington to Greene, November 17, 1779, in ibid., 23:309–11.

28. Livingston to Washington, December 7, 1779, and Washington to Livingston, December 12, 1779, both in ibid., 23:548–49, 585–86.

29. Moses White to William White, November 7, 1779, United States Revolution Collection, Box 3, Folder 30, American Antiquarian Society.

30. Oliver Rice to Jonathan Rice, November 23, 1779, Sol Feinstone Collection, DLAR.

31. Samuel Tenney to Joseph Gilman, November 29, 1779, in *Fragments of Revolutionary History*, ed. Gaillard Hunt (Brooklyn, NY: Historical Printing Club, 1892), 144–45.

32. Mayo Carrington to unknown, November 28, 1779, Ferdinand Dreer Autograph Collection, HSP.

33. Joseph Ward to Richard Varick, December 4, 1779, Richard Varick Papers, NYHS.

34. Greene to Moore Furman, November 30, 1779, in *Greene Papers*, 5:130.

35. Richards, *Diary of Samuel Richards*, 62.

36. Elijah Porter Journal, December 1779, CHS.

37. Nathan Beers Diary, December 5 and 14, Yale University Sterling Memorial Library, New Haven, CT; Ebenezer Huntington to Andrew Huntington, December 3, 1779, in Ebenezer Huntington, *Letters Written by Ebenezer Huntington during the American Revolution*, ed. G. W. F. Blanchard (New York: Chas, Fred, Hartman, 1914), 82.

38. Alexander Scammell to Stephen Peabody, December 8, 1779, Ferdinand Dreer Manuscript Collection, HSP.

39. As quoted in Friedrich Kapp, *The Life of John Kalb, Major-General in the Revolutionary Army* (New York: Henry Holt, 1870), 187. Italics are my own.

40. Friedrich Wilhelm von Steuben, *Regulations for the Order and Discipline of the Troops of the United States* (Philadelphia: Styner and Cist, 1779), 76–77.

41. Washington to Greene, November 17, 1779, in Fitzpatrick, *The Writings of George Washington*, 17:119.

42. Washington to Greene, November 17, 1779, in *PGWRWS*, 23:309–10.

43. Greene to Washington, November 17, 1779, and General Orders, November 19, 1779, both in ibid., 23:312, 338.

44. Rutsch and Peters, "Forty Years of Archaeological Research," 24.

45. Josiah Harmar Diary, March 20, 1780, Lyman Draper Manuscript Collection, Wisconsin Historical Society.

46. Almon W. Lauber, ed., *Orderly Books of the Fourth New York Regiment, 1778–1780, the Second New York Regiment, 1780–1783, by Samuel Tallmadge and Others, with Diaries of Samuel Tallmadge, 1780–1782 and John Barr, 1779–1782* (Albany: University of the State of New York, 1932), 124.

47. Joseph Walker to Samuel Blachley Webb, February 6, 1780, in Johnston, *Yale and Her Honor Roll*, 113.

48. Quoted in Kapp, *The Life of John Kalb*, 189.

49. Erkuries Beatty to Reading Beatty, December 22, 1779, in "Letters of the Four Beatty Brothers of the Continental Army, 1774–1794," ed. Joseph M. Beatty Jr., *Pennsylvania Magazine of History and Biography* 46 (1920): 205–6.

50. John Faust Pension, S. 41527, M804, RWP.

51. Martin, *Ordinary Courage*, 101.

52. William Irvine to Joseph Reed, Joseph Reed Papers, NYHS.

53. Lauber, *Orderly Books*, 816.

54. Fisher, *Elijah Fisher's Journal*, 11.
55. John Eccleston to Joseph Richardson, December 24, 1779, John Eccleston Letters, Rutgers University Alexander Library.
56. Ebenezer Huntington to Samuel Blachley Webb, December 24 and December 29, 1779, in Samuel Blachley Webb, *Reminiscences of General Samuel B. Webb of the Revolutionary Army*, ed. J. Watson Webb et al. (New York: Globe Stationery and Printing, 1882), 200–201.
57. Wright, *The Continental Army*, 142.
58. Finney, "The Walter Finney Diary," 59.
59. Greenman, *Diary of a Common Soldier*, 169.
60. Ebenezer Huntington to Samuel Blachley Webb, January 22, 1780, in Webb, *Reminiscences*, 203; Ebenezer Huntington to Andrew Huntington, February 8, 1780, in Huntington, *Letters Written*, 83.
61. Anonymous Sketch, undated, Park Collection, Morristown National Historical Park, Morristown, NJ.
62. Rutsch and Peters, "Forty Years of Archaeological Research," 24.
63. General Orders, December 12, 1779, in *PGWRWS*, 23:576.
64. Brigade Orders, April 17 and 21, 1780, Spencer's Regiment Orderly Book, Regimental Orderly Book Collection, Morristown National Historical Park.
65. Daniel Livermore, "A Journal," ed. Joseph B. Walker, in *Collections of the New Hampshire Historical Society* 6 (1850): 335; Thomas Blake Journal, in Kidder, *History of the First New Hampshire Regiment*, 54.
66. McDougall to Washington, November 6, 1779, in *PGWRWS*, 23:177–80.
67. Washington to McDougall, November 13, in ibid., 23:259–61.
68. McDougall to Washington, November 16 and 21, 1779, in ibid., 23:301–2, 386.
69. McDougall to Washington, November 25, 1779, in ibid., 23:419–20.
70. Washington to Heath, November 27, 1779, in ibid., 23:448–56; Thomas W. S. Quarterly, "Revolutionary Camps of the Hudson Highlands," *Journal of the New York State Historical Association* 2 (July 1921): 151–52.
71. General Orders, November 21, 1779, in *PGWRWS*, 23:382.
72. Heath to Paterson, December 5, 1779, in *Collections of the Massachusetts Historical Society, Seventh Series*, 10 vols., ed. Charles C. Smith et al. (Boston: Massachusetts Historical Society, 1901–15), 4:330–31, hereafter cited as *Heath Papers I*.
73. William Betts to John Fisher, December 4, 1779, John Fisher Collection, NYHS; Udny Hay to John Fisher, December 5, 1779, Udny Hay Collection, Folder 1, NYHS.
74. Heath to Washington, December 14, 1779, in *PGWRWS*, 23:607–9; Quarterly, "Revolutionary Camps," 151.
75. Benjamin Gilbert, *A Citizen-Soldier in the American Revolution: The Diary of Benjamin Gilbert in Massachusetts and New York*, ed. Rebecca D. Symmes (Cooperstown: New York Historical Association, 1980), 61.
76. General Orders, December 1, 1779, Andrew Peters Orderly Book, AAS.
77. Christopher Meng to John Fisher, November 19, 1779, Frederick Dearborn Collection, HUL.
78. Samuel Adams Diary, December 14, 1779, NYPL.
79. Glynn Narrative, 14.
80. Garrison Orders, December 22, 1779, and January 7, 1780, Andrew Peters Orderly Book, AAS.

81. William Heath to George Clinton, January 25, 1780, in *Clinton Papers*, 5:465.

82. Henry Sewall Diary, December 13, 1779, Massachusetts Historical Society, Boston, MA. Original emphasis.

83. Samuel Adams Diary, January 3 and 5, 1780, NYPL.

84. Samuel Adams to Sally Adams, January 13, 1780, Frederick Dearborn Collection, HUL.

85. Glynn Narrative, 14.

86. John Paterson to Heath, January 8, 1780, in *Collections of the Massachusetts Historical Society, Seventh Series*, 10 vols. (Boston: Massachusetts Historical Society, 1901–15), 5:4, hereafter cited as *Heath Papers II*.

87. Daniel Lyman Diary, January 10, 1780, Rhode Island Historical Society, Providence, Rhode Island.

88. Heath to Washington, January 10–11, 1780, in *PGWRWS*, 24:73–76.

89. Heath to Washington, February 4, 1780, in ibid., 24:368–70.

90. Heath to Washington, February 2–3, 1780, in ibid., 24:353–58.

91. E. Wayne Carp, *To Starve the Army at Pleasure: Continental Army Administration and American Political Culture, 1775–1783* (Chapel Hill: University of North Carolina Press, 1990), 104–13.

92. Furman to Greene, November 22, 1779, in *Greene Papers*, 5:107; Washington to Congress, December 10, 1779, in Fitzpatrick, *The Writings of George Washington*, 17:241.

93. Washington to Samuel Huntington, December 15, 1779, in *PGWRWS*, 23:622–23.

94. Bradford, "Hunger Menaces the American Revolution," 4

95. Carp, *Starve the Army at Pleasure*, 177.

96. Francis Swaine to Joseph Reed, January 6, 1780, in Linn and Egle, *Pennsylvania Archives*, 8:76; James Parker Diary, January 1780, Rutgers University Alexander Library.

97. Gilbert, *Citizen Soldier*, 62.

98. Thacher, *A Military Journal*, 181.

99. Washington to Samuel Huntington, January 4, 1780, in *PGWRWS*, 24:25–27.

100. Washington to Samuel Huntington, January 5, 1780, in ibid., 24:41–43.

101. Nathan Beers Diary, January 2, 1780, Yale University Sterling Memorial Library.

102. James Fairlie to Charles [?], January 12, 1780, John Lamb Papers, NYHS.

103. Martin, *Ordinary Courage*, 104.

104. Moses White to William White, January 2, 1780, United States Revolution Collection, Box 4, Folder 2, AAS.

105. Royal Flint to Washington, January 3, 1780, and Flint to Henry Champion, December 27, 1779, both in Johnston, *Yale and Her Honor Roll*, 115–16.

106. Washington to the New Jersey Magistrates, January 7, 1780, in *PGWRWS*, 24:49–51.

107. Washington to Heath, January 14, 1780, in Fitzpatrick, *The Writings of George Washington*, 17:395–98.

108. Joseph Lewis to Moore Furman, January 15, 1780, Joseph Lewis Letterbook, Lloyd W. Smith Collection, Morristown National Historical Park.

109. Representations from the Officers at West Point, undated but likely January 1780, *Heath Papers II*, 3.

110. Benjamin Williams Pension, Roll 2585, S31479, M8104, RWP; Greene to Benomi Hathaway, January 6, 1780, in *Green Papers*, 5:243.

111. Gilbert, *Citizen-Soldier*, 62.

112. William Shephard to William Heath, undated but likely January 1780, in *Heath Papers II*, 5; General Orders, January 7, 1780, Andrew Peters Orderly Books, AAS.

113. Joseph Walker to Samuel Blachley Webb, February 6, 1780, in Johnston, *Yale and Her Honor Roll*, 113.

114. John Patten to Caesar Rodney, January 18, 1780, in Ryden, *Letters to and from Caesar Rodney*, 332–33.

115. Washington to Heath, February 1, 1780, in *PGWRWS*, 24:343–44.

116. Nathanael Greene to Christopher Greene, February 10, 1780, in *Greene Papers*, 5:362–64.

117. Jacob Weiss to John Mitchell, April 6, 1780, in Weiss, *Jacob Weiss Letterbook*, 91.

118. Washington to Congress, March 17, 1780, in Fitzpatrick, *The Writings of George Washington*, 18:121–22.

119. John Paterson to William Heath, March 31, 1780, *Heath Papers II*, 44.

120. Philip Schuyler to Ezra L'Hommedieu, May 20, 1780, in Smith, *Letters of Delegates to Congress*, 15:165–66.

121. Washington to Jonathan Trumble, May 26, 1780, in Fitzpatrick, *The Writings of George Washington*, 18: 425.

122. James Robertson to George Germain, May 18, 1780, in *The Twilight of British Rule in Revolutionary America: The New York Letter Book of General James Robertson, 1780–1783*, ed. Milton M. Klein and Ronald W. Howard (Cooperstown: New York State Historical Association, 1983), 109–12.

123. Stephen Popp, "Popp's Journal, 1777–1783," ed. Joseph G. Rosegarten, *Pennsylvania Magazine of History and Biography* 26 (1901): 33.

124. Washington to Parsons December 13, 1779, and Washington to Maxwell, December 13, 1779, both in *PGWRWS*, 23:600, 601–2; Parsons to Horatio Gates, December 27, 1779, Horatio Gates Papers, NYHS. For illegal trade in New Jersey, see Gregory F. Walsh, "'Most Boundless Avarice': Illegal Trade in Revolutionary Essex," in *The American Revolution in New Jersey: Where the Battlefront Meets the Home Front*, ed. James J. Gigantino III (New Brunswick, NJ: Rutgers University Press, 2015), 32–53.

125. Washington to Samuel Huntington, January 18, 1779, in *PGWRWS*, 24:174–75.

126. Hazen to Washington, January 26, 1780, in ibid., 24:258–59.

127. Washington to St. Clair, January 27, 1780, in ibid., 24:296–98.

128. St. Clair to Washington, January 28, 1780, in ibid., 24:307–9.

129. St. Clair to Washington, February 11, 1780, in ibid., 24:444–46.

130. St. Clair to Washington, February 20, 1780, in ibid., 24:530–31.

131. Smith, *Winter at Morristown*, 28; Adrian Leiby, *The Revolutionary War in the Hackensack Valley: The Jersey Dutch and the Neutral Ground, 1775–1783* (New Brunswick, NJ: Rutgers University Press, 1962), 232–52; Kwasny, *Washington's Partisan War*, 259.

132. Kwasny, *Washington's Partisan War*, 258–59.

133. General Orders, February 16, 1780, in *PGWRWS*, 24:483–84.

134. Ebenezer Stanton to Thomas Goldstone Smith, February 10, 1780, in *A Salute to Courage: The American Revolution as Seen through the Wartime Writings of Officers of the Continental Army and Navy*, ed. Dennis P. Ryan (New York: Columbia University Press, 1979), 181–82.

135. General Orders, January 14, 1780, Andrew Peters Orderly Book, AAS; General Orders, May 5, 1780, Samuel Carr Orderly Book, AAS.

136. Garrison Orders, May 5, 1780, Samuel Carr Orderly Book, AAS.

137. M. M. Quaife, ed., "A Boy Soldier Under Washington: The Memoir of Daniel Granger," *Mississippi Valley Historical Review* 16 (March 1930): 555.

138. Martin, *Ordinary Courage*, 121.

139. General Orders, March 8, 1780, in *PGWRWS*, 24:659–60.

140. Regimental Orders, Hazen's Regiment, February 1, 1780, Hazen's Regiment Orderly Book, Regimental Orderly Books, Morristown National Historical Park.

141. Regimental Orders, March 5, 1780, Sherburne's Regiment Orderly Book, Regimental Orderly Books, Morristown National Historical Park.

142. Brigade Orders, March 8, 1780, Second Battalion, Artillery Brigade Orderly Book, Regimental Orderly Books, Morristown National Historical Park.

143. Brigade Orders, May 22 and May 23, 1780, Joel Smith's Orderly Book, 1779–1780, American Revolution Collection, CHS.

144. Lesser, *Sinews of Independence*, xxxi.

145. Henry Marble to Breck Parkman, May 9, 1780, United States Revolution Collection, Box 4, Folder 3, AAS.

146. Martin, *Ordinary Courage*, 109–13.

147. Smith, *Winter at Morristown*, 28–30.

148. Ibid., 30–31; Kwasny, *Washington's Partisan War*, 260–61.

149. Clinton, *The American Rebellion*, 190; Andrew Jackson O'Shaughnessy, *The Men Who Lost America: British Leadership, the American Revolution, and the Fate of Empire* (New Haven, CT: Yale University Press, 2013), 233.

150. Smith, *Winter at Morristown*, 31–32, 42; Kwasny, *Washington's Partisan War*, 261–62; Fleming, *Forgotten Victory*, 99–113.

151. Smith, *Winter at Morristown*, 42; Fleming, *Forgotten Victory*, 235–64.

152. Fleming, *Forgotten Victory*, 290–302.

153. Samuel Shaw to Nathaniel Shaw, December 25, 1779, Samuel Shaw Letters, MHS.

Chapter 7

1. Royster, *A Revolutionary People*, 255–294.

2. Washington to Pickering, November 17, 1780, in Fitzpatrick, *The Writings of George Washington*, 20:367.

3. Risch, *Supplying Washington's Army*, 306.

4. Council of War, October 31, 1780, in Fitzpatrick, *The Writings of George Washington*, 20:270.

5. Wayne to Washington, November 2, 1780, Founders Online, accessed February 15, 2019, https://founders.archives.gov/documents/Washington/99-01-02-03941.

6. Huntington to Washington, November 1, 1780, Founders Online, https://founders.archives.gov/documents/Washington/99-01-02-03778.

7. Glover to Washington, November 7, 1780, Founders Online, https://founders.archives.gov/documents/Washington/99-01-02-03848.

8. Irvine to Washington, November 1, 1780, Founders Online, https://founders.archives.gov/documents/Washington/99-01-02-03781; Hand to Washington, November 1, 1780, Founders Online, https://founders.archives.gov/documents/Washington/99-01-02-03790.

9. Howe to Washington, November 2, 1780, Founders Online, https://founders.archives.gov/documents/Washington/99-01-02-03792.

10. St. Clair to Washington, November 2, 1780, Founders Online, https://founders.archives.gov/documents/Washington/99-01-02-03793.

11. Lord Stirling to Washington, November 2, 1780, Founders Online, https://founders.archives.gov/documents/Washington/99-01-02-03794.

12. Howe to Washington, November 2, 1780, Founders Online, https://founders.archives.gov/documents/Washington/99-01-02-03792.

13. Lafayette to Washington, November 1, 1780, Founders Online, https://founders.archives.gov/documents/Washington/99-01-02-03782.

14. Stirling to Washington, November 2, 1780, Founders Online, https://founders.archives.gov/documents/Washington/99-01-02-03794; St. Clair to Washington, November 2, 1780, Founders Online, https://founders.archives.gov/documents/Washington/99-01-02-03793; Knox to Washington, November 3, 1780, Founders Online, https://founders.archives.gov/documents/Washington/99-01-02-03803.

15. Hand to Washington, November 2, 1780, Founders Online, https://founders.archives.gov/documents/Washington/99-01-02-03790.

16. Irvine to Washington, November 1, 1780, Founders Online, https://founders.archives.gov/documents/Washington/99-01-02-03781.

17. Knox to Washington, November 3, 1780, Founders Online, https://founders.archives.gov/documents/Washington/99-01-02-03803.

18. Reed to Wayne, October 31, 1780, in *The Casket: Flowers of Literature, Wit, and Sentiment* (Philadelphia: Samuel C. Atkinson, 1829), 406.

19. Washington to Heath, November 12, 1780, in Fitzpatrick, *The Writings of George Washington*, 20:336–37.

20. Washington to Moylan, November 17, 1780, in ibid., 20:361.

21. George Clinton to Alexander McDougall, October 3, 1780, in *Clinton Papers*, 6:274.

22. Dearborn, *Revolutionary War Journals*, 210; see also Thomas Blake, "Lieutenant Thomas Blake's Journal," in Kidder, *History of the First New Hampshire Regiment*, 56.

23. The Rhode Island regiment, for instance, transported timber on scows from Haverstraw to West Point to build barracks for officers in November 1780. See Greenman, *Diary of a Common Soldier*, 185–86.

24. Alexander McDougall to William Heath, November 14, 1780, *Heath Papers II*, 5:129–33.

25. Daniel Lyman to John G. Wanton, November 24, 1780, in Ryan, *A Salute to Courage*, 202.

26. Ebenezer Huntington to Samuel Blachley Webb, November 24, 1780, in Webb, *Reminiscences*, 211–12.

27. Garrison Orders, December 1, 1780, Eighth Massachusetts Regiment Orderly Book, HL, hereafter 8MROB.

28. Mary A. Stimson Mouldry, "Nathaniel Cowdrey of Reading, Mass," *The American Monthly Magazine* 4 (Jan.–July, 1894): 416.

29. Henry Sewall Diary, December 1 and December 2, 1780, MHS.

30. Nehum Parker Diary, December 3, 1780, Nehum Parker Pension, S. 112000, Roll 1874, RWP.

31. Garrison Orders, December 3, 1780, 8MROB.

32. Daniel Carthy to John Fisher, December 2, 1780, West Point Collection, NYHS.

33. Garrison Orders, December 4, 5, 6, and 9, 1780, 8MROB; Benjamin Gilbert to His Father, January 3, 1781, in *Winding Down: The Revolutionary War Letters of Benjamin Gilbert of Massachusetts, 180–1783*, ed. John Shy (Ann Arbor: University of Michigan Press, 1989), 31.

34. Hugh Hughes to Nicholas Quackenbush, November 4, 1780, and David McCarthy to Quackenbush, November 12, 1780, both in Frederick Dearborn Collection, HUL.

35. Samuel Adams Diary, December 2–4, 1780, NYPL.

36. William Lee, ed., "Constant Freeman Narrative," in *Magazine of American History* 2 (1878): 354.

37. William Pennington Diary, December 11, 1780, and January 5, 1781, New Jersey Historical Society, Newark, NJ.

38. John Hutchinson Buell Diary, December 2, 1780, Society of the Cincinnati.

39. Nathan Beers Diary, December 5 and December 15, 1780, Yale University Sterling Library.

40. Greenman, *Diary of a Common Soldier*, 188.

41. Thacher, *A Military Journal*, 240.

42. Washington to Wayne, November 14, 1780, in Fitzpatrick, *The Writings of George Washington*, 20: 344–45.

43. Wayne to Craig, November 14, 1780, in *The Casket*, 446.

44. Craig to Wayne, December 20, 1780, in ibid., 446.

45. Washington to Wayne, November 27, 1780, in Fitzpatrick, *The Writings of George Washington*, 20:406.

46. Joseph McClellan, "Diary of Events in the Army, August 1, 1780, to December 31, 1780," in Linn and Egle, *Pennsylvania Archives*, 11:583–84.

47. Wayne to William Irvine, December 6, 1780, Department of Defense, Adjutant General's Copies of Correspondence, Box 1, New Jersey State Archives.

48. McClellan, "Diary of Events," 584.

49. Wayne to Irvine, December 6, 1780, Department of Defense, Adjutant General's Copies of Correspondence, Box 1, New Jersey State Archives.

50. Wayne to Israel Shreve, December 22, 1780, Israel Shreve Papers, University of Houston Library.

51. Blaine to Washington, November 10, 1780, Founders Online, https://founders.archives.gov/documents/Washington/99-01-02-03880.

52. William Heath, *Memoirs of Major General William Heath* (New York: William Abbatt, 1901), 245.

53. Timothy Pickering to George Clinton, December 12, 1780, in Hastings, *Clinton Papers*, 6:492.

54. Hay to Washington, November 12, 1780, Founders Online, https://founders.archives.gov/documents/Washington/99-01-02-03905.

55. Hay to Washington, November 23, 1780, Founders Online, https://founders.archives.gov/documents/Washington/99-01-02-04036.

56. Washington to Clinton, November 27, 1780, in Fitzpatrick, *The Writings of George Washington*, 20:413–14.

57. Washington to Heath, November 27, 1780, and Washington to Wayne, November 27, 1780, both in Fitzpatrick, *The Writings of George Washington*, 20:405, 406–7; Risch, *Supplying Washington's Army*, 120–21.

58. Washington to Glover, November 27, 1780, in Fitzpatrick, *The Writings of George Washington*, 20:403.

59. Washington to Heath, November 28, 1780, and Washington to Samuel P. Huntington, December 13, 1780, both in ibid., 20:417, 468.

60. Ebenezer Gray to His Brother, December 22, 1780, in Johnston, *Yale and Her Honor Roll*, 128.

61. Washington to Clinton, December 10, 1780, in Fitzpatrick, *The Writings of George Washington*, 20:453–54.

62. Clinton to Washington, December 15, 1780, Founders Online, https://founders .archives.gov/documents/Washington/99-01-02-04229.

63. Washington to Heath, December 20, 1780, in Fitzpatrick, *The Writings of George Washington*, 20:505.

64. Heath to Washington, December 9, 1780, in *Heath Papers II*, 140–41.

65. Hay to Washington, December 29, 1780, Founders Online, https://founders .archives.gov/documents/Washington/99-01-02-04373.

66. Washington to Hay, December 22, 1780, in in Fitzpatrick, *The Writings of George Washington*, 21:2.

67. Hay to Washington, January 2, 1781, Founders Online, https://founders.archives .gov/documents/Washington/99-01-02-04407; Hay to Washington, January 12, 1781, Founders Online, https://founders.archives.gov/documents/Washington/99 -01-02-04515.

68. Henry Marble to Breck Parkman, January 11, 1781, United States Revolution Collection, Box 4, Folder 10, AAS.

69. Circular to the New England States and New York, January 22, 1781, and Washington to Ephraim Blaine, January 29, 1781, both in Fitzpatrick, *The Writings of George Washington*, 21:129–30, 156.

70. Garrison Orders, January 18 and 19, 1781, 8MROB.

71. Garrison Orders, January 15 and 19, 1781, ibid.

72. Heath to Washington, February 28, 1781, in *Heath Papers II*, 177.

73. The standard account of the mutinies remains Carl van Doren, *Mutiny in January* (New York: Viking, 1943).

74. Robert Howe to Unknown, January 27, 1781, Jared Sparks Collection, HUL.

75. Dirck Romeyn to Richard Varick, February 13, 1781, Richard Varick Papers, NYHS.

76. Washington to Commanding Officer of the Jersey Brigade, January 28, 1781, in Fitzpatrick, *The Writings of George Washington*, 21:150

77. Washington to Commanding Officer of the New Jersey Troops, February 7, 1781, and Washington to Rochambeau, February 15, 1781, both in ibid., 21:196–97, 229–31.

78. Washington to St. Clair, February 26, 1781, in ibid., 21:294–95.

79. Circular to Ulster and Orange County Militia Colonels, February 25, 1781, and Washington to Philemon Dickinson, March 1, 1781, both in ibid., 21:290–91, 324–35. He also called for reinforcements from the New York Brigade near Albany, see Washington to Heath, March 3, 1781, in ibid., 21:329.

80. Heath, *Memoirs*, 258.

81. Ibid., 248.

82. Ibid., 252; General Orders, January 30, 1781, and Washington to Congress, January 31, 1781, both in Fitzpatrick, *The Writings of George Washington*, 21:158–60, 165–67.

83. Loane, *Following the Drum*, 133.

84. Heath, *Memoirs*, 257; Heath to Washington, February 28, 1781, in *Heath Papers II*, 140–41.

85. Samuel Adams Diary, January 20, 23, 24, 30, 31 and February 1, 13, NYPL.

86. Heath to Washington, February 1, 1781, Founders Online, https://founders.archives.gov/documents/Washington/99-01-02-04723.

87. General Orders, February 3, 1781, Founders Online, https://founders.archives.gov/documents/Washington/99-01-02-04738.

88. Heath to Washington, February 8, 1781, Founders Online, https://founders.archives.gov/documents/Washington/99-01-02-04794.

89. Garrison Orders, March 17, 1781, Eighth Massachusetts Regiment Orderly Book, HL.

90. Garrison Orders, March 27 and 28, 1781, ibid.

91. Garrison Orders, March 28, 1781, ibid.

92. Katie Turner Getty, "Smoking the Smallpox Sufferers," *Journal of the American Revolution*, January 9, 2020, https://allthingsliberty.com/2020/01/smoking-the-smallpox-sufferers/.

93. Thacher, *Military Journal*, 308–10.

94. Heath, *Memoirs*, 260.

95. Thacher, *Military Journal*, 309.

96. Heath to Washington, April 11, 1781, Founders Online, https://founders.archives.gov/documents/Washington/99-01-02-05362.

97. General Orders, April 19, 1781, Founders Online, https://founders.archives.gov/documents/Washington/99-01-02-05453.

98. Garrison Orders, January 24, 1781, 8MROB.

99. Garrison Orders, January 30, 1781, ibid.

100. Brigade Orders, February 23, 1781, ibid.

101. Brigade Orders, March 12 and March 17, 1781, ibid.

102. Garrison Orders, March 18, 1781, ibid.

103. Israel Angell, *Diary of Colonel Israel Angell, Commanding the Second Rhode Island Regiment during the American Revolution, 1778–1781*, ed. Edward Field (Providence, RI: Preston and Rounds, 1899), 134–36; Livermore, "Orderly Book," 244.

104. Garrison Orderly, April 1, 1781, 8MROB.

105. Lieutenant Samuel Benjamin's diary notes the arrival of recruits on March 11, April 28, and May 3. Samuel Benjamin Diary, Yale University Sterling Library.

106. Regimental Orders, May 3, 1781, 8MROB.

107. Garrison Orders, May 5, 1781, ibid.

108. Garrison Orders, June 2 and 3, 1781, ibid.

109. Garrison Orders, June 18, 1781, ibid.

110. Garrison Orders, February 24, March 11, and April 17, 1783, ibid.

111. Garrison Orders, May 2, 1781, ibid.

112. General Orders, June 18, 1781, ibid.

113. Garrison Orders, June 14, 1781, ibid.

114. Washington to Benjamin Harrison, March 27, 1781, in Fitzpatrick, *The Writings of George Washington*, 23: 380–84.

115. John Fisher to John Keef, October 18, 1781, John Fisher Collection, NYHS.

116. Washington to Heath, October 29, 1781, in Fitzpatrick, *The Writings of George Washington*, 23:290–91.

117. William Heath to George Clinton, November 30, 1781, in Hastings, *Clinton Papers*, 7:529–31.

118. General Orders, January 2, 1782, in Fitzpatrick, *The Writings of George Washington*, 23:423; Greenman, *Diary of a Common Soldier*, 242–50.

119. John Hutchinson Buell Diary, November 23, 1781, Society of the Cincinnati; Greenman, *Diary of a Common Soldier*, 220.

120. Roger Welles to Solomon Welles, December 10, 1781, American Revolution Collection, Box 11, Folder J, CHS; Wild, *The Journal of Ebenezer Wild*, 85; Thomas Graton Diary, December 1781, Becca Graton Pension, W. 14824, Roll 1110, RWP.

121. Thacher, *A Military Journal*, 363.

122. James Thacher to His Brothers and Sisters, December 30, 1781, James Thacher Correspondence, HUL.

123. Washington to James Clinton, December 14, 1781, in Fitzpatrick, *The Writings of George Washington*, 23: 385–86.

124. Heath, *Memoirs*, 300.

125. Henry Sewall Diary, January 10 and 25, February 4, 1782, MHS; William Eustis to James Thacher, March 13, 1782, James Thacher Correspondence, HUL; Heath to Washington, January 10, 1782, in *Heath Papers II*, 335–36.

126. Elisha Hopkins to Samuel Blachley Webb, January 9, 1782, in *Correspondence and Journals of Samuel Blachley Webb*, 3 vols., ed. Worthington Chauncey Ford (New York: Wickersham, 1893–94), 2:382–83.

127. Heath to Washington, January 19, 1782, in *Heath Papers II*, 341–42; Heath, *Memoirs*, 303, 318.

128. Oliver Rice to Jonathan Rice, March 9, 1782, Sol Feinstone Collection, DLAR.

129. Benjamin Gilbert to Aaron Kimball, April 30, 1782, in Shy, *Winding Down*, 56–57.

130. Washington to Greene, December 18, 1782, in Fitzpatrick, *The Writings of George Washington*, 25:448.

131. Pickering to Washington, October 15, 1782, Founders Online, https://founders.archives.gov/documents/Washington/99-01-02-09892.

132. Washington to Knox, August 29 and September 17, 1782, and Washington to Benjamin Lincoln, September 19, 1782, all in Fitzpatrick, *The Writings of George Washington*, 25:91, 173, 179–80.

133. General Orders, October 28, 1782, in ibid., 25:303. Emphasis in the original.

134. Timothy Pickering, Regulations for Hutting, November 4, 1782, cited in Janet Dempsey, *Washington's Last Cantonment: High Time for a Peace* (Monroe, NY: Library Research Associates, 1987), 47; Timothy Pickering, Sketch of Hut Model, Timothy Pickering Papers, MHS.

135. Ebenezer Elmer, "Journal of Lieutenant Ebenezer Elmer," *Proceedings of the New Jersey Historical Society, First Series* 3 (1848–49): 101.

136. Washington to Hazen, November 27, 1782, and Washington to Hazen, December 6, 1782, both in Fitzpatrick, *The Writings of George Washington* 25:378–79, 400–401; John Hawkins Diary, November 1782, HSP.

137. Ebenezer Elmer to Israel Shreve, November 4, 1783, Israel Shreve Papers, University of Houston Library.

138. Oliver Rice to Jonathan Rice, October 23, 1782, Sol Feinstone Collection, DLAR.

139. Oliver Rice to Jonathan Rice, November 15, 1782, ibid.

140. Elmer, "Journal," 101.

141. Heman Smith to Thomas Woodbridge, November 29, 1782, Thomas Woodbridge Collection, CHS.

142. Swift to Woodbridge, December 9, 1782, ibid.

143. Martin, *Ordinary Courage*, 155.

144. Washington to Walter Stewart, January 18, 1783, and General Orders, February 5, 1783, both in Fitzpatrick, *The Writings of George Washington*, 26:46, 101.

145. General Orders, February 10, 1783, in ibid., 111–12.

146. Washington to Heath, February 5, 1783, in ibid., 97.

147. Robert K. Wright, "Nor Is Their Standing Army to Be Despised: The Emergence of the Continental Army as a Military Institution," in *Arms and Independence: The Military Character of the American Revolution*, ed. Ronald Hoffman and Peter J. Albert (Charlottesville: University Press of Virginia, 1984), 72.

Conclusion

1. Enos Reeves, "Extracts from the Letterbook of Enos Reeves, of the Pennsylvania Line," *Pennsylvania Magazine of History and Biography* 21, no. 4 (1897): 235.

2. Thacher, *A Military Journal*, 369.

3. Ebenezer Denny, *Military Journal of Major Ebenezer Denny* (Philadelphia: Historical Society of Pennsylvania, 1859), 50.

4. Washington to Bland, April 4, 1783, in *The Bland Papers: Being a Selection of the Papers of Colonel Theodorick Bland Jr.*, 2 vols., ed. Charles Campbell (Petersburg: Edmund and Julian C. Ruffin, 1840), 2:104.

5. Quoted in Dempsey, *Washington's Last Cantonment*, 46.

6. Francois Jean, Marquis de Chastellux, *Travels in North America in the Years 1780, 1781 and 1782*, 2 vols. (London: G. G. J. and J. Robinson, 1787), 1:42.

7. Ibid., 1:366.

8. *Pennsylvania Packet*, March 6, 1779.

9. Washington to Alexander Hamilton, October 26, 1799, in *The Papers of Alexander Hamilton*, 27 vols., ed. Harold C. Syrett (New York: Columbia University Press, 1961–79), 22:568.

10. Richard H. Kohn, *Eagle and Sword: The Federalists and the Creation of the Military Establishment in America, 1783–1802* (New York: Free, 1975), 248.

11. Hamilton to James McHenry, October 3, 1799, in Syrett, *The Papers of Alexander Hamilton*, 22:493.

12. Kohn, *Eagle and Sword*, 248.

13. Allan Everest, *The War of 1812 in the Champlain Valley* (Syracuse, NY: Syracuse University Press, 2010), 93.

14. Henry L. Scott, *Military Dictionary: Comprising Technical Definitions, Information on Raising and Keeping Troops, Actual Service, Including Makeshifts and*

Improved Materiel, and Law, Government, Regulation, and Administration Relating to Land Forces (New York: Van Nostrand, 1861), 139, 345.

15. David Gerald Orr, Matthew B. Reeves, and Clearance R. Grier, eds., *Huts and History: The Historical Archaeology of Military Encampments during the American Civil War* (Gainesville: University of Florida Press, 2006), xvi–xvii.

16. Albert Z. Conner and Chris Mackowski, *Seizing Destiny: The Army of the Potomac's "Valley Forge" and the Civil War Winter That Saved the Union* (El Dorado Hills, CA: Savas Beatie, 2016), xii–xiv.

Bibliography

Primary Sources

Manuscript Collections

American Antiquarian Society, Worcester, MA
    Samuel Carr Orderly Book
    Isaac Glynn, "A Soldier's Story, or A Journal of Soldier in the Revolutionary War"
    Andrew Peters Orderly Book
    Josiah Whiting Orderly Book
    United States Revolution Collection
American Philosophical Society, Philadelphia, PA
    Second Pennsylvania Regiment Orderly Book
Connecticut Historical Society, Hartford, CT
    American Revolution Collection
    David Avery Diary
    Elijah Porter Journal
    Second Connecticut Regiment Orderly Book
    David Smith Orderly Book
    Joel Smith's Orderly Book
    Thomas Woodbridge Papers
David Library of the American Revolution, Washington Crossing, PA
    Sol Feinstone Collection
Harvard University Library, Cambridge, MA
    Loammi Baldwin Papers
    Frederick Dearborn Collection
    Jared Sparks Collection
    James Thacher Correspondence
    Journal of the Proceedings of the Army Under the Command of Sir William Howe
        in the Year 1777
Huntington Library, San Marino, CA
    Eighth Massachusetts Regiment Orderly Books
Historical Society of Pennsylvania, Philadelphia, PA
    James Burnside Letterbook
    Ferdinand Dreer Autograph Collection
    John Hawkins Diary

Anthony Wayne Papers
William Smallwood Orderly Book
Library of Congress, Washington, DC
William Johnston Papers
McPherson Family Papers
Maryland Historical Society, Baltimore, MD
Mordecai Gist Papers
Massachusetts Historical Society, Boston, MA
Thomas Cushman Diary
Benjamin Farnum Diary
Phineas Ingalls Diary
Timothy Pickering Papers
Henry Sewall Diary
Samuel Shaw Papers
Morristown National Historical Park, Morristown, NJ
Park Collection
Regimental Orderly Book Collection
Lloyd W. Smith Collection
National Archives and Records Administration, Washington, DC
Revolutionary War Pension Applications
New Jersey State Archives, Trenton, NJ
Department of Defense, Adjutant General's Copies of Correspondence
New Jersey Historical Society, Newark, NJ
William S. Pennington Diary
New York Historical Society, New York, NY
John Fisher Collection
Horatio Gates Papers
Udny Hay Collection
John Lamb Papers
Malcolm's Additional Regiment Orderly Book
Alexander McDougall Headquarters Orderly Book
Joseph Reed Papers
Richard Varick Papers
West Point Collection
New York Public Library, New York, NY
Dr. Samuel Adams Diary
Thomas Addis Emmet Collection
Princeton University Firestone Library, Princeton, NJ
Andre de Coppet Collection
Rhode Island Historical Society, Providence, RI
Daniel Lyman Diary
Rutgers University Alexander Library, New Brunswick, NJ
John Eccleston Letters
James Parker Diary
Zacchaeus Towne Diary
Society of the Cincinnati, Washington, DC
Jacob Brower's Sixth Pennsylvania Regiment Orderly Book

John Hutchinson Buell Diary
University of Houston Library, Houston, TX
  Israel Shreve Papers
William L. Clements Library, Ann Arbor, MI
  Josiah Harmar Letterbook
Wisconsin Historical Society, Madison, WI
  Lyman Draper Manuscript Collection
Yale University Sterling Memorial Library, New Haven, CT
  Nathan Beers Diary
  Samuel Benjamin Diary

Published Primary Sources

Abbot, W. W., ed. *The Papers of George Washington: Colonial Series.* 10 vols. Charlottesville: University of Virginia Press, 1985–95.
———, et al., eds. *The Papers of George Washington: Revolutionary War Series.* 25 vols. to date. Charlottesville: University of Virginia Press, 1987–.
Angell, Israel. *Diary of Colonel Israel Angell, Commanding the Second Rhode Island Regiment during the American Revolution, 1778–1781.* Edited by Edward Field. Providence, RI: Preston and Rounds, 1899.
Armstrong, Samuel. "From Saratoga to Valley Forge: The Diary of Lieutenant Samuel Armstrong." Edited by Joseph Lee Boyle. *Pennsylvania Magazine of History and Biography* 121 (July 1997): 237–70.
Bates, Albert C., et al., *Collections of the Connecticut Historical Society.* 31 vols. Hartford: Connecticut Historical Society, 1860–1967.
Beatty, Joseph M., Jr., ed. "Letters of the Four Beatty Brothers of the Continental Army, 1774–1794." *Pennsylvania Magazine of History and Biography* 46 (1920): 193–263.
Blach, Thomas, ed. *Papers Chiefly Related to the Maryland Line.* Philadelphia: T. K. and P. G. Collins, 1857.
Boardman, Benjamin. "Diary of Rev. Benjamin Boardman." *Collections of the Massachusetts Historical Society, 2nd Series* 10 (1895–96): 400–413.
Boyle, Joseph Lee, ed. *Writings from the Valley Forge Encampment of the Continental Army.* 7 vols. Bowie, MD: Heritage, 2000–12.
Bradford, S. Sydney, ed. "A British Officer's Revolutionary War Journal, 1776–1778." *Maryland Historical Magazine* 56 (1961): 150–75.
Bradley, Stephen R. *Stephen R. Bradley: Letters of a Revolutionary War Patriot and Vermont Senator.* Edited by Dorr Bradley Carpenter. Jefferson, NC: McFarland, 2009.
Bunbury, Henry Edward, ed. *The Lee Papers.* 4 vols. New York: New York Historical Society, 1872.
Campbell, Charles, ed. *The Bland Papers: Being a Selection of the Papers of Colonel Theodorick Bland, Jr.* 2 vols. Petersburg: Edmund and Julian C. Ruffin, 1840.
Cecere, Michael, ed. *They Behaved like Soldiers: Captain John Chilton and the Third Virginia Regiment, 1775–1778.* Bowie, MD: Heritage, 2004.
Chastellux, Francois Jean, Marquis de. *Travels in North America in the Years 1780, 1781, and 1782.* 2 vols. London: G. G. J. and J. Robinson, 1787.
Chestnut, David R., et al., eds. *The Papers of Henry Laurens.* 16 vols. Columbia: University of South Carolina Press, 1968–2004.

Clark, Joseph. "Diary of Joseph Clark, Attached to the Continental Army from May 1778 to November 1779." *Proceedings of the New Jersey Historical Society* 7 (1853–54): 93–110.

Clinton, Henry. *The American Rebellion: Sir Henry Clinton's Narrative of His Campaigns, 1775–1782, with an Appendix of Original Documents.* Edited by William B. Wilcox. New Haven, CT: Yale University Press, 1954.

Craft, Benjamin. "Craft's Journal of the Siege of Boston." Edited by S. P. Fowler. *Essex Institute Historical Collections* 3 (1861): 51–57, 133–40, 167–74, 219–20.

Dann, John C., ed. *The Revolution Remembered: Eyewitness Accounts of the War of Independence.* Chicago: University of Chicago Press, 1980.

David, Ebenezer. *A Rhode Island Chaplain in the Revolutionary War.* Edited by Jeannette D. Black and William Green Roekler. Providence: Rhode Island Historical Society, 1949.

Dearborn, Henry. *Revolutionary War Journals of Henry Dearborn, 1775–1783.* Edited by Lloyd Brown and Howard Peckham. New York: Da Capo, 1939.

Denny, Ebenezer. *Military Journal of Major Ebenezer Denny.* Philadelphia: Historical Society of Pennsylvania, 1859.

Elmer, Ebenezer. "Journal of Lieutenant Ebenezer Elmer." *Proceedings of the New Jersey Historical Society, First Series* 3 (1848–49): 90–102.

Ewald, Johann. *Diary of the American War: A Hessian Journal.* Translated and edited by Joseph P. Trustin. New Haven, CT: Yale University Press, 1979.

Finney, Walter. "The Walter Finney Diary." Edited by Joseph Lee Boyle. *New Jersey History* 121 (2003): 23–81.

Fisher, Elijah. *Elijah Fisher's Journal while in the War for Independence and Continued Two Years after He Came to Maine, 1775–1784.* Augusta, ME: Badger and Manley, 1880.

Fithian, Philip Vickers. *Journal, 1775–1776: Written on the Virginia-Pennsylvania Frontier and in the Army around New York.* Edited by Robert Greenhalgh Albion and Leonidas Dodson. Princeton, NJ: Princeton University Press, 1934.

Fitzpatrick, John C., ed. *The Writings of George Washington from the Original Manuscript Sources, 1745–1799.* 39 vols. Washington, DC: US Government Printing Office, 1931–54.

Force, Peter, ed. *American Archives, 4th Series.* 9 vols. Washington, DC: Published under Authority of an Act of Congress, 1837–53.

———, ed. *American Archives, 5th Series.* 9 vols. Washington, DC: Published under Authority of an Act of Congress, 1837–53.

Ford, Worthington Chauncy, ed. *Correspondence and Journals of Samuel Blachley Webb.* 3 vols. New York: Wickersham, 1893–94.

———, ed. *Some Papers of Aaron Burr.* Worcester, MA: American Antiquarian Society, 1920.

Ford, Worthington C., et al., eds. *Journals of the Continental Congress.* 34 vols. Washington, DC: United States Government Printing Office, 1904–37.

Fuller, Archelaus. "Journal of Colonel Archelaus Fuller of Middletown." *Essex Institute Historical Collections* 46 (1910): 209–20.

Gilbert, Benjamin. *A Citizen-Soldier in the American Revolution: The Diary of Benjamin Gilbert in Massachusetts and New York.* Edited by Rebecca D. Symmes. Cooperstown: New York Historical Association, 1980.

Glasier, Benjamin. "French and Indian War Diary of Benjamin Glasier of Ipswich." *Essex Institute Historical Collections* 86 (1950): 65–92.

Green, Ashbel. *The Life of Ashbel Green.* New York: R. Carter, 1849.

Green, Samuel A., ed. *Three Military Diaries Kept by Groton Soldiers in Different Wars.* Cambridge, MA: John Wilson and Son, 1901.

Greenman, Jeremiah. *Diary of a Common Soldier in the American Revolution, 1775–1783: An Annotated Edition to the Military Journal of Jeremiah Greenman.* Edited by Robert Bray and Paul Bushman. DeKalb: Northern Illinois University Press, 1978.

Greenwood, Isaac, ed. *The Revolutionary Services of John Greenwood of Boston and New York, 1775–1783.* New York: De Vinne, 1922.

Hall, Charles S., ed. *Life and Letters of Samuel Holden Parsons: Major General in the Continental Army and Chief Judge of the Northwestern Territory, 1737–1789.* Binghamton, NY: Otsenigo, 1905.

Hastings, Hugh, ed. *The Public Papers of George Clinton, First Governor of New York.* 10 vols. New York: Wynkoop Hallenbeck Crawford, 1899–1914.

Heath, William. *Memoirs of Major General William Heath.* New York: William Abbatt, 1901.

Heth, William. "Orderly Book of Major William Heth of the Third Virginia Regiment, May 15–July 1, 1777." *Virginia Historical Society Collections* 2 (1892): 319–76.

Hitchcock, Enos. *Diary Enos Hitchcock, D.D., Chaplain of the Revolutionary Army.* Edited by William B. Weeden. Providence: Rhode Island Historical Society, 1899.

Hoyt, Edward P., ed. "A Revolutionary Diary of Captain Paul Brigham, November 19, 1777–September 4, 1778." *Vermont History* 34 (January 1966): 2–30.

Hunt, Gaillard, ed. *Fragments of Revolutionary History.* Brooklyn, NY: Historical Printing Club, 1892.

Huntington, Ebenezer. *Letters Written by Ebenezer Huntington during the American Revolution.* Edited by G. W. F. Blanchard. New York: Chas, Fred, Hartman, 1914.

Johnston, Henry Phelps, ed., *Connecticut Military Record, 1775–1748.* Hartford, CT: Adjutant General's Office, 1889.

———. *Yale and Her Honor Roll in the American Revolution: Including Original Letters, Records of Service, Biographical Sketches.* New York: Putnam and Sons, 1888.

Kidder, Frederic. *History of the First New Hampshire Regiment in the War of the Revolution.* Albany: J. Munsell, 1868.

Klein, Milton M., and Ronald W. Howard, eds. *The Twilight of British Rule in Revolutionary America: The New York Letter Book of General James Robertson, 1780–1783.* Cooperstown: New York State Historical Association, 1983.

Lauber, Almon W., ed. *Orderly Books of the Fourth New York Regiment, 1778–1780, the Second New York Regiment, 1780–1783, by Samuel Tallmadge and Others, with Diaries of Samuel Tallmadge, 1780–1782 and John Barr, 1779–1782.* Albany: University of the State of New York, 1932.

Lee, William, ed. "Constant Freeman Narrative." *Magazine of American History* 2 (1878): 349–60.

Linn, John B., and William Henry Egle, eds. *Pennsylvania Archives, Second Series.* 19 vols. Harrisburg: Pennsylvania State Archives, 1874–90.

Livermore, Daniel. "A Journal." Edited by Joseph B. Walker. *Collections of the New Hampshire Historical Society* 6 (1850): 308–35.

———. "Orderly Book of Captain Daniel Livermore's Company, Continental Army, 1780." *Collections of the New Hampshire Historical Society* 9 (1889): 201–44.

Lobdell, Jared C., ed. "The Revolutionary War Journal of Sergeant Thomas McCarty." *Proceedings of the New Jersey Historical Society* 82 (January 1964): 33–46.

Lymon, Simeon. "Journal of Simeon Lymon." *Collections of the Connecticut Historical Society* 7 (1899): 111–34.

Martin, James Kirby, ed. *Ordinary Courage: The Revolutionary War Adventures of Joseph Plumb Martin.* St. James, NY: Brandywine, 1993.

Martin, Sara, et al., eds. *The Papers of John Adams.* 20 vols. to date. Cambridge, MA: Harvard University Press, 1977–.

McMichael, James. "Diary of Lieutenant James McMichael, of the Pennsylvania Line, 1776–1778." *Pennsylvania Magazine of History and Biography* 16 (July 1892): 129–59.

Morgan, Nathaniel. "Journal of Ensign Nathaniel Morgan, April 21 to December 11, 1775." *Collections of the Connecticut Historical Society* 7 (1899): 99–110.

Mouldry, Mary A. Stimson. "Nathaniel Cowdery of Reading, Mass." *The American Monthly Magazine* 4 (Jan.–July 1894): 409–16.

Muenchhausen, Friedrich von. *At General Howe's Side, 1776–1778.* Edited by Samuel Stelle Smith. Translated by Ernst Kipping. Monmouth Beach, NJ: Philip Freneau, 1974.

Nash, Solomon. *Journal of Solomon Nash, a Soldier of the Revolution.* Edited by Charles I. Bushnell. Monmouth Beach, NJ: Philip Freneau, 1974.

Paine, Thomas. "Military Operations near Philadelphia in the Campaign of 1777–1778. Described in a Letter from Thomas Paine to Dr. Franklin." *Pennsylvania Magazine of History and Biography* 2 (1878): 283–96.

Popp, Stephen. "Popp's Journal, 1777–1783." Edited by Joseph G. Rosegarten. *Pennsylvania Magazine of History and Biography* 26 (1901): 25–41.

Prince, Carl E., et al., eds. *The Papers of William Livingston.* 5 vols. Trenton: New Jersey Historical Commission, 1979–88.

Quaife, M. M., ed. "A Boy Soldier under Washington: The Memoir of Daniel Granger." *Mississippi Valley Historical Review* 16 (March 1930): 538–60.

Rau, Louise, ed. "Sergeant John Smith's Diary of 1776." *Mississippi Valley Historical Review* 20 (September 1933): 247–70.

Reed, William B., ed. *Life and Correspondence of Joseph Reed.* 2 vols. Philadelphia: Lindsay and Blankston, 1847.

Reeves, Enos. "Extracts from the Letter Book of Enos Reeves, of the Pennsylvania Line." *Pennsylvania Magazine of History and Biography* 21, no. 1 (1897): 72–85.

Rodney, Thomas. "Diary of Captain Thomas Rodney 1776–1777." Edited by Caesar A. Rodney. *Papers of the Historical Society of Delaware* 8 (1888): 1–52.

Richards, Samuel. *Diary of Samuel Richards, Captain of Connecticut Line, War of the Revolution, 1775–1781.* Philadelphia: Leeds and Biddle, 1909.

Ryan, Dennis P., ed. *A Salute to Courage: The American Revolution as Seen through the Wartime Writings of Officers of the Continental Army and Navy.* New York: Columbia University Press, 1979.

Ryden, George Herbert, ed. *Letters to and from Caesar Rodney.* Philadelphia: University of Pennsylvania Press, 1933.

Shaw, Samuel. *The Journals of Major Samuel Shaw.* Edited by Josiah Quincy. Boston: Crosby and Nichols, 1847.

Showman, Richard K., Dennis R. Conrad, and Roger N. Parks, eds. *The Papers of Nathanael Greene*. 13 vols. Chapel Hill: University of North Carolina Press, 1976–2005.

Shy, John, ed. *Winding Down: The Revolutionary War Letters of Benjamin Gilbert of Massachusetts, 1780–1783*. Ann Arbor: University of Michigan Press, 1989.

Simcoe, John Graves. *A Journal of the Operations of the Queen's Rangers from the End of the Year 1777 to the Conclusion of the Late American War*. Exeter, UK: privately printed, 1789.

Simms, W. M. Gilmore, ed. *The Army Correspondence of Colonel John Laurens in the Years 1777–1778*. New York: Bradford Club, 1867.

Smith, Charles C., et al., eds. *Collections of the Massachusetts Historical Society, Seventh Series*. Boston: Massachusetts Historical Society, 1901–15.

Smith, Paul H., ed. *Letters of Delegates to Congress, 1774–1789*. 26 vols. Washington, DC: Library of Congress, 1976–2000.

Smith, William Henry, ed. *The St. Clair Papers: The Life and Public Services of Arthur St. Clair*. 2 vols. Cincinnati, OH: Robert Clark, 1881.

Stevens, James. "The Revolutionary Journal of James Stevens of Andover Mass." *Historical Collections of the Essex Institute* 48 (1912): 41–70.

Syrett, Harold C., ed. *The Papers of Alexander Hamilton*. 27 vols. New York: Columbia University Press, 1961–79.

Thacher, James. *A Military Journal during the American Revolutionary War, from 1775 to 1783; Describing Interesting Events and Transactions of this Period; with Numerous Historical Sketches of Several General Officers*. Boston: Cottons & Barnard, 1827.

Turner, Joseph Brown, ed. *The Journal and Order Book of Captain Robert Kirkwood of the Delaware Regiment of the Continental Line*. Wilmington: Historical Society of Delaware, 1910.

Tyler, J. E., ed. "The Operations in New Jersey: An English Officer Describes the Events of December 1776." *Proceedings of the New Jersey Historical Society* 70 (1952): 133–36.

Uhlendorf, Bernhard A., and Edna Vosper, eds. *Letters from Major Bauermeister to Colonel von Jungkenn Written during the Philadelphia Campaign, 1777–1778*. Philadelphia: Historical Society of Pennsylvania, 1935.

Vaughan, Zebulon. "The Journal of Private Zebulon Vaughan, Revolutionary Soldier, 1777–1780." Edited by Virginia Steel Wood. *Daughters of the American Revolution Magazine* (February 1979): 100–114, 256–57, 320–21, 478–87.

Wayne, Anthony. "Letter to Richard Peters, May 13, 1778." *Pennsylvania Magazine of History and Biography* 31 (1907): 240–41.

Webb, Samuel Blachley. *Reminiscences of General Samuel B. Webb of the Revolutionary Army*. Edited by J. Watson Webb et al. New York: Globe Stationery and Printing, 1882.

Webb, William Seward, ed. *General Orders of 1757, Issued by the Earl of Loudoun and Phineas Lyman in the Campaign against the French*. New York: Dodd, Mead, 1899.

Weedon, George. *Valley Forge Orderly Book of General George Weedon of the Continental Army*. New York: Dodd, Mead, 1902.

Weiss, Jacob. *Jacob Weiss Letterbook*. Edited by Melville J. Boyer. Allentown, PA: Lehigh County Historical Society, 1956.

Wild, Ebenezer. *The Journal of Ebenezer Wild*. Edited by James M. Bugabee. Cambridge, MA: John Wilson and Son, 1891.

Young, William. "Journal of Sargent William Young." *Pennsylvania Magazine of History and Biography* 8 (1884): 255–78.

Newspapers

The Casket: Flowers of Literature, Wit, and Sentiment, May 1820.
New Jersey Gazette, October 20, 1779–December 22, 1779.
Pennsylvania Packet, March 6, 1779.

Military Treatises

Anonymous. *Castramatatio*. Potsdam: publisher unknown, ca. 1780.
Bland, Humphrey. *A Treatise of Military Discipline*. 4th ed. London: Buckley, 1740.
Continho, Francisco Antonio Freire da Fonceca. *Pequeno resumo de Castrametaçao*. Lisbon: Na Typographia Nunesiana, 1792.
Crissé, Lancelot, Comte Turpin de. *Essay on the Art of War*. Translated by Joseph Otway. London: Strand, 1761.
Cuthbertson, Bennett. *A System for the Complete Interior Management and Oeconomy of a Battalion of Infantry*. Bristol, UK: Rothus and Nelson, 1776.
Fallois, Joseph de. *Traité de la Castramétation et de la Defense*. Paris: Chez G. J. Decker, 1771.
Frederick II, King of Prussia. *Military Instructions from the Late King of Prussia to His Generals*. Translated by Thomas Phillips. Harrisburg, PA: Stackpole, 1960.
Le Blond, Guillaume. *Essai sur la Castramétation*. Paris: Chez Carles-Antoine Jombert, 1748.
Lochée, Lewis. *An Essay on Castrametation*. London: T. Cadell, 1778.
Muller, Friderick Eugen Eric von. *Castrametation*. Potsdam, 1776.
Nicola, Lewis. *A Treatise of Military Exercise, Calculated for the Use of Americans*. Philadelphia: Styner and Crist, 1776.
Perrin, Benton de. *Dissertation sur les Tentes*. Paris: Chez Gonichon, 1735.
Pickering, Timothy. *An Easy Plan of Discipline for a Militia*. Salem, MA: Samuel and Ebenezer Hall, 1775.
Pirscher, Johann Dietrich Carl. *Von der Castrametation*. Berlin: Arnold Wever, 1778.
Pringle, John. *Observations on the Diseases of the Army, in Camp, and in Garrison*. London: Strand, 1752.
Reide, Thomas. *The Staff Officer's Manual*. London: T. Egerton, 1806.
Saxe, Maurice de. *Reveries, or Memoirs Concerning the Art of War*. Edinburgh, UK: Sands, Donaldson, Murray, and Cochrane, 1759.
Scott, Henry L. *Military Dictionary: Comprising Technical Definitions, Information on Raising and Keeping Troops, Actual Service, Including Makeshifts and Improved Materiel, and Law, Government, Regulation, and Administration Relating to Land Forces*. New York: Van Nostrand, 1861.
Simes, Thomas. *The Military Medley*. London, 1768.
Von Steuben, Friedrich Wilhelm. *Regulations for the Order and Discipline of the Troops of the United States*. Philadelphia: Styner and Cist, 1779.

Secondary Sources

Books

Anderson, Fred. *A People's Army: Massachusetts Soldiers and Society in the Seven Years' War*. Chapel Hill: University of North Carolina Press, 1984.

Anderson, M. S. *War and Society in Europe of the Old Regime, 1618–1789*. Guernsey, UK: Sutton, 1988.

Bilby, Joseph G., and Katherine Bilby Jenkins. *Monmouth Court House: The Battle that Made the American Army*. Yardley, PA: Westholme, 2010.

Bodle, Wayne K. *The Valley Forge Winter: Civilians and Soldiers in War*. University Park: Pennsylvania State University Press, 2002.

Bowler, Arthur. *Logistics and the Failure of the British Army in America, 1775–1783*. Princeton, NJ: Princeton University Press, 1975.

Brady, Lisa. *War upon the Land: Military Strategy and the Transformation of Southern Landscapes during the American Civil War*. Athens: University of Georgia Press, 2012.

Braisted, Todd. *Grand Forage 1778: The Battleground around New York City*. Yardley, PA: Westholme, 2016.

Brewer, John. *The Sinews of Power: War, Money, and the English State, 1688–1783*. Cambridge, MA: Harvard University Press, 1990.

Brown, Kathleen M. *Foul Bodies: Cleanliness in Early America*. New Haven, CT: Yale University Press, 2011.

Buchanan, John. *The Road to Valley Forge: How Washington Built the Army That Won the Revolution*. Hoboken, NJ: Wiley, 2004.

Carp, E. Wayne. *To Starve the Army at Pleasure: Continental Army Administration and American Political Culture, 1775–1783*. Chapel Hill: University of North Carolina Press, 1984.

Chet, Guy. *Conquering the American Wilderness: The Triumph of European Warfare in the Colonial Northeast*. Amherst: University of Massachusetts Press, 2003.

Clemens, Paul G. E., and Peter O. Wacker. *Land Use in Early New Jersey: A Historical Geography*. New Brunswick, NJ: Rutgers University Press, 1995.

Conner, Albert Z., and Chris Mackowski. *Seizing Destiny: The Army of the Potomac's "Valley Forge" and the Civil War Winter That Saved the Union*. El Dorado Hills, CA: Savas Beatie, 2016.

Corvisier, André. *Armies and Societies in Europe, 1494–1789*. Translated by Abigail T. Siddall. Bloomington: Indiana University Press, 1979.

Cox, Caroline. *A Proper Sense of Honor: Service and Sacrifice in George Washington's Army*. Chapel Hill: University of North Carolina Press, 2004.

Creveld, Martin van. *Supplying War: Logistics from Wallenstein to Patton*. New York: Cambridge University Press, 1977.

Cubbison, Douglas R. *All Canada in the Hands of the British: General Jeffery Amherst and the 1760 Campaign to Conquer New France*. Norman: University of Oklahoma Press, 2014.

Cunningham, John T. *The Uncertain Revolution: Washington and the Continental Army at Morristown*. West Creek, NJ: Down the Shore, 2007.

Curson, Daniel. *Putnam's Revolutionary War Winter Encampment: The History and Archaeology of Putnam Memorial State Park*. Charleston, SC: History, 2011.

Dempsey, Janet. *Washington's Last Cantonment: High Time for a Peace*. Monroe, NY: Library Research Associates, 1987.

D'Estrees, Marshal. *Camp Topographies of the Campaign of MDCCLVII in Westphalia*. Translated by James J. Mitchell. Valparaiso, IN: Old Battlefield, 1996.

Duffy, Christopher. *The Army of Frederick the Great.* 2nd edition. London: Emperor's, 1996.

———. *The Army of Maria Theresa: The Armed Forces of Imperial Austria, 1740–1780.* New York: Hippocrene, 1977.

———. *The Military Experience in the Age of Reason, 1715–1789.* New York: Routledge, 1987.

———. *Siege Warfare: The Fortress in the Early Modern World, 1494–1660.* New York: Routledge, 1979.

Eames, Stephen C. *Rustic Warriors: Warfare and the Provincial Soldier on the New England Frontier, 1689–1748.* New York: New York University Press, 2011.

Everest, Allan. *The War of 1812 in the Champlain Valley.* Syracuse, NY: Syracuse University Press, 2010.

Fenn, Elizabeth A. *Pox Americana: The Great Smallpox Epidemic of 1775–1782.* New York: Hill and Wang, 2002.

Fischer, David Hackett. *Washington's Crossing.* New York: Oxford University Press, 2003.

Fischer, Joseph R. *A Well-Executed Failure: The Sullivan Campaign against the Iroquois, July–September 1779.* Columbia: University of South Carolina Press, 1997.

Fleming, Thomas. *Forgotten Victory: The Battle for New Jersey, 1780.* New York: Reader's Digest Press, 1973.

French, Allen. *The First Year of the American Revolution.* Boston: Houghton Mifflin, 1934.

Gerlach, Larry R. *Prologue to Independence: New Jersey in the Coming of the American Revolution.* New Brunswick, NJ: Rutgers University Press, 1976.

Gigantino, James G., II, ed. *The American Revolution in New Jersey: Where the Battlefront Meets the Home Front.* New Brunswick, NJ: Rutgers University Press, 2014.

Gutmann, Myron P. *War and Rural Life in the Early Modern Low Countries.* Princeton, NJ: Princeton University Press, 1980.

Higginbotham, Don. *The War of American Independence: Military Attitudes, Policies, and Practice, 1763–1789.* New York: MacMillan, 1971.

Hoffman, Ronald, and Peter J. Albert, eds. *Arms and Independence: The Military Character of the American Revolution.* Charlottesville: University of Virginia Press, 1984.

Houlding, J. A. *Fit for Service: The Training of the British Army, 1715–1795.* Oxford, UK: Clarendon, 1981.

Jones, Archer. *The Art of War in the Western World.* Urbana, IL: University of Chicago Press, 1987.

Kapp, Friedrich. *The Life of John Kalb, Major-General in the Revolutionary Army.* New York: Henry Holt, 1870.

Kohn, Richard H. *Eagle and Sword: The Federalists and the Creation of the Military Establishment.* New York: Free, 1975.

Kwasny, Mark. *Washington's Partisan War.* Kent, OH: Kent State Press, 1996.

Lee, Wayne E. *Barbarians and Brothers: Anglo-American Warfare, 1500–1865.* New York: Oxford University Press, 2014.

Leftkowitz, Arthur. *The Long Retreat: The Calamitous Defense of New Jersey, 1776.* New Brunswick, NJ: Rutgers University Press, 1999.

Leiby, Adrian C. *The Revolutionary War in the Hackensack Valley: The Jersey Dutch and the Neutral Ground, 1775–1783.* New Brunswick, NJ: Rutgers University Press, 1961.

Lender, Mark Edward, and Gary Wheeler Stone. *Fatal Sunday: George Washington, the Monmouth Campaign, and the Politics of Battle.* Norman: University of Oklahoma Press, 2017.

Lengel, Edward G. *Washington: A Military Life.* New York: Random House, 2005.

Lesser, Charles H. *Sinews of Independence: Monthly Strength Reports of the Continental Army.* Chicago: University of Chicago Press, 1976.

Loane, Nancy K. *Following the Drum: Women at the Valley Forge Encampment.* Washington, DC: Potomac Books, 2009.

Lockhart, Paul. *The Drillmaster of Valley Forge: Baron de Steuben and the Making of the American Army.* New York: HarperCollins, 2008.

Luvaas, Jay. *Frederick the Great on the Art of War.* Cambridge, MA: Da Capo, 1999.

Lynn, John A., ed. *Feeding Mars: Logistics in Western Warfare from the Middle Ages to the Present.* Boulder, CO: Westview, 1993.

———. *The Giant of the Grand Siècle: The French Army 1610–1715.* New York: Cambridge University Press, 2008.

Martin, James Kirby, and Mark Edward Lender. *A Respectable Army: The Military Origins of the Republic, 1763–1789.* Wheeling, IL: Harlan Davidson, 1982.

Mayer, Holly A. *Belonging to the Army: Camp Followers and Community during the American Revolution.* Columbia: University of South Carolina Press, 1999.

McConnell, Michael N. *Army and Empire: British Soldiers on the American Frontier, 1758–1775.* Lincoln: University of Nebraska Press, 2004.

McCurdy, John Gilbert. *Quarters: The Accommodation of the British Army and the Coming of the American Revolution.* Ithaca, NY: Cornell University Press, 2019.

McNeill, John R. *Mosquito Empires: Ecology and War in the Greater Caribbean, 1620–1914.* New York: Cambridge University Press, 2010.

Meier, Kathryn Shively. *Nature's Civil War: Common Soldiers and the Environment in 1862 Virginia.* Chapel Hill: University of North Carolina Press, 2013.

Middlekauff, Robert. *The Glorious Cause: The American Revolution, 1763–1789.* New York: Oxford University Press, 1982.

Miller, Charles E., Jr., Donald V. Lockey, and Joseph Visconti Jr. *Highlands Fortress: The Fortification of West Point during the American Revolution.* West Point, NY: United States Military Academy, 1988.

Mitnick, Barbara J., ed. *New Jersey in the American Revolution.* New Brunswick, NJ: Rutgers University Press, 2005.

Neimeyer, Charles Patrick. *America Goes to War: A Social History of the Continental Army.* New York: New York University Press, 1997.

Nelson, Paul David. *The Life of William Alexander, Lord Stirling.* Tuscaloosa: University of Alabama Press, 1987.

Olsen, Charles E., Jr., ed. *Images of the Recent Past. Readings in Historical Archaeology.* Lanham, MD: Rowman Altamaria, 1996.

Orr, David Gerald, Matthew B. Reeves, and Clearance R. Grier, eds. *Huts and History: The Historical Archaeology of Military Encampments during the American Civil War.* Gainesville: University of Florida Press, 2006.

O'Shaughnessy, Andrew Jackson. *The Men Who Lost America: British Leadership, the American Revolution, and the Fate of Empire.* New Haven, CT: Yale University Press, 2013.

Palka, Eugene J., and Francis A. Galgano. *The Historical Geography of the Hudson Highlands.* 2nd edition. West Point, NY: United States Military Academy, 2006.

Paret, Peter, ed. *Makers of Modern Strategy: From Machiavelli to the Nuclear Age.* Princeton, NJ: Princeton University Press, 1986.

Peckham, Howard H. *The War for Independence: A Military History.* Chicago: University of Chicago Press, 1958.

Prince, Carl. *Middlebrook: The American Eagle's Nest.* Somerville, NJ: Somerset, 1957.

Quarles, Benjamin. *The Negro in the American Revolution.* Chapel Hill: University of North Carolina Press, 1961.

Risch, Erna. *Supplying Washington's Army.* Washington, DC: Center of Military History, United States Army, 1981.

Royster, Charles. *A Revolutionary People at War: The Continental Army and the American Character 1775–1783.* Chapel Hill: University of North Carolina Press, 1979.

Skaggs, David Curtis, and Larry L. Nelson, eds. *The Sixty Years' War for the Great Lakes, 1754–1814.* East Lansing: Michigan State University Press, 2001.

Smith, Samuel Stelle. *The Darkest Winter: Morristown, 1780.* Monmouth Beach, NJ: Philip Frenau, 1980.

Spring, Mathew H. *With Zeal and Bayonets Only: The British Army on Campaign in North America, 1775–1783.* Norman: University of Oklahoma Press, 2008; reprint, Norman: University of Oklahoma Press, 2010.

Stansfield, Charles A., Jr. *A Geography of New Jersey: The City in the Garden State.* 2nd edition. New Brunswick, NJ: Rutgers University Press, 1988.

Taaffe, Stephen R. *Washington's Revolutionary War Generals.* Norman: University of Oklahoma Press, 2019.

Thibaut, Jacqueline. *In the True Rustic Order: Material Aspects of the Valley Forge Encampment, 1777–1778.* Washington, DC: National Parks Service, 1980.

———. *Logistics, Supply, and the Continental Army at Valley Forge.* Washington DC: National Parks Service, 1980.

Trussell, John. *Birthplace of an Army: A Study of the Valley Forge Encampment.* Philadelphia: Pennsylvania Historical Society, 1976.

Van Buskirk, Judith L. *Standing in Their Own Light: African American Patriots in the American Revolution.* Norman: University of Oklahoma Press, 2017.

Van Doren, Carl. *Mutiny in January.* New York: Viking, 1943.

Wade, Herbert T., and Robert A. Lively. *This Glorious Cause: The Adventures of Two Company Officers in Washington's Army.* Princeton, NJ: Princeton University Press, 1958.

Ward, Christopher. *The War of the Revolution.* 2 vols. New York: MacMillan, 1952.

Wright, Robert K. *The Continental Army.* Washington, DC: Center of Military History, United States Army, 1986.

Articles

Angelekos, Peter. "The Army at Middlebrook." *Proceedings of the New Jersey Historical Society* 70 (January 1952): 97–120.

Becker, Ann M. "Smallpox in Washington's Army: Strategic Implications of the Disease in the American Revolutionary War." *Journal of Military History* 68 (April 2004): 381–430.

Bodle, Wayne K. "Generals and 'Gentlemen': Pennsylvania Politics and the Decision for Valley Forge." *Pennsylvania History: A Journal of Mid-Atlantic Studies* 62 (Winter 1995): 59–89.

Bolton, Reginald Pelham. "The Military Hut-Camp of the War of the Revolution on the Dyckman Farm, Manhattan." *New York Historical Society Quarterly* 2 (1918, 1919): 89–97, 130–36.

Bradford, S. Sydney. "Hunger Menaces the Revolution, December 1779–January 1780." *Maryland Historical Magazine* 61 (1966): 1–23.

Brier, Mark A. "Tolerably Comfortable: A Field Trial of a Recreated Soldier Cabin at Valley Forge." Valley Forge National Historical Park, 2004.

Curson, Daniel. "Archaeology of an Enlisted Man's Hut at Putnam Memorial State Park." *Bulletin of the Archaeological Society of Connecticut* 63 (2001): 41–58.

Fenn, Elizabeth A. "Biological Warfare in the Eighteenth Century: Beyond Sir Jeffery Amherst." *Journal of American History* 86 (March 2000): 1552–80.

Fisher, Charles L. "The Archaeology of Provincial Officers' Huts at Crown Point State Historic Site." *Northeast Historical Archaeology* 24 (1995): 65–86.

Greene, Jack P. "The South Carolina Quartering Dispute, 1757–1758." *South Carolina Historical Magazine* 60 (October 1959): 193–204.

Herrera, Ricardo A. "Foraging and Combat Operations at Valley Forge, February–March, 1778." *Army History* 79 (Spring 2011): 7–29.

Higginbotham, Don. "The Early American Way of War: Reconnaissance and Appraisal." *William and Mary Quarterly* 44 (April 1987): 230–73.

Hsiung, David C. "Food, Fuel, and the New England Environment in the War for Independence, 1775–1776." *New England Quarterly* 80 (December 2007): 614–54.

Lee, Wayne E. "Early American Ways of War: A New Reconnaissance." *Historical Journal* 44 (March 2001): 269–89.

Mayer, Holly. "From Forts to Families: Following the Army into Western Pennsylvania, 1758–1766." *Pennsylvania Magazine of History and Biography* 130 (2006): 5–43.

McNeill, John R. "Woods and Warfare in World History." *Environmental History* 9 (July 2004): 388–410.

Newcomb, Benjamin H. "Washington's Generals and the Decision to Camp at Valley Forge." *Pennsylvania Magazine of History and Biography* 117 (October 1993): 309–29.

Parker, Geoffrey. "The Military Revolution 1550–1650—A Myth?" *Journal of Modern History* 48 (June 1976): 195–214.

Poirier, David A. "Camp Reading: Logistics of a Revolutionary War Winter Encampment." *Northeast Historical Archaeology* 5 (1976): 40–52.

Powers, Sandra L. "Studying the Art of War: Books Known to American Officers and their French Counterparts in the Late Eighteenth Century." *Journal of Military History* 70 (July 2006): 781–814.

Quarterly, Thomas W. S. "Revolutionary Camps of the Hudson Highlands." *Journal of the New York State Historical Association* 2 (July 1921): 141–55.

Rogers, J. Alan. "Colonial Opposition to the Quartering of British Troops during the French and Indian War." *Military Affairs* 34 (February 1970): 7–11.

Rutsch, Edward S., and Kim M. Peters. "Forty Years of Archaeological Research at Morristown National Historical Park, Morristown New Jersey." *Historical Archaeology* 11 (1977): 15–38.

Seidel, John L. "Archaeological Research at the 1778–1779 Winter Cantonment of the Continental Artillery, Pluckemin, New Jersey." *Northeast Historical Archaeology* 12 (1983): 7–14.

Thrusfield, Hugh. "Smallpox in the American War of Independence." *Annals of Medical History* 3 (1940): 312–18.

Zimmerman, John J. "Governor Denny and the Quartering Act of 1756." *Pennsylvania Magazine of History and Biography* 91 (July 1967): 266–81.

Unpublished Dissertations

Seidel, John. "The Archaeology of the American Revolution: A Reappraisal and Case Study of the Continental Army Artillery Cantonment of 1778–1779, Pluckemin, New Jersey." PhD Diss., University of Pennsylvania, 1987.

Online Sources

Barbieri, Michael. "Winter Soldiering in the Champlain Valley." *Journal of the American Revolution*, October 19, 2015. https://allthingsliberty.com/2015/10/winter-soldiering-in-the-lake-champlain-valley/.

Burns, Alex. "Valley Forge vs. the Bunzelwitz Position." *Kabinettskrieg*, July 6, 2016. http://kabinettskriege.blogspot.com/2016/07/valley-forge-vs-bunzelwitz-position.html.

Childs, John. "Barracks and Conscription: Civil-Military Relations in Europe from 1500." *European History Online*, August 1, 2001. http://ieg-ego.eu/en/threads/alliances-and-wars/war-as-an-agent-of-transfer/john-childs-barracks-and-conscription-civil-military-relations-in-europe-from-1500#Militaryaccommodation.

George Washington Papers. Founders Online. https://founders.archives.gov/.

Getty, Katie Turner. "Smoking the Smallpox Sufferers." *Journal of the American Revolution*, January 9, 2020. https://allthingsliberty.com/2020/01/smoking-the-smallpox-sufferers/.

INDEX

Page numbers in *italic* typeface indicate illustrations.

CPSIA information can be obtained
at www.ICGtesting.com
Printed in the USA
LVHW030138180321
681772LV00004B/39